Klimt's Women

Klimt's Women

Edited by

Tobias G. Natter and Gerbert Frodl

Texts by

Neda Bei
Hans Bisanz
Marian Bisanz-Prakken
Alessandra Comini
Franz Eder
Lisa Fischer
Gerbert Frodl
Daniela Hammer-Tugendhat
Jeroen van Heerde
Hansjörg Krug
Tobias G. Natter
Monika Pessler
Regine Schmidt
Thomas Trummer
Heidemarie Uhl
Angela Völker

DUMONT

This catalogue has been published to accompany the Millennium exhibition "Klimt und die Frauen", 231st temporary exhibition of the Österreichische Galerie Belvedere, Vienna, from 20 September 2000 to 7 January 2001.

Exhibition

Concept
Tobias G. Natter

Curators
Tobias G. Natter, Regine Schmidt

Exhibition assistant
Christiane Böker

Exhibition architecture
Dimitris Manikas
Doris Kristandl (Assistant)

Exhibition construction
Wolfgang Mahr and Gerhard Davit,
Christian Kochmann, Georg Lucina,
Helmut Messaros, Mario Nitsch,
Herbert Pitzer, Norbert Stocker,
Franz Zwickelsdorfer
and Artex, Vienna

Art restoration
Elisabeth Foissner, Erhard Stöbe,
Bettina Urban

Public Relations
Klaus Pokorny,
Sandra Maria Ziegerhofer (Assistant)

Art mediation
Petra Schröck, Tamara Loitfellner,
Christian Huemer

Sponsoring
Hannelore Talburg

Catalogue

Catalogue editors
Tobias G. Natter, Christiane Böker

Copy editing
Carmen Söntgerath

Translations
Nikolas Bertheau, Pauline Cumbers, Michael
Eldred, Ishbel Flett, Eileen Martin

Design
Birgit Haermeyer

Production
Peter Dreesen, Marcus Muraro

Colour separations
Litho Köcher, Cologne
Eichhorn, Frankfurt

Printing
Rasch, Bramsche

Binding
Bramscher Buchbinder Betriebe

Library of Congress Card Number
00-108343

A Catalogue record for this book is available
from the British Library

© 2000 Österreichische Galerie Belvedere,
Vienna, and DuMont Buchverlag, Cologne
© on the texts the authors
Responsible for the content: Gerbert Frodl,
director of Österreichische Galerie Belvedere
© VG Bild-Kunst, Bonn 2000, on the works
of Giovanni Boldini, Oskar Kokoschka, Henri
Matisse, Edvard Munch, Kees van Dongen

Distributed by Yale University Press,
New Haven and London

Printed in Germany
ISBN 0–300–08796–9

Acknowledgements

Tania Adams, London
Dr. Wladimir Aichelburg, Vienna
Dr. Karl Albrecht-Weinberger, Vienna
Maria Altmann, Los Angeles
Renata Antoniou, Vienna
Masahiro Aoki, Toyota
Paul Asenbaum, Vienna
Prof. Peter Baum, Linz
Dr. Felix Baumann, Zurich
Dr. Reinhold Baumstark, Munich
Dr. Monika Bernold, Vienna
Dr. Marian Bisanz-Prakken, Vienna
Torill Bjordal, Oslo
Dr. Antonia Boswell, Vienna
Nicholas Booth, London
Claire Both, Paris
Dr. Christian Brandstätter, Vienna
Cécile Brunner, Zurich
Anne Buddle, Edinburgh
Wolfgang Büche, Halle a. d. Saale
Michael Clarke, Edinburgh
Dir. Timothy Clifford, Edinburgh
John B. Collins, Ottawa
Barbara Creaghan, Montreal
Dr. Gudrun Danzer, Graz
Dir. Agnès Delanoy, Saint-Germain-en-Laye
Dir. Dr. Helga Dostal, Vienna
HR Dr. Günter Düriegl, Vienna
Judith Durrer, Berne
Franz Eder, Salzburg
Mag. Viola Eichberger, Vienna
Heike Eipeldauer, Baden bei Wien
Jasminka Ekkeren, Oslo
Dr. Gottfried Fliedl, Wolfpassing/Zeiselmauer
Gloria G., Vienna
Georg Gaugusch, Vienna
Robin Gibson, London
Dir. Dr. Heide Grape-Albers, Hanover
Nehama Guralnik, Tel Aviv
Prof. Erich Gusel, Langenzersdorf
B. Heimberg, Munich
Dir. Allis Helleland, Copenhagen
Beatrice Hosegood, London
Dir. Nicole d'Huart, Brussels
Univ. Prof. Dr. Clemens Jabloner, Vienna
Otto von Jacobs, Purbach
Erika Jakubovits, Vienna
Dr. Annegret Janda, Berlin
Dipl. Ing. Erich Jiresch, Vienna
Dr. Andrea Jungmann, Vienna
Marianne Kirstein-Jacobs, Vienna
Claudia Klein-Primavesi, Vienna
Gerhard von Knobelsdorff, Berlin
AR Herbert Koch, Vienna
HR. Dr. Michael Krapf, Vienna
Dr. Almut Krapf-Weiler, Vienna
Dr. Carl Kraus, Innsbruck
Dr. Hansjörg Krug, Vienna
Mag. Wolfgang Krug, St. Pölten

Prof. Dr. Rudolf Leopold, Vienna
Mag. Michaela Lindinger, Vienna
Dir. Henri Loyrette, Paris
Caroline Mathieu, Paris
Patrice Mattia, MA, New York
Univ. Prof. Dr. Siegfried Mattl, Vienna
Mag. Monika Mayer, Vienna
Univ. Prof. HR Dr. Lorenz Mikoletzky, Vienna
Hanne Moller, Copenhagen
Jean-Paul Monory, Saint Tropez
Kyoko Moronaga, Vienna
Christian Müller, Solothurn
Monika Müller, Halle a. d. Saale
Dr. Lutz Musner, Vienna
Kazuo Nakabayashi, Tokyo
Dr. Christian M. Nebehay, Vienna
Dir. Peter Noever, Vienna
Dr. Elisabeth Nowak-Thaller, Linz
Silke Oldenburg, Hamburg
Claudia Österreicher, Vienna
Dr. Cornelia Pallavicini, Vienna
Dr. Erika Patka, Vienna
Dir. Dr. Gianna Piantoni, Rome
Dir. Dr. Bianca Alessandra Pinto, Rome
Dr. Roswitha Preiß, Salzburg
Dir. Renee Price, New York
Richard Primavesi, Montreal
Gen. Dir. Dkfm. Gerhard Randa, Vienna
Dir. Otto Hans Ressler, Vienna
Dr. Christopher Riopelle, London
Dir. Giandomenico Romanelli, Venice
Dr. Arthur Saliger, Vienna
Peter Sátor, Vienna
Dir. Dr. Katja Schneider, Halle
Dir. Dr. Klaus-Albrecht Schröder, Vienna
Dir. Dr. Karl Schütz, Vienna
Mag. Romana Schuler, Vienna
Dr. Flavia Scotton, Venice
Gen. Dir. HR Dr. Wilfried Seipel, Vienna
Dir. Tone Skedsmo, Oslo
Mag. Dr. Franz Smola, Vienna
Kathleen Soriano, Edinburgh
Dir. Werner Spies, Paris
Waltraud Stangl, Vienna
HR Mag. Erhard Stöbe, Vienna
Dir. Toni Stooss, Berne
Dr. Ursula Storch, Vienna
HR Mag. Dr. Alice Strobl, Vienna
Elisabeth Sturm-Bednarczyk, Vienna
Dir. Mitsuhiko Tera, Toyota
Dir. Tetsuo Tsujimura, Tokyo
Dir. Dr. Christoph Vögele, Solothurn
Herlinde Weiß, Vienna
Dir. Eliane de Wilde, Brussels
Dr. Christian Witt-Döring, Vienna
Univ. Prof. Dr. Gotthart Wunberg, Vienna
Univ. Doz. Dr. Pavel Zatloukal, Olomouc
Univ. Prof. Dr. Thomas Zaunschirm, Vienna

Lenders

Albertina, Vienna
Bank Austria, Vienna
C. Bednarczyk, Vienna
Fondation Roi Baudouin, Brussels
Galleria d'Arte Moderna Ca' Pesaro, Venice
Galleria Nazionale d'Arte Moderna e
 Contemporanea, Rome
Galerie Welz, Salzburg
Historisches Museum der Stadt Wien
Christine Kugler, Vienna
Kunsthaus Zurich
Kunsthistorisches Museum, Vienna
Kunstmuseum Berne
Kunstmuseum Solothurn
L' Annonciade – Musée de Saint Tropez
MAK, Museum für angewandte Kunst, Vienna
Musée d'Ixelles, Brussels
Musée Départemental Maurice Denis –
 "Le Prieuré", Saint-Germain-en-Laye
Musée d'Orsay, Paris
Musées Royaux des Beaux Arts de Belgique,
 Brussels
Nasjonalgalleriet, Oslo
National Gallery of Scotland, The Mound,
 Edinburgh
National Museum of Modern Art, Tokyo
National Portrait Gallery, London
Neue Galerie am Landesmuseum Joanneum,
 Graz
Neue Galerie der Stadt Linz
Niedersächsisches Landesmuseum,
 Hanover
Sammlung Dichand, Vienna
Sammlung Leopold Privatstiftung, Vienna
Staatliche Galerie Moritzburg, Halle a.d. Saale
Statens Museum for Kunst, Kopenhagen
Theatermuseum Vienna
Toyota Municipal Museum of Art, Toyota

We thank the private collectors who wish to
remain anonymous.

Preface

"Gustav Klimt and European Female Portraiture" (Gustav Klimt und das europäische Frauenbildnis) was the original working title for this project, before eventually settling on the simpler and at the same time more inclusive title of "Klimt's Women" (Klimt und die Frauen). The choice of title reflects the fact that, rather than merely paying homage yet again to an already widely revered artist—an increasingly fraught undertaking given the fragility of many surviving works—this publication seeks to place Klimt's portraits of women within the broader context of European art and shed some light on the lives of his sitters.

The focus of the catalogue, then, is on the women Klimt portrayed in the course of his successful career. Painstaking research has uncovered much information on their hitherto little-known lives, fleshing out their personalities and indicating what became of them later, particularly in the Nazi period. It is largely to these women, albeit indirectly, that Klimt owes his reputation as a seminally important artist at the forefront of one of the most exciting and innovative periods in Viennese art.

Accordingly, the spectrum of works presented is somewhat broader than the original working titled suggested. They range from the late nineteenth-century swagger portrait to the symbolic and allegorical depiction of woman, from the tranquil early works to the famous golden paintings and the later innovative vibrancy of colour melding with ornament to the point of dissolution. In recent years, so many exhibitions have addressed the theme of "Fin-de-siècle Vienna" that, with a few notable exceptions, most of the relevant publications have fallen short of placing Klimt's oeuvre within a wider context that actually ventures beyond his Viennese links. This catalogue intends to redress the balance by providing a long overdue and more multifaceted evaluation of Gustav Klimt's art.

Mounting a major Klimt exhibition in Vienna—the first in many years and unprecedented in scope and thematic focus—does have certain advantages. After all, not only is this the original setting, but Vienna is also the home of several permanently installed monumental early works by Klimt, which permit comparisons to be drawn with his later work and bear eloquent witness to his creative development. Finally, even today, a full century later, Vienna with its Ringstrasse, its Secession building, and its countless reminders of the Klimt era, still provides the perfect setting for an exhibition of this kind, enhancing its appeal and providing far more incidental information than any other venue could.

An undertaking such as this involves the work of many people. I would like to take this opportunity to thank them all for their dedication and personal commitment. The smooth cooperation between the various teams and individuals and the careful coordination of their tasks deserve special mention and more detailed reference is made to this at the relevant points in the publication.

Sincere thanks are also due to the lenders for their willingness to place their works of art at our disposal for the duration of the exhibition, and not least to the companies whose generous support contributed greatly to the realisation of this project.

Gerbert Frodl

Gustav Klimt—Painter between the Times

GERBERT FRODL

Gustav Klimt's art is unique. For all its originality, however, his painting is part of a general European development that led to different formal and thematic emphases in the different centres—though not necessarily at the same time.

Vienna's special circumstances produced the phenomena in painting that are only incompletely and cursorily described as "Vienna around 1900" or "secessionism". The situation was dominated by Klimt as the outstanding artistic personality.

The Künstlervereinigung Secession was founded in 1897 with Klimt as its first president and its spokesman and figurehead until he resigned in 1905. Its express and clear objective was to bring Austrian art closer to the international art world. The domestic artists were thus called upon to give up their cosy self-sufficiency, to which they had accustomed themselves and their public for many years. The manifold activities launched by the Secession in subsequent years, particularly in the exhibition sector, were impressive proof of these intentions. Foreign contacts were flourishing, the exhibitions in J. M. Olbrich's new building made history, and friendships were formed with artists in other countries that also influenced the art scene at home. This has been extensively described and acknowledged in literature and in numerous exhibition catalogues.

In his painting from the time immediately before the founding of the Secession as well as in his later works, a wide knowledge of European contemporary art reveals Gustav Klimt's international quality. Nevertheless, the results of this process remained unmistakably Viennese, faithful to domestic traditions and critical of, though not impervious to, new influences. When considering his pre-Secessionist oeuvre we notice several things: on the one hand, there is the enormous productivity of the painters' collective consisting of Klimt, his brother Ernst, and Franz Matsch that existed between 1882 and 1892, as well as the changes that took place in this period, which, of course, was partly due to the artists' increasing maturity. On the other hand, there is the clear break following the death of the brother Ernst Klimt (1864–1892), which brought the successful co-operation to an end. Strokes of fate afflicting the family (the father died in the same year) have probably increased the intensive wish to shake off obsolete artistic ties. As the strongest of the three, Gustav Klimt must have thought for a long time about becoming more independent and emancipating himself from the group and its patrons, who still inclined towards historicism. Moreover, after so many successes, the financial considerations, which had certainly once encouraged the three painters to work together, must have become less important, leaving room for individual developments.

In continuation of the "Maler-Compagnie's" proven activity and their earlier historicist decoration programmes, Gustav Klimt and Franz Matsch in 1894 were commissioned by the university of Vienna to create paintings for its ballroom. Klimt was given the subjects *philosophy, medicine* and *jurisprudence.* His handling of these themes unleashed a wave of indignation and quarrels in subsequent years, showing him very clearly how precarious it was to be a committed artist in an atmosphere that had not been sufficiently prepared, even by the Secession and its intentions. Since there are almost no extant writings from Klimt's hand, except for a short curriculum vitae dating from 1893, and remarks about him are only from others, we must rely on assumptions and deductions. As usual, Ludwig von Hevesi's descriptions and judgements are very helpful; a special case is the interview that Berta Zuckerkandl held with the painter in 1905, at a time when he was being strongly attacked. These *faculty pictures*—tragically destroyed at the end of the Second World War—are known only from black-and-white reproductions (except for a single detail reproduced in colour). Here for the first time a Gustav Klimt is speaking to us who is now openly assimilating new impressions from outside. This has nothing in common any more with the allegorical paintings, including his own, in various Ringstraße palais; for the first time in Klimt's work we see the mannerism and ambiguousness of monumental Jugendstil, expressing itself not only formally, but also in the interpretation and the choice of allegorical figures. These monumental allegories, which transpose the given subjects into the realm of mysticism, symbolise the final stage of historicism. At the same time, they can be considered as an attempt to overcome it. The artist's individuality triumphs over the patron and the historicist programme laid down for these Ringstraße buildings. The mystics Jan Toorop (Netherlands), Fernand Khnopff, and Jean Delville (Belgium) who were deeply admired by the Secessionists, clearly form the background, and in the context of the faculty pictures we should also remember Ferdinand Hodler's monumental allegorical compositions (*The Night*). Rather than art at the "service of the human society" (H. Read) in the old sense, this is a dialogue with the individual self, which is not primarily aimed at being accepted by the patrons and the public.

The above-mentioned year of 1892 marks a turning point: Klimt had undoubtedly been convinced that he must shake off the ties of a long-proven and accepted style, and he must have been aware of the fact that he had long since reached the limits of this style and the contents conveyed by it. (He was probably not aware that rather than propagating an old "worn-out" style, he was putting forward another one that would be doomed to the same destiny even during his lifetime.) At that time, there was not much artistic life in Vienna, and foreign contacts were rare. The external circumstances that have been briefly described made 1892 into a crucial year for the thirty-year-old. A little earlier, stylistic tendencies appear in some work for the staircase of the Kunsthistorisches Museum, which can be traced back to Victorian English salon painting. The question of why Klimt first turned to this, and then became interested in the mythologising, symbolistic painting from Belgium and Holland in particular can only be answered by his environment and his being rooted in historicism. French impressionism's "pure painting", the "intellectual" pointillism of Georges Seurat and others must have been unfamiliar to him at that time. Later it was only in the large landscapes of Lake Atter that it became evident that he needed Monet's example, and that his pictures were inconceivable without preparation by the "domestic" Stimmungsmalerei of an artist like Emil Jakob Schindler and his "descendants". Klimt was never a painter of fleeting impressions though his early landscapes (around 1900) might be interpreted as such. At the time of the "Maler-Compagnie" as well as in the period before the founding of the Secession, he worked on scenic, historic subjects, thus following "the trend", so what would be more natural than looking at other fashionable currents, not least for the sake of being up-to-date? (The yearly summer stays at Lake Atter, artistically devoted only to landscape painting, are to be seen as "hors concours" in this context.) The English pre-Raphaelites such as Edward Burne-Jones or Dante Gabriel Rossetti with their effusively poetic painting seeking spiritual depth and creating stereotypical faces and figures became an example. Other, slightly younger English artists also made an impression: highly fashionable painters of the time such as Sir Frederic Leighton, Lawrence Alma-Tadema, or John William Waterhouse, whose works Klimt hardly knew in the original but had seen as reproductions. Not only their generous interpretations of traditional "historicist" subjects, projections of an idealised daily idyllic life, seem to have fascinated the Viennese, also did a trick that was widely used in the late nineteenth century, that of painting on the frame and thus drawing the observer into the composition (also Franz v. Stuck from Munich, Fernand Khnopff, and others such as Hans Makart sometimes used the frame as a support for painting). All this was to be found, unchanged, at the end of the nineteenth century while beside it a new kind of painting emerged, unimpressed by the old developments, that laid the foundation for so-called "modernism".

The commitment to the Viennese painting tradition, which can easily be explained by his ten-year career as a "Ringstraße painter", was temporarily overlaid by intense new impressions and influences, but never extinguished. This tradition had a catalysing effect to the extent that in Klimt's work, impressions and external influences were transformed into an unmistakably personal approach. Rather than being innovators in the sense of "classical modernism", the Secession's foreign favourites were great individualists and mystics representing the end of the old painting in indisputable highlights: Jan Toorop and Fernand Khnopff have already been mentioned, and Max Klinger, Ferdinand Hodler, Edvard Munch, and others also made use of the achievements of the new, not yet fully established Paris "scene". The Secession's penchant for monumental art also manifested itself in the admiration shown for Klinger, Hodler, or Puvis de Chavannes. In the crucial years from 1897 to 1905, the Secession introduced its public to the new European art at a moment when—one could say—there was a breathing space. Impressionism and neo-impressionism were established in a certain sense, though not yet anchored in everybody's awareness, the "Fauves" in Paris and the "Brücke" in Dresden developed at almost the same time in 1905—just as Klimt and the most important Secessionists were already leaving the community.

As a painter of figural compositions, Klimt remained committed to historicism to the extent that he liked to refer to older approaches to the equivalent pictorial themes without caring about the original function. This included allegories as well as prestigious portraits of ladies.

He never tried to describe a woman's grace and beauty, for instance, by the sound of colours or by the movement in space, he always used all his painting talent to represent the sweetness of a skin surface or a look. However he did make use of the symbolism inherent in a colour or a coloured area. The sometimes disquieting beauty of a face, a hand, a shoulder, achieved in this way, with contrasts increasing its effect, is opposed to an ornamentalised garment, a form, abstract in its two-dimensional quality and motionlessness, that seems to be placed in front of a screen rather than in space.

This ambiguity proves to be a dilemma—and that is Klimt's great and unmistakable achievement—though the two elements are never balanced.

Fritza Riedler or *Adele Bloch-Bauer* are nearer to Diego Velázquez's infanta Maria Teresa (middle of the seventeenth century) or to the mosaic with the princess Galla Placidia in front of her gold background from the sixth century in San Vitale, Ravenna, than to Edouard Manet's *Nina de Callias* (1873–74) or Claude Monet's *Danseuse* (1876). In these paintings from the late nineteenth century, the ladies are not represented as being in the space, but they create the space by their movement, which seeks to connect with the observer. Gustav Klimt's female portraits couldn't form a sharper contrast to that. It is no coincidence that the word "icon" has often been used in order to describe the *Judith* picture or the first, golden portrait of Adele Bloch-Bauer. These women are rendered hieratic, like queens in their richest jewelry, in precious raiment—distant, motionless, as objects of adoration. The discrepancy between the content and the tools of composition couldn't be greater. In Gustav Klimt's first female portrait, *Sonja Knips*, 1898, the immobility still seems to be anticipatory, as if the quietness in the studio were only temporary. The influence of the "European" American James Abbott McNeill Whistler (1834–1903) is as apparent as that of Hans Makart, and one is even reminded of Anton Romako (*Portrait of Mathilde Stern*).

Without intending to explain the phenomenon we want to point out the immense difference between the drawings that indeed have an extremely intimate (not only erotic) character and the paintings that try to create a distance from the observer. Is the intimacy followed by raising the subject onto a pedestal? An explanation can probably be found in Klimt himself, in his—if one believes contemporary reports—strength of personality, his effect on women. Around one generation earlier, Hans Makart (1840–84) exerted a similar attraction, with the erotic element, suitably to its period, being lasciviously and more than clearly hidden "between the lines". Makart must be seen as a forerunner of Klimt in another respect as well: The glorification of artistry by the media and the public ("Malerfürst", prince of painters) that wasn't natural around 1870/1880 contributed considerably to the painter's success. The other aspect is the painting itself, relying on the effect of contrasts, on the virtuoso simultaneousness of the tenderest skin surface and the wild impasto of garments and other decorative elements. This was Hans Makart's own, special achievement, distinguishing him from the traditional representative style of an artist like F. X. Winterhalter for instance (*Portrait of the Empress Elisabeth in great ball robe,* 1865). Superficially, Klimt had been near to his admired hero when young, later only internally, when he himself had become the "painters' prince"—of the Secession—who approached familiar subjects in an unfamiliar way.

In the great female portraits we frequently notice—besides the deliberate use of contrasting effects—the attitude, also shown by Makart, of glorifying the woman with the means of painting. This is representation in the traditional sense as well as stylistic and societal Zeitgeist. All this took place in the Viennese hothouse through whose windows one gazed only now and then.

Around 1900, Paris was undoubtedly the centre of the arts and for a great number of young artists from all over Europe the measure of all things. Impressionism and pointillism were acknowledged—though not generally—and had already gained entry into big international exhibitions: The Viennese Secession also included them—at least once (1903)—in its exhibition programme, but they were not used as models. Paris became a centre of attraction for only a few late nineteenth-century Viennese artists, none of whom ever dealt with impressionism in such a way that it left noticeable traces (although, Theodor v. Hörmann should be mentioned as a small exception). There was not a single Austrian among the many painters trying their luck in Paris around 1900 and participating in the realisation of new ideas.

It remains a strange though explicable fact that the Secession's protagonists, first and foremost Gustav Klimt, remained committed to more traditional approaches themselves while presenting new (not the newest) trends of the fine arts in exhibitions that later became famous (for most Viennese this was the first contact with such work). The avant-garde of the early years of the century had lost its importance for them. It is only in Klimt's later works, when he had turned his back on the colour gold, that elements of expressionism show up, in the choice of colours traces of the "Fauves", a "touch" of Henri Matisse and—more palpably—a dialogue with the Japanese art of coloured wood-engravings. The latter was, since its "discovery" by Europe's painters in the 1870s and later a source of trend-setting inspiration both, superficially, in the motifs and, more profoundly, in the compositional arrangement or in how space is represented by using planes. Also in this context, Klimt's large female portraits are contradictory in themselves and in complete accordance with his art's two-sidedness. This is expressed in his life-long penchant for creating allegories, for symbolism and also for naturalism on the one—traditional—side, and the frequent inclination to an abstraction that in the last years of the nineteenth century began to play a role in a whole variety of formulations. Thus even in Klimt's works on the threshold of a new age we find the dualism between reality and identity that has dominated most of the art of the nineteenth century. Compared with Gerstl, Schiele or the German and French expressionists, this link with the old century, to which Klimt owed much of his career, becomes particularly obvious.

.

Fin-de-siècle Vienna and the Ambivalence
of Modernism

HEIDEMARIE UHL

1   Cf. Allan Janik, "Vienna 1900: Reflections on Problems and Methods" in Emil Brix, Patrick Werkner (eds.), *Die Wiener Moderne. Ergebnisse eines Forschungsgespräches der Arbeitsgemeinschaft Wien um 1900 zum Thema »Aktualität und Moderne«*, Vienna/Munich 1990, p. 156.—Janik emphasises the prominence of Paris—»if any city is the birthplace of modernism it has to be Paris«—and sees Vienna's contribution to modernism as being the development of a critical stance (»critical modernism«).
2   Allan Janik/Stephen Toulmin, *Wittgensteins Wien*, Munich/Vienna 1984, p. 9.– For an analysis of the intellectual-artistic milieu from a more long-term "Austrian" perspective cf. William M. Johnston, *The Austrian Mind. An Intellectual and Social History 1848–1938*, Berkeley/Los Angeles/ London 1972.
3   On the uncertainty as regards terms and dates cf. Dagmar Lorenz, *Die Wiener Moderne*, Sammlung Metzler 290, Stuttgart/Weimar 1995.—The strongest focus has been on the artistic, intellectual and scientific achievements in the period from 1890 to 1910. Cf. Gotthard Wunberg (ed.), *Die Wiener Moderne. Literatur, Kunst und Musik zwischen 1890 und 1910*, Stuttgart 1981. 4 Ernst Topitsch, "Wien um 1900—und heute", in Peter Berner, Emil Brix, Wolfgang Mantl (eds.), *Wien um 1900. Aufbruch in die Moderne*, Vienna 1986, p. 28.
5   Jacques Le Rider, *Das Ende der Illusion. Die Wiener Moderne und die Krisen der Identität*, Vienna 1990, p. 20f.
6   Michael John/Albert Lichtblau, *Schmelztiegel Wien—einst und jetzt. Zur Geschichte und Gegenwart von Zuwanderung und Minderheiten*, Vienna/Cologne 1990, p. 12.
7   Cf. Renate Banik-Schweitzer, Gerhard Meißl, *Industriestadt Wien. Die Durchsetzung der industriellen Massenproduktion in der Habsburgerresidenz*, Vienna 1983.
8   Cf. Carl E. Schorske, *Fin-de-Siecle Vienna: Politics & Culture*, London 1981, and Franz Baltzarek/Alfred Hoffmann/Hannes Stekl, *Wirtschaft und Gesellschaft der Wiener Stadterweiterung, Die Wiener Ringstraße 5*, Wiesbaden 1975.

Since its "discovery" in the early 1980s—at the latest with the publication of Carl E. Schorske's study *Fin de siècle Vienna: Politics and Culture* (1980), turn-of-the-century Vienna has come to be regarded as an essential part of the agenda of a new understanding of modernism. Fin de siècle Vienna assumed a great fascination as an illustrative example of the contradictions, discontinuities and ambivalences in the process of modernisation in the early modern era: The main question raised by scholars continues to be how a city with so little faith in progress, wracked by political and economic crises, and lagging ever further behind in the dynamics of modernisation could possibly become a "birthplace of modernism"[1] and the scene of "one of the most fruitful, original and creative periods in the realms of art and architecture, music and literature, psychology and philosophy"?[2] The continued interest in fin-de-siècle Vienna thus focuses on the interaction between the creative potential of Viennese modernism—a designation which also first asserted itself in the 1980s[3]—and the city's "anti-modern" social climate of Catholic conservativism, anti-Semitism and virulently nationalistic politics, even at local government level, following the loss of power of the Liberals and the election victory of the Christian Socialists under Karl Lueger in the mid–1890s. Today's nostalgic reminiscences of a "glorious past" on which Austria can look back "with pride"[4] are countered by the fact that the protagonists of Viennese modernism felt their situation to be "more a hindrance, exile almost" and saw Vienna not as the centre of modernism but as a "bastion of all that is archaic".[5]

This perception can be based mainly on three developments: Vienna was lagging more and more behind in the competition between the major urban centres; the ultimately insoluble tensions between a multi-ethnic migration society and the political concepts of national homogeneity ("German Vienna"); and the politico-cultural predominance of an anti-Semitic, anti-Slav, German-nationalist mentality which became stylised as the "typical Viennese" folk character. Concepts such as that of a supra-national, multi-ethnic metropolis, which corresponded more to the Habsburg concept of state, remained for the most part marginal, or were doomed to failure.

This diagnosis of Vienna as retrograde and provincial seems at first to contradict its development into a large modern city during the second half of the nineteenth century. Like other major European cities, Vienna in the prosperous years of the *Gründerzeit* experienced a population explosion (the number of inhabitants in the greater Viennese municipal area, calculated according to today's territorial area, rose from 900,998 in 1869 to 2,083,630 in 1910[6]), by structural modernisation and by industrialisation.[7] More than anything else, the projects for expanding the city were the visible expression of this spectacular modernisation boom. In 1857, despite the military's reservations,

Kaiser Franz Joseph ordered that the fortifications separating the medieval town centre from the suburbs be razed to the ground, and thereby created the prerequisite for the city's expansion into an urban metropolis. The social modernisation processes found symbolic expression in the stately buildings along the Ringstrasse—as a "projection of values in space and stone" and as a medium of cultural self-representation, the street stood for the political emancipation and social rise of the liberal bourgeoisie. The City Hall, the parliament buildings, the university, the Burgtheater, and the Hofoper signalled the assertion of the bourgeois system of liberal values. "Not palaces, fortifications or churches dominated the Ringstrasse, but centres of constitutional government and an enlightened culture".[8]

The fact that Vienna still felt it was lagging behind in the dynamics of urban modernisation had to do with its relative backwardness compared to Paris or London, and, above all, with the rise of the new German capital Berlin to the status of a modern metropolis and a rival in the German-speaking world. The dynamic "cosmopolitan city" of Berlin, its effective government administration, and the modernity of the life-style there constituted a counter-image and as such became a benchmark by which Vienna was perceived as an increasingly provincial "old imperial town on the Danube".[9] Robert Musil's retrospective characterisation of a backward "Kakanien" became the topos of this self-image: "There, in Kakanien ... there was tempo, but not too much tempo ... Of course, cars ran along those streets, but not too many cars! ... But the capital city was somewhat smaller than the other large cities in the world, yet considerably larger than large cities usually are ..."[10] Both the regionally different speeds of economic growth[11] and, above all, the permanent political crises caused by the unsolved national question[12] made the Austro-Hungarian Empire seem like the essence of backwardness, like a "European China".[13] Accordingly, enormous importance was attached to culture, especially theatre, on which the aspiration to a position of cultural importance in the German-speaking region continued to be based.[14]

Even within the Austro-Hungarian Empire, competition between the large cities had nationalist-political connotations: Both Budapest, nurtured as the capital of the Hungarian half of the empire after the *Ausgleich* (settlement) of 1867,[15] and Prague developed into nationally-defined cities, whose self-image thrived on their being culturally and politically different from Vienna.

The main problem for Vienna at the close of the nineteenth century, however, was the national question, against the backdrop of the migration of ethnically, nationally and religiously heterogeneous groups. A large portion of the immigrants came from non-German-speaking regions in the empire; Vienna was attractive above all for Jews.[16] In this central European region marked by ethnic, linguistic and cultural pluralism, urbanisation and demographic revolution thus resulted not only in a socially differentiated, but also an ethnically and culturally heterogeneous population.[17] With the strengthening and radicalisation of nationalist movements, national conflicts began to prevail over the urgency of social issues such as the situation of the working class.[18] In the second half of the nineteenth century, Vienna, like other central European cities, developed not so much into a "melting pot" as a "battlefield of nationalist chauvinisms, ethnic and social opposites, racism of all kinds, and anti-Semitism."[19]

In contrast to Germany and France, the policy of national homogenisation in the crisis zone of Central Europe had the effect not of melding ever wider strata of people

9   Cf. Juliane Mikoletzky, "Die Wiener Sicht auf Berlin, 1870–1934" in Gerhard Brunn, Jürgen Reulecke (eds.): Metropolis Berlin. Berlin als deutsche Hauptstadt im Vergleich europäischer Hauptstädte 1871–1939, Bonn/Berlin 1992, pp. 471–528.

10   Quoted from Walter Weiss, "Zur Kulturgeschichte der Zeit Franz Josephs in Österreich" in Das Zeitalter Kaiser Franz Josephs. 2. Teil: 1880–1918 Glanz und Elend. Niederösterreichische Landesausstellung, Schloss Grafenegg 1987, p. 174.

11   On the different pace of growth in advanced and underdeveloped regions in the Habsburg Empire cf. David F. Good, "Ökonomische Ungleichheit im Vielvölkerstaat. Zur Rolle der Metropole Wien" in Jürgen Nautz, Richard Vahrenkamp (eds.), Die Wiener Jahrhundertwende. Einflüsse—Umwelt—Wirkungen, Studien zu Politik und Verwaltung 46, Vienna/Cologne/Graz 1993, pp. 720–746.

12   On the nationalities issues cf. Robert A. Kann, "Zur Problematik der Nationalitätenfrage in der Habsburgermonarchie 1848–1918. Eine Zusammenfassung" in Adam Wandruszka, Peter Urbanitsch (eds.), Die Habsburgermonarchie 1848–1918. Bd. 3: Die Völker des Reiches, Vienna 1980, pp. 1304–1338; Gerald Stourzh, "Ethnisierung der Politik in Altösterreich" in Wiener Journal 7 (1999), pp. 35–40.

13   Weiss 1987, p. 174.

14   Cf. Mikoletzky 1992, pp. 517ff.

15   Cf. Zsuzsa L. Nagy, "Transformations in the City Politics of Budapest: 1873–1941" in Thomas Bender, Carl E. Schorske (eds.), Budapest and New York. Studies in Metropolitan Transformation 1870–1930, New York 1994, pp. 35–54; Gerhard Melinz, Susan Zimmermann (eds.), Wien—Prag—Budapest. Blütezeit der Habsburgermetropolen. Urbanisierung, Kommunalpolitik, gesellschaftliche Konflikte (1867–1918), Edition Forschung, Vienna 1996.

16   In 1910, 175,318 Jews lived in Vienna, and their percentage of the overall population was 8.6%. Cf. Marsha L. Rozenblit, Die Juden Wiens 1867–1914. Assimilation und Identität, Forschungen zur Geschichte des Donauraumes 11, Vienna/Cologne/Graz 1988, p. 24.

17   Cf. Moritz Csáky, "Die Vielfalt der Habsburgermonarchie und die nationale Frage" in Urs Altermatt (ed.), Nation, Ethnizität und Staat in Mitteleuropa, Buchreihe des Institutes für den Donauraum und Mitteleuropa 4, Vienna/Cologne/Weimar 1996, pp. 44–64.

18   Hubert Ch. Ehalt, Gernot Heiß, Hannes Stekl (eds.), Glücklich ist, wer vergisst? Das andere Wien um 1900, Kulturstudien 6, Vienna/Cologne/Graz 1986.

19   Jacques Le Rider, Mitteleuropa. Auf den Spuren eines Begriffes. Essay, Vienna 1994, p. 78.

20 In the *Kronprinzenwerk* the description of the Viennese only includes the "genuine Viennese", "direct, true and unsullied descendants of the original tribe": "for this reason, and regardless of the strong invasion of representatives of other races, tribes and nationalities, when one speak of "Vienna and the Viennese" in their totality, one can and will only have in mind by the latter mostly the real Viennese." Friedrich Schlögl, "Wiener Volksleben" in *Die österreich-ungarische Monarchie in Wort und Bild. Wien und Niederösterreich*, Vienna 1886, p. 92.
21 Cf. Brigitte Hamann, *Hitlers Wien. Lehrjahre eines Diktators*. 2nd edition, Munich 1998, pp. 437ff.
22 Cf. Johannes Hawlik, *Der Bürgerkaiser. Karl Lueger und seine Zeit*, Vienna/Munich 1985, p. 193.—On Lueger's cultural and political ideas cf. Günther Berger, *Bürgermeister Dr. Karl Lueger und seine Beziehungen zur Kunst*, Frankfurt/M. a. o. 1998.
23 The number of Viennese Czechs cannot be established precisely as it was estimated differently, depending on the national interests and conflicts; even the everyday use of language registered in the census does not provide an exact image because in Vienna, as in other cities, ethnic or national minorities adapted under social pressure. John and Lichtblau assume that there were about 250,000 to 300,000 Czechs and Slovaks in Vienna at the turn of the century. Cf. John/Lichtblau 1990, p. 18.—On the situation of the Czechs in Vienna cf. Monika Glettler, *Die Wiener Tschechen um 1900. Strukturanalyse einer nationalen Minderheit in der Großstadt*, Vienna 1972.—On ambivalent depictions of Vienna from the view of the "others" cf. Gertraud Marinelli-König, Nina Pavlova (eds.), *Wien als Magnet? Schriftsteller aus Ost-, Ostmittel- und Südosteuropa über die Stadt*, Österreichische Akademie der Wissenschaften. Veröffentlichungen der Kommission für Literaturwissenschaft 17, Vienna 1996.
24 Cf. Steven Beller, "Die Geschichte zweier Städte. Herzls Wien, Hitlers Wien" in *Transit. Europäische Revue*, 10 (1995), pp. 79–94.
25 Cf. Lisa Fischer, Emil Brix (eds.), *Die Frauen der Wiener Moderne*, Vienna-Munich 1997; Harriet Anderson, *Vision und Leidenschaft. Die Frauenbewegung im Fin de Siècle Wiens*, Vienna 1994; David F. Good, Margarete Grandner, Mary J. Maynes (eds.), *Frauen in Österreich. Beiträge zu ihrer Situation im*

into one imagined national community, but of intensifying the competition between rivalling national identities. Concepts of national "purity", which dominated public debate and political culture in Vienna even before the election victory of Karl Lueger's anti-Semitic and anti-Slav Christian Socialist Party, were mobilised mainly against the Czech and Jewish populations. The strategies of excluding these "foreign" or "alien" groups from all that had been established as specifically "Viennese" ranged from the normative self-descriptions of the city and its population, as laid down in the *Kronprinzenwerk*,[20] via the clerical and German-nationalist press and the anti-Semitic and racist caricatures presented in satirical periodicals such as *Kikeri*,[21] to specific political measures such as Karl Lueger's introduction of a citizen's oath that swore to preserve the "German character" of the city.[22] Political pressure and the ostracisation of everything "alien" meant that only a minority of those Viennese who originated from the non-German-speaking regions of the empire acknowledged their native tongue.[23]

The constantly propagated threat of "Überfremdung" (domination by foreign influences) particularly affected the Jewish population, for whom orientation around the ideal of enlightenment and liberal German culture had become a defining moment in bourgeois emancipation. The eagerness for education, above all, of the "second generation" of Viennese Jews, who were much more strongly represented in secondary schools and universities than their percentage of the population would have led one to expect, signalled a willingness by the Jewish population to be assimilated. Social integration was denied them, however, by an anti-Semitic environment. It was the omnipresent anti-Semitism in turn-of-the-century Vienna that convinced Theodor Herzl of the vanity of all attempts at assimilation and the need for a Jewish state; it also politically influenced Adolf Hitler.[24]

The current interest in fin-de-siècle Vienna sees in the faults and paradoxes of the modernisation process—expressed in the tense relationship between artistic modernism and the "antimodern" social context—an affinity to current experiences with our crisis-ridden, ambivalent and fragmented modernisation process. The declining confidence in progress, the "postmodern" criticism of the notions of a teleological "project of modernism", found in fin de siècle Vienna a sounding board for a collective and individual consciousness of crisis and of the contradictions in the prevailing gender-specific identities.[25]

The reconstructions of fin-de-siècle Vienna which, since the 1980s, have shaped the scholarly and cultural image of the city at the end of the Austro-Hungarian Empire, can thus be read as *lieux de mémoire*, as an attempt to make Vienna relevant to today's cultural memory, influenced by many and varied current horizons of experience.

This tension between current socio-political issues and a perspective on the past is also reflected in the different approaches taken in explaining the enormous creative energy of the artistic-intellectual milieu in fin-de-siècle Vienna. According to Carl E. Schorske, it was the crisis of liberalism and the political disillusion of the bourgeoisie at the end of the liberal era that triggered a tendency to seek out the cultural sphere as a place of refuge from a reality perceived as increasingly threatening, and the pursuit of cultural and creative activity as a surrogate for potential political action.[26] For Jacques Le Rider[27] and Steven Beller[28], the creative potential of fin-de-siècle Vienna was engendered by the search for identity of the intellectual Jewish elites in anti-Semitic surroundings, while Moritz Csaky points, above all, to the relevance of the cultural-ethnic pluralism of the Central European region; a large number of the artists and intellectuals did not come from Vienna, but from other parts of the multi-ethnic empire.[29] The contradictory national and cultural identifications, and the problem of developing an Austrian cultural identity distinct from the German culture are the coordinates around which Michael Pollak bases his analysis of the phenomenon of fin-de-siècle Vienna,[30] and on which Hermann Bahr's thesis of the construction of a specific Austrian modernism rests, according to Peter Sprengel and Gregor Striem in a comparative analysis of modernism in Berlin and Vienna.[31]

The negative relationship between art and society still forms the common horizon for the different perceptions of Viennese modernism and its individual and collective experiences: "Modernism in art pointed to the other side of modernisation. Everything that was suppressed or restrained in order to promote the process of modernisation was brought to the light of day by modernism: the dream of a beautiful aesthetic life, the unfathomable depths of man's drives, the anxiety, the potential for violence. What Viennese modernism achieved was to highlight the ambivalence of modernisation" (Ernst Hanisch).[32]

Despite the tendency to present fin-de-siècle Vienna as a new classical era in a glorious cultural legacy—since the exhibition "Traum und Wirklichkeit. Wien 1870–1930 (Dream and Reality in Vienna 1870–1930)"[33] the fin de siècle has become "a determining factor in the Austrian image of itself and of the Other"[34]—it must still be acknowledged that the Vienna of Klimt, Schnitzler, Freud and Wittgenstein, to mention just the most prominent icons in an image of Vienna that has even penetrated the everyday world of commodities, is inseparably linked with the negative potential of modernism, the Vienna of Lueger and Hitler.

19. und 20. Jahrhundert, Vienna/Cologne/Weimar 1993.
26 Cf. Schorske 1994, p. 8.
27 Cf. Le Rider 1990.
28 Cf. Steven Beller, Wien und die Juden 1867–1938, Böhlaus zeitgeschichtliche Bibliothek 23, Vienna/Cologne/Weimar 1993, and Robert S. Wistrich, Die Juden Wiens im Zeitalter Kaiser Franz-Josephs, Anton Gindely Reihe 4, Vienna/Cologne/Weimar 1999, pp. 405ff.
29 Cf. Moritz Csáky, "Die Wiener Moderne. Ein Beitrag zur Theorie der Moderne in Zentraleuropa" in Rudolf Haller (ed.), nach kakanien. Annäherung an die Moderne, Studien zur Moderne 1, Vienna/Cologne/Weimar 1996, pp. 59–102; Moritz Csáky, Ideologie der Operette und Wiener Moderne, Ein kulturhistorischer Essay zur österreichischen Identität, Vienna/Cologne/Weimar 1996.
30 Michael Pollak, Wien 1900. Eine verletzte Identität, Edition discours 6, Konstanz 1997, p. 22.
31 Peter Sprengel, Gregor Streim, Berliner und Wiener Moderne. Vermittlungen und Abgrenzungen in Literatur, Theater, Publizistik. With an article by Barbara Noth. Literatur in der Geschichte, Geschichte in der Literatur 45, Vienna/Cologne/Weimar 1998.
32 Ernst Hanisch, Der lange Schatten des Staates. Österreichische Gesellschaftsgeschichte im 20. Jahrhundert. Österreichische Geschichte 1890–1990, Vienna 1994, p. 261.
33 Traum und Wirklichkeit. Wien 1870–1930, 93rd Special exhibition at the Historische Museum der Stadt Wien, 28 March to 6 October 1985.
34 Susanne Breuss/Karin Liebhart/Andreas Pribersky, Inszenierungen. Stichwörter zu Österreich. With a preface by Anton Pelinka, Vienna 1995, pp. 131–134 (keyword Fin de siècle).

The Habsburg State and Gustav Klimt
Scenes from a fruitful Relationship

JEROEN VAN HEERDE

Gustav Klimt's Vienna, the "k.k. Reichshaupt- und Residenzstadt" (imperial and royal capital), was mainly a creation of the Habsburg emperors, who for centuries had functionalised art and architecture to enhance their reputation, legitimise their power and preserve their memory for posterity. When Gustav Klimt founded the Künstler-Compagnie in 1879, together with his brother Ernst and his student friend Franz Matsch, Vienna was in the throes of one of the Habsburgs' most comprehensive restructuring projects: the construction of the Ringstrasse. Having survived the revolution of 1848, Vienna was to be transformed into a splendid metropolis and the focal point of a united empire, corroborating and substantiating the supreme majesty and function of the emperor in outward forms. Public buildings, complete with the emperor's double eagle and monogram, were to demonstrate the power of the re-established dynasty. "It is my will ..." are the opening words of the decree of 1857 by which Kaiser Franz Joseph ordered the city fortifications to be razed to the ground and an imposing boulevard street built in their stead.

From the late eighteenth century onwards, art patronage by the royal dynasty, the nobility and the church had declined sharply. Now, state commissions offered great opportunities for artists and craftsmen. In the 1880s, even such young artists as the Klimt brothers received their first important state commissions, in the broadest sense of the term: the decoration of various theatres, ceiling paintings for the Empress Elisabeth's Hermes Villa (1885), the paintings for the two main staircases in the Hofburgtheater (1886). The painting *The Auditorium of the Old Burgtheater* (ill. p. 63), commissioned by the Vienna city council, was awarded the highly prestigious Kaiserpreis, or Imperial Prize, donated by the Kaiser at the annual exhibition of the Künstlerhaus in 1890.

When the Künstler-Compagnie was commissed to paint forty works for the spandrels of the staircase of the Kunsthistorisches Museum in 1890, it was clear that the Klimt brothers had finally established themselves. Not only was the museum intended to accommodate the art collection of the imperial house, but also the decorative theme of the building itself was to illustrate the dynasty's passion for collecting and its patronage of the arts over the centuries—a patronage that now helped to provide Gustav Klimt with recognition, success, and a secure income.

Until 1897, the world of Austrian art was clearly organised: arts and crafts schools, museums, the Akademie der bildenden Künste and the Künstlergenossenschaft, all interlinked and financed and controlled by the state, produced art that was appropriate for representational use by the state. The founding of the Secession in 1897 was not just a revolution of the avant-garde, led by Gustav Klimt and proclaiming a new art and a new task for art in society, but also signified a splintering of the art scene. In the years that followed, this caesura was further intensified by the foundation of other associations, both in Vienna (Hagenbund, Wiener Werkstätte, Klimt-Gruppe) and in the Crownlands.

Of major importance in the philosophy of the Secessionist artists, alongside the presentation of works of modernism from other countries, was their resolve to lend an "honest" expression to their own time. This "honest art", a reunification of art and craft (*gesamtkunstwerk*), was allotted an important, almost missionary social task: to provide an aesthetic solution to social problems. If art were to be integrated into people's everyday lives, it would exert a harmonising and unifying force.

The Secessionists were aware of the fact that their ambitious mission was only feasible with the support of the state. In 1901, Carl Moll wrote on behalf of the Secession to the "hohe k.k. Regierung" (high imperial and royal government), "Only the state, rather than the art-loving private citizen, can do justice to the strong tendency towards monumentality in our art."[1]

Where was the Habsburg state when modernism emerged in Austria and turned the world of art upside down? How did the Habsburgs and their officials, the greying monarch and his guardians "of the golden age of security" (Stefan Zweig) react to the renewal proclaimed by the representatives of the avant-garde? Surely with mistrust, rejection and exclusion, intent as they were on preserving the time-honoured useful iconography of historicism. This likely but false estimation is to be found repeatedly in the historical literature.[2]

18th Secession exhibition, Vienna 1903. Room with Klimt's paintings *Medicine* and *Philosophy*. Bildarchiv Österreichische Nationalbibliothek, Wien.

From the standpoint of the Habsburg state, the views and objectives of the secessionists had many positive aspects: they showed respect for Austrian art of the past and they underscored what was "pan-Austrian, patriotic", that is to say, they were—like the Habsburg concept of state itself—absolutely supranationalist. They endorsed the existing social structure and, what is more, were extremely loyal to the Habsburgs. The praised heaped on the art of the Secession abroad enhanced the international prestige of the Habsburg state. The modern ornamentation could demonstrate the vitality and powers of renewal of the old state form, something to which the optimism radiating from the new art also contributed. The Secession aimed to address everyone, irrespective of their social or ethnic origins, and thus represented a trend that ran counter to the centrifugal forces in the country. Furthermore, the new design was able to provide new impulses for the local crafts and for industrial production.

As a result, the Habsburg state did not hesitate at all to embrace the avant-gardists. The Habsburg administration purchased their works, awarded commissions and positions, presented titles and orders. The "young wild ones" were thus successfully integrated into the existing politico-social system. This policy was part of a series of state-guided modernisation efforts aimed at renewing and reforming social, economic and political life, and characterised the last decades of the Austro-Hungarian Empire. The concept of state that prevailed in that era is reflected in its arts policy: the Habsburg state, based on the rule of law, formed the secure pluralist framework for the progress

1   *Ver Sacrum*, No. 20, 15. 10. 1901. For a detailed outline of the Habsburgs' promotion of the arts at the turn of the century and an analysis of their motives see Jeroen Bastiaan van Heerde, *Staat und Kunst. Staatliche Kunstförderung 1895 bis 1918*, Vienna, Cologne and Weimar 1993.
2   Some examples are Maria Rennhofer, *Kunstzeitschriften der Jahrhundertwende in Deutschland und Österreich, 1895–1914*, Vienna and Munich 1987, p. 15: "The new art was more or less ignored by the officials", Renata Kassal-Mikula, "Der Historismus", in *Wien um 1900: Kunst und Kultur*, Vienna 1985, p. 12: "Official recognition and support was not granted to the 'stylist' art and the representatives of the Secession...", Lucian Meysels, *In meinem Salon ist Öster-*

of all the nations of the empire. The Secession, and other new artists' associations founded shortly afterwards, was integrated into the state promotion of the arts and constituted a tool for maintaining that state, as had been the case until then with the Künstlergenossenschaft.

For their part, the Secessionists were happy to place their works at the disposal of the state. There can be no doubt that modernism in Austria had much to gain from the positive attitude of the government. Apart from the many and varied state commissions and opportunities for artists to make their mark at various official exhibitions at home and abroad or in teaching institutes, the approval given to modern art by the state or the Kaiser in the public domain must be regarded as highly significant, above all, in a society where the ruling class enjoyed considerable prestige.

On behalf of the Secession, Gustav Klimt, Rudolf von Alt and Carl Moll wrote to the Kaiser requesting "... most respectfully that ... the Emperor ... glorious patron of all that is noble and beautiful ... deign to grant the highest endorsement to their first step towards achieving their objectives ..."[3] They were granted an audience, and on 6 April 1898 Kaiser Franz Joseph made his famous visit to the first Secession exhibition. The Hagenbund Exhibition of 1903 was also given the honour of an imperial visit, as was Galerie Miethke in 1905. The situation in the German Reich was totally different. There, modern art struggled long and hard under the rule of Kaiser Wilhelm II, who rejected any kind of experimental modern art. State patronage was reserved almost exclusively for the traditional camp. When the Berlin Secession opened its first exhibition in 1898, the commanding officer of the city forbade his officers to visit the gallery in uniform, thereby equating the Secession with an "establishment of dubious repute."[4]

In Austria by contrast, the Minister of Education, Wilhelm Ritter von Hartel, spoke in 1901 of a "fresh and spirited wind", of the "capital city of the Habsburgs joining forces with the latest efforts in art", and of a "thriving artistic life that was beginning to pulsate in all the regions of our fatherland".[5] Words were followed by actions. Representatives of modernism were invited to advise officials and could thereby exert an influence on state decisions to promote the arts. In 1900, four of the twelve members of the Ministry of Education's art commission were representatives of modernism: Otto Wagner, Carl Moll, Felician Freiherr von Myrbach and Friedrich Ohmann.

By nominating several members of the Secession to the preparatory commission for the World Exposition in Paris in 1900 the Ministry did not hesitate to push aside the long-standing "monopoly" of the Künstlergenossenschaft. From then on, pluralism was a typical feature of presentations of Austrian art abroad. This also applied to the World Exposition in St Louis in 1904, where Austria was present in "secessionist style". Arts and crafts schools and artists' associations from all over the Austro-Hungarian Empire showed their works.[6] The message was clear: Inside the Habsburg state was a multiplicity of flourishing national cultures which constituted Austria's strength; in terms of progressiveness, Austrian art (that is, Austria) was in no way lagging behind other states.

Similarly, modernism gained entrance to the major art academies. A typical example of this is the Viennese Kunstgewerbeschule (Arts and Crafts School), which passed into secessionist hands within a few years.[7] The Austrian Museum of Art and

Industry also became a power base of the avant-garde with the nomination in 1897 of Arthur von Scala as its director.

The foundation of a museum of contemporary art was an important objective of the secessionists in the context of their efforts to make modern art more easily accessible to the general public. Though positive in its response to the idea, the Ministry of Education was unable to allay the reservations of the Ministry of Finance. On 13 April 1903, however, the enterprise was given a considerable boost by the publication of a letter written by Kaiser Franz Joseph, in which he ordered the foundation of a Modern Gallery in Prague opining that, "It would be a further important signal of progress if easily accessible collections existed in those capital cities [of the Crownlands] ..."[8] The Modern Gallery in Prague and the Landesmuseum in Sarajevo were soon established, thanks to an imperial donation and a state loan. Financing a Modern Gallery in Vienna remained a problem, however. In the end it was again the emperor who made rooms available provisionally in the Lower Belvedere, so that "... the best works by modern artists, with particular emphasis on local production" could be preserved "as a spiritual legacy for future generations".[9]

The name Moderne Galerie was altered to Österreichishe Staatsgalerie in 1912, as the task of the gallery was to present a representative survey of developments in Austrian art. The space problem was only solved after the demise of the monarchy, when both the lower and the upper belvederes were refurbished.

Many of the works purchased by the state after 1850 were housed at the Moderne Galerie after it opened in 1903. Furthermore, works then began to be acquired specifically for the new museum. Until the 1890s, state purchases of art were undertaken mainly during the major Viennese art exhibitions (particularly those of the Künstlergenossenschaft). Now the art officials and members of the art commission also visited exhibitions by the Secession, the Hagenbund, the Künstlergenossenschaft etc., the most important galleries (above all, Miethke[10] and Pisko in Vienna and Cassirer in Berlin), as well as auctions. Over the years, the Ministry of Education acquired numerous works by Austrian and foreign artists, including many modernist works. For example, it bought Klimt's *After the Rain* (Novotny-Dobai No. 107) in 1900, *On the Attersee II* (Novotny-Dobai No. 116a) in 1901, *The Kiss* (ill. p. 231) in 1908, *Farmhouse* (Novotny-Dobai No. 173) in 1912, and twelve figurative drawings in 1915. This new state purchasing policy contributed to the fact that in 1918 there were significant public art collections in all the regions of the empire, and these were characterised by diversity, ethnic multiplicity, and modernity. In Vienna, the foundations for today's famous collection in the Belvedere had been laid—not least thanks to the Klimt brothers.

Modernism, just one of several art movements in Habsburg Austria around 1900, was able to corner a prominent position in the country's art world within only a few years due to the unusually munificent promotion by the state. The importance of this victory soon becomes obvious when compared with the limited social acceptance the new art received, as Gustav Klimt was to experience personally. One hundred years later, the so-called Klimt Affair, a "cause célèbre" in Vienna at the turn of the century, is still interesting in that it illustrates the discrepancy that had arisen between the state espousal of modernism and the reactions of the broader Austrian public.[11]

When Klimt's *Philosophy*, the first of the so-called "faculty paintings" commissioned from him for the university by the Ministry of Education, was exhibited publicly

reich. Berta Zuckerkandl und ihre Zeit, Vienna and Munich 1984, p. 95: "... the k.k. Ministry of Education had decided, by way of exception, to grant a state commission to one of the ostracised Secessionists.", Renate Redl, *Berta Zuckerkandl und die Wiener Gesellschaft*, Diss. Vienna 1978, pp.113f.: "Bureaucratic decision-making in matters of art focused on tried-and-tested tradition cultural works and rejected thematic and formal innovation.", Heinz Rieder, *Geburt der Moderne. Wiener Kunst um 1900*, Graz and Vienna 1964, p. 117: "...Modernism provokes the rational Philistine to the extreme, a final, helpless antidote!—police prohibition, 'degenerate art', literature and music."

3   Allgemeines Verwaltungsarchiv (AVA), Ministerium für Kultus und Unterricht (KUM), Präsidium Unterricht (PU), Inventory Number (Inv. No.) 927/1898.

4   Peter Paret, *Die Berliner Secession. Moderne Kunst und ihre Feinde im kaiserlichen Deutschland*, place of publication not given, 1981, S. 101.

5   Address by Wilhelm von Hartel at the 1st Session of the Arts Council, AVA, KUM, Inv. No. 22591/1900, minutes of the meeting of the Arts Council on 25. 5. 1901.

6   After disagreements about the selection of its contribution, the Secession withdrew.

7   In the satirical magazine *Die Fackel*, Karl Kraus (correctly) claimed that the Austrian state had granted modernism entry to the arts and crafts schools firstly, for economic reasons and secondly, in order to "modernise" its image: "Almost concomitant with this revolution in artists' circles, an upheaval in the arts and crafts was initiated from above ... in this field we in Austria are officially modern." *Die Fackel*, No. 29, January 1900, pp. 18f.

8   AVA, KUM, PU, Inv. No. 910/1901.

at the Secession in March 1900, it caused a scandal. The Ministry ignored the criticism, some of it from the university professors, and in doing so gained the strong approval of the Secessionist circles. That same year in fact, the Ministry even decided to include *Philosophy* in the Paris World Exposition, where it was awarded the Grand Prix, and also purchased Klimt's *After the Rain* at the exhibition of the Künstlergenossenschaft.[12] In 1901, Klimt's second university mural, *Medicine*, unleashed an even greater controversy. At that point, the state's arts policy became a political issue and had to be defended before parliament by the minister responsible, Wilhelm Ritter von Hartel, when deputies asked if this was now "official Austrian art". The minister made reference to "the complete freedom of the creative artist", albeit without actually rebuking Klimt's opponents, much to the disappointment of Klimt's supporters.[13] When the university rejected the Klimt paintings in 1905, the ministry did not oppose the decision, whereupon Klimt kept the faculty paintings, because, as he claimed, the ministry was no longer "on the side of the artist" and had made it clear that the latter "had become an embarrassment to it."[14]

Von Hartel's speech in parliament in 1901 is often evaluated as a turning point in the state's arts policy, indicating that an "official cooling" had set in as regards modern art.[15] This interpretation is not confirmed by contemporary sources. So as to avoid further controversy, and under pressure from parliament and the public, the state may well have distanced itself from Klimt to a certain extent, but this was only superficial and temporary, and did not effect the avant-garde in general. Even in the years after the so-called Klimt Affair, the Ministry of Education still showed an interest in purchasing the artist's works. Thus at the Secession exhibition in March 1901 it bought Klimt's *On the Attersee* (Novotny-Dobai No. 116a). In late 1903, the art officials tried to buy *Emilie Flöge* (ill. p. 101) for the Moderne Galerie, despite the fact that at that point in time the three university paintings on show were at the centre of such heated debate. The purchase attempt failed in the end because of the high price.[16] Throughout the whole affair, the Ministry continued to acknowledge the artistic value of the university paintings, as is clear from a report dated 1903 by the art official Ritter von Wiener to the minister: "There can be absolutely no doubt that, apart from certain eccentricities, the large ceiling paintings by Klimt are artistic achievements of the first order. What must be doubted, however, is whether the understanding of the broader public today is mature enough to be able to grasp such creations with impartiality."[17] The Klimt Affair was a lesson not so much for the state as for the Secessionists. However much they may have been willing to defend their artistic mission, it was clear that modern art would only be accepted by the general public with reservations. At that point in time, the goal of the secessionists to exert a harmonising influence on society through a widely disseminated contemporary art must have seemed if not unrealistic, then at least problematic. Even their motto "To every age its art, to art its freedom" proved difficult to realise, especially as the Secessionists on the one hand demanded freedom for art, while on the other expecting help from the state in case of opposition.

Even after 1903, the avant-garde could still count on the support of the state. This was evident at the Kunstschau 1908, an initiative of the Klimt Group, for which Klimt held the opening speech. This presentation of modern art and design was only possible with the help of considerable state subsidies: the Ministry of the Interior made the area on Karlsplatz available, the Ministry of Education gave a subsidy of 54,000 Crowns, which amounted to more than the revenue from the exhibition. The Ministry

9   Petition by the most obedient Minister Wilhelm von Hartel to the Emperor dated 19.IV.1903. AVA, KUM, PU, Inv. No. 842/1903 and HHStA, KZ, Zl. 1010/1903.
10   Cf. the important contribution by Tobias G. Natter, "Ausstellungen der Galerie Miethke, 1904–1912" in *Carl Moll, Österreichische Galerie Belvedere*, 10.9–22. 11. 1998, ed. by Tobias G. Natter and Gerbert Frodl, Salzburg, not dated.
11   On the Klimt Affair cf. Christoph Doswald, "Die Fakultätsbilder" in *Gustav Klimt, Kunsthaus Zürich*, 11.9–13. 12. 1992, ed. by Toni Stooss and Christoph Doswald, Ostfildern 1992; James Shedel, *Art and Society. The new Art Movement in Vienna, 1897–1914*, Palo Alto 1981, pp. 109–134; Jane Wiegenstein, *Artists in a Changing Environment: The Viennese Art World 1860–1918*, Diss. Bloomington 1980, pp. 241–251; Peter Vergo, *Art in Vienna 1898–1918. Klimt, Kokoschka, Schiele and their contemporaries*, London 1975, pp. 49–62, Werner Hofmann, *Gustav Klimt und die Wiener Jahrhundertwende*, Salzburg 1970, chapter VI; Alice Strobl, "Zu den Fakultätsbildern von Gustav Klimt" in *Albertina Studien*, Vol. II (1964), pp. 138–169.
12   AVA, KUM, Inv. No. 9552/1900.

also purchased the work *The Kiss* (ill. p. 231) from Klimt for the Moderne Galerie for the extravagant sum of 25,000 Crowns.[18]

There can be no doubt that in the first thirty years of his artistic career Gustav Klimt profited significantly from the Habsburgs' promotion of the arts, not least because it gained him access to Viennese society. However, after the Klimt Affair he no longer sought public commissions, which he also no longer needed, for he had reached a position (and found a loyal clientele) that guaranteed him independence. He was disappointed that the state, intent on preserving the principle of pluralism, did not regard avant-garde art as the only worthy art. But he was surely even more disillusioned by the lack of acceptance of his art on the part of the broader public. But one cannot speak of Klimt as having generally distanced himself from the state, as proven by his application for state support for the Kunstschau 1908. He also fully approved of his works being purchased for the state collections.

Gustav Klimt's attitude to the state did not differ essentially from that of most other Austrian—traditional and progressive—artists of his time, who had one thing in common, although for various reasons: They all maintained a remarkable attitude of loyalty to the state and oriented themselves around the Habsburg system of rule even in their works. In this they focused not only on the financial advantage of a state commission or purchase, but also on the attention, recognition and applause of the government (in the form of awards, titles, etc.). There are countless example of this, ranging from Adolf Loos's design in black and yellow of 1908 for the War Ministry, Josef Hoffmann's and Heinrich Lefler's collaboration on the Kaiser Jubilee Parade, also in 1908, Friedrich Ohmann's plans for a Habsburg Museum in 1916, Schiele's and Klimt's "Kunsthalle Projekt" of 1917, and the artists' flaunting of titles such as "k.k. Hofkammermedailleur" (Rudolph Marschall), "k.k. Oberbaurath" (Otto Wagner) or new noble titles such as "Ritter von" (Edmund Hellmer).

The loyalty of many Austrian artists to the Habsburgs was evident to the last in their great personal commitment to the state during the First World War, when art was utilised for propaganda or charitable purposes. Among them, Stefan Zweig, Franz Léhar, Robert Oerley, Hermann Bahr, Hugo von Hofmannsthal and Rainer Maria Rilke all showed a dedication to the cause that was acknowledged in the form of prestigious awards.

The fact that Austria made representations to the German occupational force in Belgium in November 1917 illustrates that the Habsburg state regarded the art of Viennese modernism as an important constituent of Austria's cultural legacy. The occupying forces intended to requisition the metal in the Palais Stoclet in Brussels, for which Klimt had created the famous frieze, among other things. With some success, Austria requested that they refrain from doing this, on grounds that the Palais Stoclet "constitutes a highly representative achievement not only of Austrian architecture, but also of all the fine and applied arts of Austrian modernism ... of particular art historical significance for the development of our national art, which originated in the Viennese Seces-

"Oh, the poor Viennese artists! It looks as if Viennese women have not really got what it takes to be models." Caricature of the presentation of modern Austrian art at the World Exposition in Paris 1900. In *Der Floh*, No. 18 (1900), p. 7.

sion at the turn of the century and reached its apex in the Wiener Werkstätte group of artists."[19]

On the accession to power of Kaiser Karl, art was used as a propaganda vehicle primarily to present Austria as a peace-loving and highly cultivated country. In order to demonstrate to people abroad the high quality of Austrian art, the Habsburg state launched a touring exhibition, featuring Austrian painting of the turn of the century as an important component. In Amsterdam, Stockholm, Copenhagen and Zurich, fifteen paintings by Klimt, including *Death and Life* (Novotny-Dobai 183), *The large Poplar* (Novotny-Dobai 111) and the *Portrait of Adele Bloch-Bauer* (ill. p. 117), occupied a central position in this show. While, shortly before its demise, the Austro-Hungarian Empire was again utilising Viennese modernism in this way for its own particular purposes, Gustav Klimt died, on 6 February 1918, indebted to the Habsburgs' promotion of the arts for his own rise to fame, in the "k.k. Reichshaupt- und Residenzstadt" which he had helped to shape and which would very soon be an "imperial royal city" no more.

13 Stenographer's minutes of the sessions of the House of Deputies of the Austrian Imperial Council, Vienna 1901, 25th gathering in the 17th session. The exhibition of the third painting *Jurisprudenz* (Jurisprudence) in 1903 again caused a controversy. The fact that the Ministry acquiesced in Klimt's request to be allowed to exhibit *Jurisprudenz* in public bears witness to its unwavering stance.
14 Berta Zuckerkandl-Szeps, *Zeitkunst Wien 1901–1904*, Vienna and Leipzig 1908, pp. 163–168.
15 This view stems mainly from the influential work by Carl E. Schorske, *Fin-de-siècle Vienna, Politics and Culture*, New York 1981, pp. 243.
16 AVA, KUM, Inv. No. 4197/1904, Klimt's letter of 17. 1. 1904
17 AVA, KUM, Inv.No. 33219/ 1903. Gottfried Fliedl's interpretation of the university paintings as representing a "clash between Klimt's artistic world view and the aspirations of the commissioner as regards the depiction of the rational and social achievements of the sciences" is not tenable. Gottfried Fliedl, "Geste und Blick" in *Gustav Klimt*, Kunsthaus Zürich, 11.9–13. 12. 1992, ed. by Toni Stooss and Christoph Doswald; Ostfildern 1992, p. 17.
18 AVA, KUM, Inv. No. 32554/1908.
19 AVA, KUM, Inv. No. 43304/ 1918, Representation by the k.u.k. commissioner in Belgium, Baron Franckenstein, to the German Generaloberst Freiherr von Frankenhausen dated 10. 11. 1917.

Of Sweet Young Things and Femmes Fatales
Gustav Klimt and Women around 1900
A Path to Freedom

REGINE SCHMIDT

To many of his contemporaries Gustav Klimt was a magical figure who exerted a particularly strong fascination on women of all social classes, not only because he was an outstanding artist. His origins and background placed him somewhere between the "ordinary citizens" and the bourgeoisie. His clients, without exception, were from the aristocracy and the haute bourgeoisie.

Though he was by no means handsome, he possessed an air of such assured masculinity that not even his famous painter's smock could make him seem unmanly or ridiculous. He wore a beard and his hair began to thin at a fairly early age. His heavy neck and highly coloured complexion gave him the look of one who spent much of his time out of doors.

He had beautiful, piercing eyes, and his manner was quite direct. To Vienna's socialites, he was "interesting" both as an artist and as an individual, yet at the same time there was something rather unnerving about him, especially because of the thick Viennese dialect he spoke. Let me relate a small episode from the childhood memories of my mother, who was born in 1908. One of her aunts, an acquaintance of Gustav Klimt, decided to call on him with little Grete, the first-born and the apple of the family's eye, possibly hoping that she might obtain a sketch of the child. At any rate, my mother was told that they were going to visit "a nice friendly uncle". The first fright my mother got was the sight of a huge and uncanny-looking suit of armour in the dark ante-chamber, and then Klimt himself appeared—enormous, bearded and strangely attired. One glance at him was enough for my mother to start crying at the top of her voice, at which Klimt retorted "Bring des blazerte bangert weg!" ("Take that blasted bastard away!")

Gustav Klimt in his painters coat. Vienna, Historisches Museum der Stadt Wien

My mother never forgot those words, for in a typical middle-class Viennese home before the first world war, only a slight dialect was spoken and strong language was never used.

Given that my mother's family lived near Schönbrunn, and she had walked to the studio, it must have been the studio on Feldmühlgasse that Klimt used from 1912 onwards. From Hietzinger Platz, looking towards Feldmühlgasse, Klimt could still see the sixteenth-century roadside cross that was walled in to the parish church of Hietzing in 1919. Having been involved in decorating many buildings on Ringstrasse, he had witnessed an incredible boom in new buildings, especially in Hietzing. Villa after villa was built, including such famous edifices as the Skywa-Primavesi villa at Gloriettegasse 14–16. Straightening the river course in 1898 and building the urban railway system brought enormous changes to many parts of Vienna.

Klimt loved the Schönbrunn area and every morning he would start the day with a visit to "Meierei Tivoli". At the foot of the "Grüner Berg" Klimt would acknowledge the XAIPE of the villa at Grünbergstrasse 2, which the people of Vienna, not necessarily versed in Ancient Greek, simply called the Villa Xaipe.[1] The Meierei Tivoli, of which I have the fondest childhood memories, and which was a favourite haunt of my mother's, was a cafe and restaurant with a large terrace offering fine views, set in a broad expanse of park-like gardens. Unfortunately, this former idyll no longer exists and the Grün-

Meierei Tivoli. Vienna, Historisches Museum der Stadt Wien

bergstrasse rumbles noisily past the place where Klimt used to savour his coffee with whipped cream while enjoying the view.[2] For a while, Egon Schiele, too, could be seen in the area, for he kept a studio at Grünbergstrasse 31 from October 1910 until 13 May 1911.

Around 1900 life and death were still closely interwoven and were experienced far more directly than today. Women bore their children at home, and many died in the process; their wake would be held at home. Many children died in infancy and early childhood. Although Ignaz Semmelweis, who saved so many lives by proving that prophylactic hygiene measures could prevent puerperal infection or "childbed fever", had presented his groundbreaking thesis in 1847, his prominent contemporaries showed little understanding for his theory. The following passage in the novel *Der Lauf der Asdur* by Princess Mechtilde Lichnowsky, an author held in high esteem by Karl Kraus, is clearly based on her own childhood memories around 1900: "When the door opened, she did not recognise the room, half garden, half

Villa XAIPE, Photograph by
Bruno Reiffenstein. Vienna,
Historisches Museum der Stadt
Wien

church, where only her mother's bed normally stood at the left behind the screen. Her first thought was a vague 'no that isn't our home' but at the same time, she recognised the ivory face, immobile and framed with cushions, like a sculpture, as the face of her mother, a mother of breathtaking unfamiliarity, whose hands folded over her breast expressed the piety of a holy image of martyrdom. And there was something by her side, a tiny, closed face, white like a wooden doll's head washed by the rain."

Klimt, as a man so closely in touch with nature and the father of several children, could understand full well the cycle of life in portrayals of the ages—birth, marriage, old age and death. In the outlying districts of the city, nature was more or less on the doorstep, and the meadows, hedges and fields gave out a sweet scent unadulterated by chemicals. In the immediate vicinity of the "Tivoli", the "Gatterhölzel" and the so-called "Flohberg" there was a veritable ocean of flower-strewn meadows bursting with sweet peas, bindweed and violets until about 1918. At night, the sound of nightingales could be heard, and by day the voices of countless children playing. Yet they had to learn at an early age that they could not play with "anybody". Class differences were closely guarded by the parents. The following scene from Thomas Mann's *Buddenbrooks* is certainly comparable with social life in Vienna at the time, even though it is set in the northern German port of Lübeck: "But if other children came up to them on the Mill-wall, when she had sat down with Hanno, Fräulein Jungmann would get up almost at once and take her leave on grounds of being late for something or troubled by the breeze."[4]

Such mores clearly also applied when Arthur Schnitzler met Gustav Klimt in private circles. Schnitzler respected Klimt as an artist and even bought two drawings from him. Yet their friendship remained no more than the superficial acquaintance of two men from very different social and educational backgrounds. Schnitzler belonged to the liberal and educated haute bourgeoisie, and had attended the prestigious Akademisches Gymnasium. In 1885 he took his doctorate in medicine at the University of Vienna. Klimt was born in Baumgarten, far from the feudal Praterstrasse (formerly Jägerzeile) where the young Schnitzler grew up. In Schnitzler's diaries, Klimt is mentioned only in passing, as in this entry of 1909: "Evening alone Loewe concert society, Dohnanyi a Mozart concerto, Mahler's 5th, affected me more strongly than ever ... behind me, behaving appallingly, Frau Bertha Zuckerkandl: 'Mahler doing well in America'. To Klimt, who accompanied her, she said: 'Do you know Dohnanyi, I get goosebumps when he plays ... a genius ... like Liszt'. Unfortunately, Schnitzler does not record Klimt's reply. Another brief entry for 20 October 1911 states "Saw Klimt's mosaic for the Villa Stoclet at Pappenheimstrasse". On 5 December 1912 he writes "...Evening at Zuckerkandls. With Nedbal and O. Brahms songs for viola and piano accompaniment ... sat between Hofrätin and Mrs Zuckerkandl. Spoke to Hofrätin about Bernhardi. Klimt, not unlike a lively faun, sat opposite me." Schnitzler's observation is witty and not entirely inaccurate, but the very fact that he says it to himself speaks volumes. Klimt's superficial manliness may well have contributed to a latent and unacknowledged animosity. Yet in their art and their nature they were not dissimilar. Paul Willhelm wrote of Schnitzer in 1908: "He has clad his poet's soul in everyday attire. He is a very pleasant and modest person who likes to close his window shutters against the loud voices of the public. ... His favourite landscape is forest—compare Klimt's 'Beechwood'—for that is his notion of summer, and of beautiful, calm maturity."[5] He had a distinctly bourgeois notion of art, and admired the artists of the renaissance, especially Leonardo da Vinci. As a student, he had built up a collection of drawings and watercolours by Rudolf von Alt—and his purchase of two drawings by Klimt were an exception to this bourgeois rule.

Arthur Schnitzler, Vienna 1915. Photography by d'Ora. Vienna, Bildarchiv Österreichische Nationalbibliothek

The prosperity of the decade prior to the first world war coincided with the apex of Schnitzler's literary success. It also marks the high point of Klimt's creativity both in female portraiture and in his allegories. Schnitzler's turn-of-the-century work "addresses the emotional stimuli and insoluble tensions that were also described by Strindberg and Chekov. Tormenting oneself and others while one laughs and makes jokes, despairing and yet dancing, dying and yet wanting to be beautiful, fleeing from life into music, dance and art—these are the Viennese themes at the turn of the century."[6]

Gustav Klimt's work was and is such that one can lose oneself in it. His women, ladies and girls are mere forms of nature itself, flowers, as it were, that he drew and painted as they budded, blossomed and withered. His approach to women was elementary. He is Zeus approaching Danae, he is a breath expiring over poppy-strewn meadows and summer gardens, a breath of life that knows death and invites it in. He is the groom

1   In Klimt's day the Villa XAIPE was at Schönbrunnerstrasse 309.
2   Long before Klimt's day the Tivoli was an attraction in Vienne. Around 1830 "Tout Vienne spoke about the Tivoli that was to be a great source of amusement". Ferdinand Raimund parodies the Tivoli in Viennese dialect in his *Gefesselten Fantasie*. See Günther Berger, *Das Tivoli in Meidling*, Meidlinger Kulturverein, Vienna 1989.
3   Mechtilde Lichnowsky, *Der Lauf der Asdur*, Vienna 1936.
4   Thomas Mann, *Buddenbrooks. Verfall einer Familie*, Berlin 1901, Part 8, chapter 8.
5   Paul Wilhelm, *Bei Arthur Schnitzler*, 190.8
6   Heinrich Schnitzler/Christian Brandstätter, *Arthur Schnitzler*, Frankfurt/M. 1981.

embracing the smiling, dreaming bride, the ominpresent seducer on the wedding night, the father of children and the helpmeet in old age and death. He is all these things, albeit with neither literary detachment nor with classification in such categories as "sweet young things" and "femmes fatales" although they also presented themselves to him in this way in outward life, and although he met the limits of his Zeus-like existence in Emilie Flöge, his Hera, whom he never married, but who kept him earth-bound in what was, to all intents and purposes, the extension of a strong maternal bond, even though she was the one who inspired him to symbolic portrayals of an "unearthly" love.

Gustav Klimt in his garden. Vienna, Historisches Museum der Stadt Wien

As a painter, he was a creative demiurge, but in mortal life the women of his day were classified according to rigid prevailing distinctions: the family members such as mother, sister and niece, the members of the middle classes and haute bourgeoise who were his clients—usually by way of their husbands—and the Viennese girls of the lower classes who came to him as models. Generally, the girls who posed nude for him earned their living as artists' models. Their negative image in society is described in great detail by Marco Brociner in his 1911 comedy set in Vienna.[7] In the very first act, set in the studio of the sculptor Hans Bach, whose door is draped with a Japanese costume, the sculptor announces "And all because of the narrow-minded jealousy of a woman who refuses to understand that an artist does not see a female model with the same eyes as any other man. Yesterday I explained to her at length that woman is my domain, that I had my first success with female nudes. I must go back to woman." As he is clearly less successful than he has been, the art dealer Grünberg advises him, "You should have a studio like Makart! And commissions you cannot cope with if you had a dozen hands. And a 60 hp automobile! And a villa of your own! And a family tomb at the main cemetery! In a word—woman is your money, your goldmine!" According to the rakish and cynical painter Reinhold, "The day finally came for me to make my reckoning! Floating around society, hypocritical and sycophantic, just to sell a picture or paint a portrait of the honourable woman and her delightful daughter, kow-towing to some ignorant patron!" Waldner says, "An artist, as long as his creative power is fresh and original, must have no ties, must be free as a bird in the air. He should regard woman only as an episode, as a *quantité négligeable*. As a sweet plaything. Should he marry, he will have a bothersome nuisance in his home, his concentration will lack the inner calm from which great works are born." And the sculptor claims "But I need a model!" To which Waldner replies: "I have one, a magnificent specimen of a woman. Slender, russet blonde, sculpturally built, a women such as nature forms in a good mood." Erna, the wife of the sculptor, has discovered a photograph of a former model. "What a bold décolleté!" Hans: "A little sugar-baker!" Erna: "Aha—a sweet young thing!" The sculptor: "I have to have a living woman before me. One immerses oneself with deep and sacred earnestness in contemplation of the forms." Monica, a model: "That is ridiculous! I, a model, should teach you something? First of all, I am not a professional model. Good-

7   Marco Brociner, *Vor dem Sündenfall*, a comedy in three acts, Vienna 1911.
8   Ibid.
9   Susanna Partsch, *Gustav Klimt. Maler der Frauen*, Munich 1994, p. 74f.
10   See note 2.
11   Richard von Schaukal, *Von Kindern und Tieren*, 1905–1915.
12   Lou Andreas-Salome, *Lebensrückblick*, Zurich/Wiesbaden 1951.

ness me, one is pretty, young, poor, full of life, one works all day for little joy, but the heart cries out for happiness! Then an artist approaches you one fine evening and you grasp the little bit of happiness you can get without a second thought. And so you become his mistress, his model because he needs a model just now. But you needn't be bad if your heart is in the right place."[8]

Klimt undoubtedly had little trouble finding models, and beautiful ones at that. The women whose portraits he painted—and more besides, it is said—were beautiful too. These were married women of Viennese society and additional clandestine meetings were probably difficult enough to arrange. For untouched girls from respectable homes, who were not allowed to be alone at all, they were virtually impossible. This would certainly explain Klimt's behaviour towards Alma Schindler and the fact that he even travelled to Venice to see her. Alma, who was mature for her age, was carefully guarded by her stepfather Moll and her mother.[9]

An interesting encounter of the period is described by Mechtilde Lichnowsky in *Der Lauf der Asdur*.[10] As the chaperone Georgina relates, "Something was always needed, it seems, and I acted as though I was convinced of the fact, for I knew that the done thing was to incline one's head modestly and blushing if one happened to see Mr So-and-so or Mr Such-and-such approaching. Mr Such-and-such or Mr So-and-so (details of names not having been fed to the wastepaper bin) would doff his hat as he passed by, and that was all. And quite a lot it was too, for no appointment had been made. It was a question of organised chance on both sides." Even if the man and woman in question, like Klimt and Alma, were introduced to one another at some social event, this did not meet that they could simply meet up with one another unaccompanied in future. For the young society ladies were not only expected to make a good match, but also to marry "Mr Right" in terms of social standing. Above all, it was not done for a young woman to make a "mistake". Such "mistakes" were the preserve of the kind of women Alma described as "wertlose Frauenzimmer" ("worthless females").

Alma Schindler and her sister Grete. Vienna, Bildarchiv Österreichische Nationalbibliothek

This problem and the lot of women from various different social classes can all be found in Schniztler's oeuvre, especially the mature married woman and the so-called *süsses Mädel* or "sweet young thing" who, as a result, generally became a "poor creature". In his *Autobiographie Jugend in Wien* Schnitzler admits: "Seduction and adultery were prohibited and dangerous, affairs with cocottes and actresses risky and expensive. Then there was a decent sort of girl who had already strayed from the path of virtue, but with whom one might still "get ensnared" just as one would with any woman one seduced. That left only the whores." And they were at the very bottom rung of the ladder. In *Reigen*, Schnitzler has the husband speak in derogatory terms of the women available for "love": "That which is generally referred to as love is made utterly repulsive to us, for what creatures are those to whom we must turn?" Richard von Schaukal arrogantly pigeon-holes women in *Kindheit und Jugend:* "Now I am one of those old-fashioned people who hates, from the very bottom of his soul, everything that even so much as hints at the much-vaunted emancipation of women. To me, woman is a little like art, for she is purposeless and beautiful—an ugly woman has failed her vocation in my opinion—and on the other hand a creature destined to serve freely and devotedly. I do not deny that there are some attractive women beyond the bounds of virtue and constraint. But no man with any self-respect would choose such a wildflower as a helpmeet..."[11]

Nothing in Klimt's work suggests that he despised women. Like the later work of Franz Wiegele, his oeuvre is a constant homage to woman. To Klimt, they were erotic creatures. The erotic atmosphere of Vienna is described by Lou Andreas-Salome in her autobiography as follows: "If I were to describe the atmosphere of Vienna in comparison to other major cities, I would say that it seemed to me at the time to be the most strongly marked by its blend of intellect and eroticism. What would elsewhere distinguish the rake from the businessman or intellectual took on an element of grace that even promoted the *süsses Mädel* into the realms of heightened eroticism..."[12]

Gustav Klimt, Phothography by Pauline Hamilton. Vienna, Historisches Museum der Stadt Wien

For all his love of women, Klimt still uses antagonistic terms of reference for the female sex: "The aesthetic-erotic sphere in which artists place woman ignores the social side whose existence is proclaimed by socialists and feminists."[13] This dualism within the man and the artist himself is lucidly recognised by Peter Altenberg, who claims that, as a painter who looks at things, you are at the same time a modern philosopher, a thoroughly modern poet. By painting, you suddenly transform yourself in an almost fairytale manner into a "modern person" that you might not necessarily be in the real world of daily life.[14] The difference between the "woman as painted figure" and reality is described by Felix Salten in 1903: "The women he paints are in reality perhaps a little different, in reality they may not be quite so poetic, not quite so exaggerated. Yet it is precisely in his way of painting women that the wondrous sensuality of Klimt's temperament is reflected."[15] In 1913, Hermann Bahr described the multiplicity of the essence of Klimt's women: "This mutability of appearances in which none of the creatures is empowered in itself, but can be imposed on any one of the others, troubles him. He paints a woman as though she were a jewel. She merely glitters, but the ring on her hand seems to breathe, and her hat has more life in it than she herself. Her mouth is like a blossom, but one does not imagine it can talk—yet her dress seems to whisper."

These ambivalent creatures who appear as Danae or water nixies in metamorphosis are the subject of Dörmann's homage in his Donaunixe verses: "I love the hectic, slender Narcissi with the blood-red mouth: I love the tormented thoughts, the heart pierced and wounded; I love the wan and the pale, the women with tired faces in which the smouldering signs of all-devouring sensuality speak. I love the shimmering snakes, so supple and malleable and cool. I love the plaintive trepidation, the songs of death."[17] To these poets, the boundaries of love, eroticism and death are blurred, and while his sense of eroticism is no less than Klimt's, he cirumscribes the appealing and repulsive magnificence of the female body in bold verse: "*Auf üppig weichen Eisbärfellen, ruht / Ein schlankes Weib die Lippen halberbrochen, / Mit leicht umblauten, müden Schwärmeraugen, / Und träumt und träumt von zügellosem Schwelgen, trunknem Rasen, / Von einem hochgepeitschten Taumelreigen / Die abgestrumpften, wurzelwelken Nerven, / Von einem letzten, nie gekannten Glück, / Von einer Wonne, die der Wonnen höchste. Und doch nicht Liebe heißt und träumt und träumt*". ("On sumptuous white bearskins lies / a slender woman, her lips half open, / with bluish rings beneath her tired, eager

13 Nike Wagner, *Geist und Geschlecht. Karl Kraus und die Erotik der Wiener Moderne*, Frankfurt/M. 1982.
14 Peter Altenberg, cited by Carl. E. Schorske in *Fin-de-Siecle Vienna: Politics and Culture*, London 1981 (paraphrased).
15 Felix Salten, *Gustav Klimt. Gelegentliche Anmerkungen*, Vienna and Leipzig 1903.
16 Hermann Bahr, *Essays*. Selected by Heinz Kindermann, Vienna 1962.
17 Helmut Schneider, *Felix Dörmann, Eine Monographie*, Vienna 1991.

eyes, / and dreams and dreams of unfettered revelry, drunken wildness, / a whipped-up delirium of ecstasy / the deadened, faded nerves / of one last, unknown happiness / of a pleasure that is the highest of all pleasures / and yet is not called love and dreams and dreams.") Felix Dörmann, born in Vienna eight years after Klimt, was highly controversial. His first volume of poetry was seized. Broch described him as a "*platonischer Wüstling*" (platonic roué). Karl Kraus dismissed him. Yet he was an insightful portrayer of the way women were seen in that era, as reflected in dreams, fears and hopes.

By rendering visible the various manifestations of "woman" it was these three—Schnitzler, Klimt and to some extent Dörmann—who came tantalisingly close to defining the "modern woman" as independent and in control of her own eroticism. The women's movement was to lead girls and women through the revolution of their daily lives, but it was artists, especially Gustav Klimt, who led "sweet young things" and "femmes fatales" alike towards the "path to freedom" by recognising the power of eroticism and lifting its taboo.

Gender Asymmetries in Viennese Modernism

LISA FISCHER

Truth is a woman. And it is to naked truth that Gustav Klimt would seem to be holding up a mirror. This *nuda veritas*, however, was not recognised by her portrayer, but merely depicted. We let her come to life again and, through her eyes, we set and keep in motion the *trompe l'oeil* image of Viennese modernism. We give back to the model the way of seeing that the master's male gaze tried to destroy. We lend a voice to the truth inherent in those pictures that shine and burn brightly behind the projections, awaiting the moment when their language will be deciphered. Truth steps out of the shadow of its myth at that moment when the longings and anxieties projected upon it become tangible. Then, woman is ready for presence. Historical memory is called upon to make a new offer to recollection. Structures of dominance are reflected in contemporary interpretations. In gazing at them, dull mirrors begin to shine.

The naked truth is that the self-fashioning of women in Viennese modernism was confronted with consistent destructive efforts by men. The crisis of the ego was a crisis of the male subject. Women dared to set out on the path to self-discovery, forced their way as never before onto the labour market and into male art domains, where they posed a threat as rivals. In politics, they demanded the right to vote and access to education. They thus became part of that mood of upheaval and crisis that marked the cheerful apocalypse.[1] Efforts towards emancipation and a criticism of the patriarchy were essential driving forces for the creative milieu of the fin de siècle; the gender issue became an all-pervasive theme. The conflicts between being and appearance, between Thanatos and Eros, were heightened and advanced on the battlefield of eroticism.

This crisis of identity and the quest for freedom, however, were not peculiar to the turn of the century; they had already been essential topoi in the nineteenth century. They were omnipresent as symbolic politics in the person of the Austrian Empress Elisabeth. In her struggle with self-renunciation and self-assertion, Elisabeth's uncompromising individuality mirrored a collective process of female self-development.[2] The life and death of the poetess-empress became the backdrop, as it were, against which the creative milieu of Viennese modernism staged itself anew. This intellectual and accomplished sportswoman, who, instead of supporting her husband the emperor in her function as "Landesmutter", preferred to absent herself from the court and refused to fulfil her duties, making it unmistakably clear at the highest echelons of state that the roles ascribed to women were no longer automatically accepted. Elisabeth, the distant beauty, even kindled male fantasies and anxieties. After her murder in 1898, a veritable Elisabeth-cult began in Vienna, above all, among artists. That slim, androgynous woman mutated into an unattainable, but constantly longed for ideal. In the minds of men who stylised themselves as gods, women, as ethereal beings, advanced to become the symbol, as it were, of a new womanhood, behind which real women were deliberately made to disappear. Male creators tried to master their feelings of helplessness and their fear of failure by producing idealised art works and new myths of womanhood, by mastering the world of appearances. A large number of the male representatives of modernism and of art nouveau, who had opposed their fathers as revolutionaries, were themselves astonishingly reactionary when it came to the relationship between the sexes.

Woman was either idealised as a Madonna, degraded to the role of a malleable girl, functionalised as a practical muse, or disparaged as a whore. In this way, female independence was either deliberately destroyed or requisitioned by males for their own creative efforts. Thus, in his famous pre-marital letter to Alma Schindler, Gustav Mahler demanded of his musically highly talented composer-fiancée that she give up composing, once she had become his wife, for reasons of competition. He writes: "From now on you have only one vocation: to make me happy. You must give yourself up to me unconditionally, make the shaping of your future life, in all its facets, dependent on my inner needs, and wish nothing more in return than my love."[3] Alma complied, and was successful, not as a composer, but as the muse of famous men: Klimt, Kokoschka, Gropius and Werfel enabled her to become famous too, in a typical female role, promoting the male genius at the price of her own fame as an artist. The strategies developed for hindering or requisitioning female creativity were altogether intricate and an integral component, indeed precondition, of male creativity. Adolf Loos, the renewer of architecture, writes to his future wife Lina, whom he referred to simply as Mädi (girlie) and who was attending drama school at the time: "For God's sake, fail resoundingly. You don't need that crowd, but I need you."[4] Lina Loos was successful, however. She became an actress and divorced her husband after two years of married life. She did not want either to be stylised as a child-women, or transformed into a work of art. She preferred to be an artist herself and thus fiercely resisted male attempts to hinder or manipulate her. She preferred her freedom. Through his marriage to Lina, the homeless architect had not only gained access to bourgeois circles, but a flat of his own, through Lina's parents, who managed the famous café Casa Piccola. He continued to live in that flat even after their divorce, indeed, until he died. Whereas Lina Loos subsequently began her own carer and liberated herself from the clutches of a Pygmalion, Loos remained true to the principle of the child-woman as a fountain of youth; he married again, twice, and the age difference between him and his second wife was twenty-nine years, between him and his third thirty-four.[5]

Egon Friedell summaries the attitude of his artist colleagues to women in a rather pointed form: "For the thinker and artist, women are nothing more than chance stimuli, which he cleverly uses so as to promote his own spiritual metabolism, as temporary firewood which he burns so as to fuel his own fire. He actually has no inner relationship to the women. For him, they are the same as alcohol, nicotine, black coffee. He needs them for a moment, but he uses them up completely, and once they have provided him with the necessary catalyst for his powers, they no longer exist for him. They are only there to make him richer and stronger. All he draws from them is himself, his own power of loving or hating, thinking or shaping."[6]

Gustav Klimt fits in smoothly to the male system of anti-modernism in Viennese modernism. His life and works provide the proof, and Klimt himself issues the invitation to analyse them: "Whoever wants to know something about me—the artist, who alone is

Gustav Klimt, Nuda Veritas, 1898 (cf. p. 239)

worthy of observation—should look carefully at my works and try to recognise in them what I am and what I want."[7] With this statement, and contrary to his own concept, given that he regarded himself as a representative of the *gesamtkunstwerk*, Klimt would seem to want to separate the man from the artist, although through the painter the man speaks that telling language which demands to be heard. By bringing together man and work, historical memory is awakened and receives that recollection which protects it from the compulsion to repeat which is part of forgetting.

Klimt was a master of separation. The verbosity of his paintings contrasts strikingly with a mysterious silence as to his person. Whereas he skilfully displays the male gaze upon the female, his eye blurs when it comes to observing his own person. Here, the sources are mute. He thus succeeds in prising himself, as human being and man, out of the historical and social contexts into which he was only willing to be integrated as an artist. As a genius on a lonely mission, as herald of a sacred spring, *Ver Sacrum*, he adhered to ancient traditions in which the master alone is called upon to set up a new community with a group of his chosen ones.[8] He stylised himself as an apostle and was widely called St Peter.[9] He adeptly separated his private and his public life. Human frailty was not to dilute his reputation as an artist of genius, and as saint and leader of an elite group of artists. Only after his death, according to Nebehay, did it transpire that he had fathered fourteen illegitimate children. Four mothers were compensated, the others renounced their claims.[10] In addition to idealised art worlds, the man also produced children, whose real worlds were located beyond gold ornamentation. Interestingly enough, only two Gustav juniors are officially known and no girls' names have been handed down. Furthermore, the mothers and models too, remained strangely silent.

Klimt's creativity was dependent on, indeed a consequence of the dedication shown by women. While Emilie Flöge, socially well situated and a successful business woman in her own right, functioned as his official partner in life, Klimt availed himself of socially disadvantaged girls from the suburbs, not only as nude models, but also as sex objects. With them, he lived out his faun-like desires, an abuse of the female body, yet with the agreement of the respective woman, coerced by the misery of her social condition and the illusion of love. Maria Ucicka, a washerwoman from Prague, was only seventeen when she became pregnant by him.[11] Their son Gustav later achieved some fame as the film director Ucicky, through his collaboration with the National Socialists. To judge by their correspondence, his affair with Maria Zimmermann may well have lasted from 1899 to 1903. Whereas Klimt financially supported his lover and their sons Gustav and Otto, he was altogether opposed to their mother's (he called her "child") attempts to paint: "I am sure nothing will come of your painting—What you should do, above all, is really recuperate, really learn to look, that's how you start—then there will surely be an opportunity somehow to have more time to paint."[12] It is still hard to imagine how the young single mother was to achieve that, between looking after the children, requesting money, and being emotionally involved with the father of her children.

The role allocation was clear. Divide et impera. Klimt spent the winters and weekdays in his studio with his models, Sundays and summer were spent with Emilie in the Salzkammergut. The "Mizzis" from the lower class, obliterated as individuals and transformed into a cliché by Schnitzler in the figure of the *süsses Mädel* or "sweet little thing", and as models reduced by Klimt in his nude drawings to a sexual body and left

1   Cf. Lisa Fischer/Emil Brix, *Die Frauen der Wiener Moderne*, Vienna 1997.
2   Cf. Lisa Fischer, *Schattenwürfe in die Zukunft, Kaiserin Elisabeth und die Frauen ihrer Zeit*, Vienna 1998.
3   Francoise Giroud, *Alma Mahler, oder Die Kunst geliebt zu werden*, Paris 1989, pp. 54f.
4   Lisa Fischer, *Lina Loos, oder wenn die Muse sich selbst küsst*, Vienna 1994, p. 81.
5   Op. cit., p. 102.
6   Egon Friedell to Lina Loos. Handwritten. Wiener Stadt und Landesbibliothek. Manuscript collection. I.N. 127.000, in Fischer 1998, p. 23.
7   Christian Nebehay, *Gustav Klimt*, Vienna 1969, p. 40.
8   Gottfried Fliedl, *Gustav Klimt*, Cologne 1989, p. 64.
9   Berta Zuckerkandl, "Einiges über Gustav Klimt" in *Volkszeitung*, 6. 2. 1936.
10   Christian Nebehay, *Die goldenen Sessel meines Vaters*, Vienna 1983, p. 114.
11   Susanna Partsch, *Gustav Klimt Maler der Frauen*, Munich 1994. The age given here is based on the date of birth of Maria Ucicka as stated by Partsch. As the date of birth of Gustav's son varies between 1898 und 1899, she can also have been eighteen; p. 58.
12   Christian Nebehay, "Gustav Klimt schreibt an eine Liebe" in *Mitteilungen der österreichischen Galerie*, Jg. 22/23, 1978/79, No. 66/67. pp. 101–118, p. 107.

alone with the children after a short affair, are kept separate from his platonic love Emilie, whom he called "Midi". So the Mizzis and Midis had distinctive functions; the one to sensually reproduce and inspire him, the other to stimulate him artistically and build up his spirit when he was gripped by the fear of falling victim to fits of depression. His countless cards, sometimes two a day, speak volumes about his male narcissism, his constant anxieties about his health and his creative crises, all of which he tried to keep in check by reporting them to his lady friend.[13] Parallel to this, he courted women from the haute bourgeoisie. Whereas his attempts to conquer the young Alma Schindler, later Mahler, were foiled by her parents, as of 1899 he had an affair with his patron Adele Bloch-Bauer.[14] Between all these women, he was cared for on a daily basis by his mother and two unmarried sisters, with whom he lived all his life. They cooked his evening meals for him and relieved him of the more tedious aspects of everyday life.[15]

Maria Zimmermann,
Photograhy, c. 1910, Vienna,
Private collection

Secure in the moorings of these female anchors, the artist Klimt could be creative at his ease, something which would have been inconceivable without that comprehensive supply network. At the same time, he gained access through these women to a network of social relationships that supported his economic advancement. From a poor background himself, Klimt was admitted to the world of the bourgeoisie through his brother's marriage to Hermine Flöge. Klimt's father died in 1892 and his brother Ernst the same year. Klimt was appointed guardian to his niece Helene. As uncle and brother-in-law, he advanced to become a recognised member of the Flöge family. Flöge senior died in 1897. Klimt thus received many and varied substitute functions in two fatherless households, that of his mother and that of his "mother-in-law". Here too, there is a dual line-up, this time in the form of two households. In 1904, Emilie and her sisters opened a fashion shop in Casa Piccola on Mariahilferstrasse 1B, which, under exclusively female management, soon became a successful enterprise. Emilie was not only the creative force, but also acted as mannequin. Her wide-ranging advertising campaigns in the leading journals of the day using fashion photographs bearing Klimt's emblem were in no way detrimental to the artist's public reputation, which had been tainted by the scandal about the so-called faculty paintings. It was around this time that Kolomann Moser succeeded in purchasing two of the controversial university paintings with money provided by his wife Editha, née Mautner Markhof.[16] Alma Mahler-Werfel introduced Klimt to the circle around Gustav Mahler, despite the fact that in her biography she says of him that "he had a habit of playing with people's feelings".[17] Serena Lederer, whose portrait he painted in 1899, got him a whole series of other commissions.[18] It was she who, after his death, purchased en bloc the complete exhibition of his drawings.[19] Finally, Berta Zuckerkandl, the grande dame of the Viennese Salon, brought him and Rodin together, and took the trouble to promote the artist when and wherever she could.

The women surrounding Klimt fulfilled the most varied of functions, making a decisive contribution to the creative milieu and to his artistic production as patrons, mentors, mothers, muses or objects of desire. Both as a man and as an artist Klimt was dependent on women. He used them in his life and abused them in his work by concealing their real diversity behind a uniform artistic façade. Is it any wonder then that his

13   Cf. Wolfgang Georg Fischer, *Gustav Klimt und Emilie Flöge*, Vienna 1987, pp.169–189.
14   Partsch 1994, p. 73.
15   Rosa Poor-Lima, "Eine alte Wiener Künstlerfamilie. Das Erbe des Maler-Apostels Gustav Klimt" in *Neues Wiener Tagblatt*, 29 December 1940.
16   Christian Nebehay, *Gustav Klimt*, Vienna 1976, p. 83, p. 156.
17   Alma Mahler-Werfel, *Mein Leben*, Frankfurt/M. 1960, p. 27.
18   Christian Brandstätter, *Gustav Klimt und die Frauen*, Vienna 1994, p. 54.
19   Nebehay 1969, p. 143.
20   Op. cit., p. 287.

greatest fear after suffering a stroke was that he would be helplessly at the mercy of caring women?[20]

Emilie Flöge certainly played the most varied role in Klimt's life. She knew his secrets, and also that he had syphilis[21], which was surely what made their relationship a platonic one. Emilie Flöge was not only his most important conversation partner, but his main point of reference. She was also helpful to him in his art. When work on the sketches for the Stoclet frieze came to yet another standstill during the summer months spent on the Attersee, Emilie Flöge rose at five in the morning and got to work herself. Klimt's comment: "Yes Midi, you can do that better than I."[22] Emilie was taller than Gustav, much as the empress Elisabeth was taller than Franz Joseph. But she also seems to have towered over him in many other ways. It comes as no surprise, therefore, that she was dissatisfied with the portrait Klimt painted of her. She preferred instead to have any likeness of herself created in the photography studio of Madame D'Ora, who, unlike Klimt, really knew how to present her personality.

Klimt's *Portrait of Margarethe Stonborough-Wittgenstein* (ill. p. 109) gives us an insight into the enormous difficulties he had in accepting women's independence if he could not requisition it for his own artistic or sexual purposes. Margarethe was the daughter of a rich industrialist and patriarch. Three of her older brothers committed suicide, while her brother Ludwig, seven years her junior, was plagued by depression. Margarethe was born in 1882 and grew up to become an imposing woman of beauty and intelligence. "Her kindness, her knowledge, her many and varied talents, and finally her beauty and her contempt for conventions" made her a compelling personality.[23] She undertook studies in mathematics, worked in a chemical laboratory in Zurich, drew after nature,[24] ran a salon, and was open-minded towards all that was new. She exerted a considerable intellectual influence on her younger brother and played an important part in his career as a philosopher. What is more, she was very protective towards him when he was plagued by death fantasies. It was as a therapeutic prescription, so to speak, that she entrusted Ludwig and the architect Engelmann with the design of her town palace in Vienna.

The portrait Klimt painted of her in 1905 clearly shows the artist's failure. In it, he merely depicted his male fantasies, not an intelligent and self-aware women. "Klimt tried in vain to render Margarethe harmless, a pliant figure in a stylised atmosphere."[25] His attempt presents a Margarethe who is strangely lacking in colour. Only her head seems to display any contour, though this does no justice to her actual beauty. In the background between her neck and face is a broad white rectangle forming a division between head and body. Thus beheaded, we are presented with a woman whom Klimt could not render erotic, and whose intellectuality he failed to depict. It is not surprising that Margarethe was so dissatisfied with the result that she banished the portrait to the attic, despite having paid a high price for it.[26]

Yet the work would seem to have introduced a new turning point in the forms Klimt used to present female figures. In his subsequent golden period, Klimt totally concealed the character of the women, making it disappear behind idealised forms and thus asserting himself as the demiurge of a world of appearances. Hidden behind gilt ornamentation, Eros degenerates into an icon,[27] and woman into the symbol of his obsessions. In *The Kiss*, the woman's image is literally inscribed into the man's, and subjected to the principle of manhood.[28] She is thus turned into a figure that can be mastered. In

21 Thomas Zaunschirm, "Der Mythos Klimt" in *Gegenwelten. Gustav Klimst Künstlerleben im Fin de siècle.* Munich 1996. According to Zaunschirm, this is confirmed by unpublished letters between Emilie and her mother, owned by Alfred Weidinger.
22 Memoires of Herta Wanke, a former apprentice in 'Salon Flöge', in Fischer 1987, p. 197.
23 Thomas Zaunschirm, *Gustav Klimt Margarethe Stonborough-Wittgenstein*, Frankfurt/M. 1985, p. 53.
24 Op. cit., p. 54.
25 Op. cit., p. 77.
26 Nebehay 1969, p. 270, according to a report by her son Thomas Stonborough.
27 Petra Renneke, *Körper Eros und Tod, Gustav Klimt im Kontext der Ästhetik des Fin de siècle*, Essen 1995, p. 178.
28 Fliedl 1989, p. 118.

his nude drawings, which largely remained concealed from the public, he perpetuated his voyeuristic gaze at women. Depicted in swift strokes, Klimt reduces woman to sexuality. He paints her as a body, of which he once said that "the bottom is more beautiful and intelligent than many another's face".[29] Klimt produced some 4,000 drawings, as opposed to his 222 paintings.[30] There is a separation here too, between the private nude drawings that reduce woman to a symbol of lust, and the publicly exhibited stylised icon. The common denominator, however, is a destructive variant of a male fantasy that strives to master woman by reducing her to a symbol. Under the guise of eroticism, Klimt lends his drawings of the female the character of objects by which he tries to protect himself from female subjectivity. He is thus an integral component of the system of those fin de siècle artist heroes who did not wish to solve social, political or personal conflicts in the real world, but who instead stylised themselves as gods and fled the real world by creating art worlds. With anti-modernist tendencies such as these, the laboratory of modernism has remained an experimental phase, to this very day. In it, Klimt became what he was: smug and narcissistic as a person, thoroughly conventional as a painter in his interpretation of the female. In this combination, his art reproduced a contemporary trend that linked him with many others. Such male fantasies were part of the spirit of the time, then as now, and their aspiration to dominance can only be refracted in the mirror of historical analysis. Only then can woman, *nuda veritas*, recover the gaze of which she has been robbed and allow truth to shine and burn brightly before contemporary eyes.

29   Arthur Roessler, "Klimt und seine Modelle", *Arbeiterzeitung* 15. August 1953.
30   Nebehay 1969, p. 35.

"Alma, my Alma"—
Gustav Klimt and Alma Schindler

HANSJÖRG KRUG

When Alma Mahler-Werfel claimed in her memoirs,[1] published in 1960, that Gustav Klimt had been the first great love of her life, few were inclined to lend credence to the tales told by this old lady who died in New York in 1964—of her love affair at the age of twenty with the then thirty-seven-year-old Gustav Klimt, of their kiss in Genoa and of his

Gustav Klimt, Photography by Pauline Hamilton, c. 1900. Vienna, Bildarchiv Österreichische Nationalbibliothek

hasty words of love to her in St Mark's Square in Venice.[2] Yet once a letter from Gustav Klimt to Alma's stepfather Carl Moll dated 19 May 1889 came to light[3] and once Alma's Diaries[4] from the years 1898–1902 were published, there could be little doubt any more as to the truth of what she herself described as her "Klimt affair" and her "novel".[5] What we do know, however, is that things did not happen exactly the way Alma Mahler-Werfel told it in her memoirs, and that it was all somewhat less dramatic. We can certainly believe that Alma Schindler shed many a tear over Gustav Klimt, and that it was to Klimt she owed her sexual awakening,[6] yet Alma's emotional sensibilities, her feelings and her lovelorn sorrows were a vast terrain indeed.

Bruno Walter, who was, at the time, the Kapellmeister at the Vienna Opera House wrote to his parents on 30 September 1901, saying that "Alma Schinder … is tall and slender and a dazzling beauty, the most beautiful in all Vienna; from a very good family and very rich."[7] The latter claim may have been a rumour, for Alma was not "very rich". "Men felt they might drown in her deep blue eyes. She was not only beautiful, but also intelli-

1 Alma Mahler-Werfel, *Mein Leben* (1960), Frankfurt/M. 1988, p. 28.
2 Mahler-Werfel, *Mein Leben*, p. 26.
3 J. A. Stargardt, Marburg, auction catalogue 624, 1981, no. 514, with an illustration of the first page of the letter, now held by the Bibliothèque Musicale Gustav Mahler, Paris. Exerpts from the letter are cited in Christian M. Nebehay, *Gustav Klimt, Von der Zeichnung zum Bild*, 1992, pp. 251–253. The quotations here are from the (not entirely correct) printing of the thirteen-page letter in *Ein Glück ohne*

gent in the most exacting way. She was witty and erudite."[8] Alma was skilled at disguising her slightly impaired hearing, and anyone who did not know of her disability "gained the impression by the way she leaned forward that she was particularly interested in the conversation."[9] On 28 December 1901, Alma confided to her diary, "According to the '-Fremdenblatt', I am brilliant. Lord—and whatever else!"[10] That same day the Neue Freie Presse reported that "the news of the engagement of Director Mahler with Miss Alma Schindler, daughter of the late and outstanding painter Emile Schindler… has aroused the interest of Viennese society… the widow of the artist Schindler had married the painter Moll in 1892 after the death of her first husband."[11] From all quarters, the opera director's fiancée was showered with gifts and good wishes. "Letters, telegrams, flowers …"[12] wrote Alma of the evening of the 28 December, though she did not mention whether Gustav Klimt had congratulated her. ("This morning, Mama called on Klimt. That doesn't bother me at all"[13] she wrote in her diary on 21 December. This is the last time Klimt's name is mentioned, little more than a week before the first "terribly sad" sexual encounter between Alma and Gustav Mahler on New Year's Day 1902. "Words cannot express what I today have undeservedly suffered."[14] According to Alma's diary the "Klimt affair" began on 26 January 1898 as unpretentiously as it was to end. "Carl (Moll) had a meeting and told us that Klimt was not there because he had a bad cough."[15] She wrote the name the way she pronounced it: Klimpt; later deleting the 'p'. From January 1898 until December 1901 Alma mentions Gustav Klimt in her diary on no fewer than one hundred and seventy-three days. Forty-seven times in 1898, seventy-nine times in 1899, thirty-three times in 1900 and fourteen times in 1901. These diary entries give a fairly precise reconstruction of events, though this does not mean that the events, actions, and conversations really did happen exactly as Alma describes them, for some of her lengthy conversations with Klimt in May 1899 in Venice were written down later, perhaps to justify her own actions, and perhaps also to make a clean break and work out the sorrows of love after the final separation.

The description of events in Gustav Klimt's letter to Carl Moll corresponds more or less to Alma's diary. Perhaps, in his verbose justification, he was unable to speak the whole truth, for he does not seem to have been entirely sure himself as to what exactly he wanted and what actually happened. "Surely you can understand," Klimt wrote to Moll, "that there are moments with regard to her when the brain's activity becomes rather irregular and muddled. Are we humans perfect?"[16] Alma's parents, her step-father Carl Moll and, in particular, her mother Anna Moll, found Klimt's explicit and implicit overtures unwelcome right from the start. She often wrote in her diary that she had been "teased about Klimt".[17] Gustav Klimt, who was a regular guest at the Moll home, sought Alma's company whenever the opportunity arose. Once, when Carl Moll had wanted to invite Klimt, but hadn't seen him to extend an invitation, Josef Maria Olbrich, who knew this, "out of spite, asked him: Tell me Klimt, are you going to the Molls' on Sunday too? He replied, very pointedly: I haven't been invited. Whereupon O. replied: For sure, you don't always have to go.."[18] Did Alma merely please Gustav Klimt "the way a pretty child pleases us painters"?[19] On 14 February 1899, following a dinner invitation at Friedrick Victor Spitzer's, Klimt and Alma "went out to his cab in the dark, [and] he said: A.S., have you ever thought of visiting me in my studio…just you, on your own? A tremor went through my whole body. I don't remember what I answered …"[20] Alma's diary gives no indication as to whether Klimt repeated the question. They met often at exhibitions of the Secession. Once, they were both standing in front of a painting called *Sunset* by a now forgotten French painter called Pierre Lagarde, which, according to Alma, was "one of the loveliest paintings I know. I told Klimt as much, and he looked at me and said: Do you really mean that. I said yes. I wouldn't have expected that of you; after all, you're not depressive … for my taste too, it's one of the loveliest pictures at the exhibition. He came closer and said: It's so disconsolate …"[21]

In March 1899, the Moll family travelled to Italy and visited Naples, Pompeii, Capri and Rome. Gustav Klimt was to travel to Florence at the end of April, and they planned to continue the journey with him via Genoa, Verona and Padua to Venice. Yet he must have been indecisive and unsure of how to respond, for he intended to write to Carl Moll to say that he could not come. "But the longing to get out of my dull hole in the wall and see something new, new works of art, new stimulation, and the thought of travelling in such pleasant company all helped to change my mind—then your telegram arrived—I travelled there—not quite myself."[22] On the evening of 24 April 1899, Gustav Klimt arrived in Florence.[23] Decades later, Carl Moll was to recall meeting Klimt at the

Ruh', Die Briefe Gustav Mahlers an Alma, edited and with a commentary by Henry-Louis de La Grange and Günther Weiß, Munich 1997, pp. 473–476.
4   Alma Mahler-Werfel, *Diaries 1898–1902*, selected and translated by Antony Beaumont, London 1998. [The English translation, published one year after the German edition, is abridged.]
5   *Diaries*, p. 153, 1. 12. 1898; p. 235–236, 16. 4. 1899.
6   Mahler-Werfel, *Mein Leben*, p. 27.
7   *Ein Glück ohne Ruh'*, p. 120.
8   Françoise Giroud, *Alma Mahler oder die Kunst, geliebt zu werden* (1988), Munich 2000, p. 10.
9   *Ein Glück ohne Ruh'*, p. 41.
10 *Diaries*, p. 465.
11 *Ein Glück ohne Ruh'*, p. 119.
12 *Diaries*, p. 465.
13 *Diaries*, p. 462
14 *Diaries*, p. 467
15 Alma Mahler-Werfel, *Tagebuch-Suiten, 1898–1902*, edited by Antony Beaumont and Susanne Rode-Breymann, Frankfurt/M. 1997, p. 5. [This is the full text of Alma Mahler-Werfel's diaries. This quote does not appear in the English edition.]
16 *Ein Glück ohne Ruh'*, p. 475.
17 *Tagebuch-Suiten, 1898–1902* p. 69, 19. 6. 1898; *Diaries* pp. 39–40, 24. 6. 1898; pp. 40–41, 6. 7. 1898; p. 101, 5. 3. 1899.
18 *Diaries*, pp. 81–82, 11. 12. 1898.
19 *Ein Glück ohne Ruh'*, p. 473, Klimt's letter to Moll.
20 *Diaries*, p. 95.

railway station. "Having received a telegraph announcing his arrival, I rushed to the station and, since the exits from the building are difficult to oversee, waited for him at the outer gate. The disembarking passengers streamed out—but Klimt was not among them. I assumed that he had missed his train and set about making enquiries about the next train from Austria. None was expected that day. I looked everywhere and left the

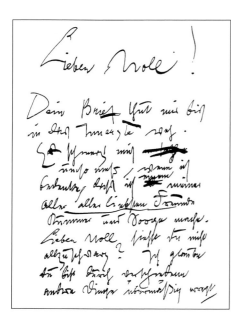

The first page of Gustav Klimt's letter to Carl Moll, May 1899

station, instinctively wandering through all the waiting rooms. Klimt was sitting there forlorn on a bench with his bag. At the hotel he was jubilantly greeted by my family. Klimt enjoyed the risotto and the Asti Spumante; next day we were in the best of sorts to enjoy all the wonders of the city."[24] A few hours before Klimt's arrival, Carl Moll had "lectured" his step-daughter Alma that she should "keep out of Klimt's way. He put it very sweetly, but he does not know me well."[25] They travelled to Fiesole and Klimt sat with Alma alone in a coach , "Like a married couple, he said, and cuddled up closer. On the way home he was sitting opposite me, and our knees touched. I couldn't sleep the night for excitement, sheer physical excitement."[26] When Klimt and Alma went to see frescos by Domenico Ghirlandaio behind an altar in the Church of Santa Maria Novella, he said, "Well, at least we've stood behind an altar".[27]

On 29 April 1899, they travelled on to Genoa, "changing trains at Pisa. Kl[imt] was sitting in a different compartment and was furious at not being with us any longer. In Genoa, towards evening, I was standing alone in my room. Kl[imt] came in: Are you on your own? Yes. And before I realized it, he'd taken me in his arms and kissed me. It only lasted a tenth of a second, for we heard a noise in the room next door. We went downstairs. That moment will remain indelibly imprinted on my mind. Halfway down, I turned round and went back up again. It's indescribable; to be kissed for the first time in my life, and that by the only person in the whole world that I love. In the evening we went for another stroll. When I came downstairs, Kl[imt] came up to me and whispered: Alma, my Alma. Mama couldn't understand what was ailing me—I looked so dreadful."[28] Two days later, in Verona, Klimt kissed her again when she "brought him his blouses" in the morning. "We were both terribly agitated."[29] Yet all her life, Alma was to remember that first kiss in Genoa.

Later, however, the love story does not seem to have been dramatic enough for her, for in her memoirs, Alma Mahler-Werfel writes that her mother "cruelly destroyed our romance. Day after day she broke her word of honour, studied the stammerings in my diary and thus kept track of the stations of my love. And in Genoa—oh horrors!—she read that Klimt had

Page from a visitors' book (25 September 1903), bearing signatures of Gustav Mahler, Alma Mahler and Klimt. Christian M. Nebehay Ges.m.b.H, Antiquariat und Kunsthandlung, Vienna

kissed me!"[30] Gustav Klimt, she claims, was then forbidden to speak to her at all. This particular detail was a figment of her imagination and an invention that even misled one of the editors of her diaries enough to draw false conclusions.[31] When one of Alma's biographers writes that Anna Moll demanded that Klimt should "disappear immediately, and from then on he secretly met with Alma in the narrow alley ways of Venice," this has as little to do with the real course of events as Klimt's promise "to abduct" Alma.[32] Gustav Klimt and the Moll family continued to travel together from Genoa to Verona and, during the journey Klimt inscribed a Latin quotation taken from Büchmann's *Geflügelten*

Worten in Alma's notebook: *Quos deus/perdere vult/prius dementat.*[33] Alma then tore Klimt's writing from her notebook and stuck in her diary. "Mama and Carl [Moll] had fallen asleep. I had manuscript paper on my lap and was composing. It was tremendously amusing."[34] In Padua, Klimt and Alma were sitting opposite each other in a coach "… our legs up close. A gentle pressure from time to time, we'd look at each other and enjoy at least a brief moment of happiness. … Mama was sitting beside me. Had she noticed? I don't know—but suddenly she said: Alma, move up closer to me, there's no room for Kl[imt]. Both of us assumed an expression of utter innocence …"[35]

On the evening of 2nd May 1899, Klimt and Alma arrived in Venice,[36] on the last stage of their journey together. There is not a word in Alma's diary about her meeting Klimt secretly in the alley ways of Venice. They went to the lido[37] and strolled through the city. Three weeks later, after her "Klimt affair" had already ended, Alma recalled a stroll by night. "Once, in Venice, we were standing on a bridge, staring into the black canal (it was night-time), in front of us the magnificent arch of the Bridge of Sighs. We were leaning on the parapet. Kl[imt] standing at my side, the others further off. Suddenly I could feel Kl[imt]'s fingers pulling, tearing at my collar. As I was leaning on the stone, the neckline tightened. Before I could realize what he was about, everyone moved on, and we had to start walking too, but further behind. As was his wont, he pinched my arm, whispering: Silly girl, Alma, I could have put my hand on your heart—easily. A cold shiver went through me, my heart missed a beat. He wanted to feel my breasts! Or did he want to know how fast my heart was beating?"[38] What really did happen in Venice on 4 and 5 May remains somewhat unclear in spite of Alma's detailed diary entries. Klimt apparently did go too far during an evening meal on 4 May and aroused Carl Moll's anger. "Kl[imt] was muttering venemously, and later, on the way to St Mark's Square, he suddenly barred my way, seething with rage and trembling with agitation."[39] Klimt himself described his dinner in his letter to Carl Moll: "Then came that evening in Venice. I am a bitter man and that sometimes expresses itself in an evil I later deeply regret. As I do now. I had drunk more quickly than I should have. I do not wish to excuse myself by that, but I was less careful in my choice of words than I should have been and what you heard probably led you to draw conclusions that are too extreme and too black. Your intervention made it clear that a life is not dreamed, but has to be lived with open eyes. The situation was quite clear, there were no doubts."[40] So Carl Moll intervened, ending Alma's "novel" in Venice. Her world fell apart. "I went to bed, I don't know how … lay all night open-eyed, thinking of nothing but that I should softly open the window and throw myself into the lagoon … And yet one clings to life!"[41] On Friday 5 May, Alma met Klimt several times on St Mark's Square and, if what she wrote in her diary is true, she swore to love Klimt "for ever" and he replied, "Alma, dear Alma, would that I'd never set eyes on you."[42]

"Kli[mt] is behaving very correctly,"[43] noted Alma on 6 May in her diary, the day when Klimt was to leave Venice at 2 a.m. "Previously we had a lunch with Asti at the Cavaletto. He sat far away … Then he had to go and fetch his luggage. Softly he said: Farewell, Alma … Then we all went off to buy Kl[imt] farewell presents … sweets, wine, flowers, sandwiches etc. Then the moment arrived for me to shake his hand, for him to look at me for the last time. I felt the ground trembling beneath my feet, the whole world darkening before my eyes."[44] Carl Moll wrote in his memoirs "We put him on a direct carriage and supplied him with all the things he liked."[45]

21 *Diaries*, pp. 68–69, 12. 11. 1898; second Secession exhibition (12. 11.—28. 12. 1898), the first in the new building. In *Ver Sacrum*, issue no. 1, January 1899, Lagarde's painting is not mentioned in the list of works sold at the 2nd exhibition; Pierre Lagarde (1853–1910) was a corresponding member of the Secession.
22 *Ein Glück ohne Ruh'*, p. 475.
23 *Diaries*, p. 123.
24 Carl Moll, "Meine Erinnerungen an Gustav Klimt", *Neues Wiener Tagblatt*, 24 January 1943; Christian M. Nebehay, *Gustav Klimt, Dokumentation*, Vienna 1969, p. 494.
25 *Diaries*, p. 123, 24. 4. 1899.
26 *Diaries*, p. 124, 26. 4. 1899.
27 *Diaries*, p. 124, 27. 4. 1899.
28 *Diaries*, p. 125.
29 *Diaries*, p. 125, 1. 5. 1899.
30 Mahler-Werfel, *Mein Leben*, cited in Antony Beaumont's introduction to the *Diaries*, p. xiii
31 Diaries, p. XII.
32 Giroud, *Alma Mahler*, p. 27.
33 *Diaries*, p. 280. "To him whom the gods have ordained to suffer, evil seems good". According to G. Büchmann, *Geflügelte Worte*, 1871, p. 239, this is from a translation "in poor latin" of the verses of an unknown Greek tragic dramatist on verses 621–623 of Sophocles' *Antigone*. The note in *Diaries*, p. 147, that the verses are a quote from *Antigone*, is incorrect.
34 *Diaries*, p. 147, written on 30. 5. 1899.
35 *Diaries*, p. 144, written on 24. 5. 1899.
36 *Diaries*, p.129.
37 *Diaries*, p. 129.
38 *Diaries*, pp. 143–144.
39 *Diaries*, p. 129.
40 *Ein Glück ohne Ruh'*, p. 475.
41 *Diaries*, p. 130.
42 *Diaries*, p. 132.
43 *Diaries*, p. 132.
44 *Diaries*, p. 133.
45 Nebehay, *Klimt, Dokumentation*, p. 494.
46 Wolfgang G. Fischer, *Gustav Klimt und Emilie Flöge*, Vienna 1987, p. 170, no. 8.
47 Emilie Flöge was the sister of Klimt's sister-in-law Helene Klimt, the wife of his brother Ernst, who died young. Klimt had begun a romance with Emilie Flöge in the spring and was to maintain a close relationship with her throughout his life. See Hansjörg Krug, "Liebe Midi, Ein Liebesbrief Gustav Klimts", in *Parnass*, special issue on Gustav Klimt, June 2000, pp. 22–23. Carl and Anna Moll knew of Klimt's circumstances. On 4 August 1898 Anna Moll pointed out to her daughter for the first time that Klimt was "involved with his sister-in-law," and mentioned this again

Before leaving Venice, Gustav Klimt sent a telegram to Emilie Flöge saying "arriving sunday morning then to you. gustav".[46] On Sunday morning, Gustav Klimt was back home with his Midi, as he fondly called Emilie Flöge.[47] We do not know what he thought or felt about his Italian adventure. When Klimt wrote to Carl Moll in May 1899, saying that he did not know his situation himself and that the only thing he was sure of was that he was a pure fool,[47] he may possibly have had in mind the fact that two young women were expecting his children. On 6 July 1899, Maria Ucicky, a laundry maid from Prague, gave birth to a son, Gustav Ucicky, who was later to become a famous film director[49] and in August 1899, Maria Zimmerman bore a son to Klimt, who was also christened Gustav.[50] As for Alma Schindler, Gustav Klimt was to prove right in saying "I do not think she will find it difficult to forget. Let us hope that time will quickly heal."[51] In February 1900, Alma met Alexander von Zemlinsky at the home of Friedrich Victor Spitzer.[52] She fell in love with the 28-year-old composer and, on 28 July 1901, Alma made a remarkable admission in her diary: "My longing is boundless. I believe he's the only man I can ever love—that I ever loved. My love for Kl[imt] was a thin gruel compared to the thick broth of my present feelings."[53]

on several occasions (*Diaries*, pp. 49, 63, 105, 124). Alma never mentions a name in her diary, but always speaks of the "sister-in-law". A conversation between Klimt and Alma on a boat trip in Venice, which she recorded some time later, provides an interesting insight (*Tagebuch-Suiten*, p. 294, 8. 6. 1899). Alma seems to have confused Helene Klimt with Emilie Flöge, whom she did not know and who she saw for the first time on 3 November 1900 at the opening of the 8th Secession exhibition. "Later they pointed out his sisters-in-law to me. They're in all his pictures. One of them—the younger—is unique. Strange eyes. Experienced, sad, floating. He wasn't there." (*Diaries*, p.338.) The woman she was describing was Emilie Flöge.
48   *Ein Glück ohne Ruh'*, p. 474.
49   Nebehay, *Klimt, Von der Zeichnung zum Bild*, pp. 272–273, Strobl, Vol. 4, No. 3315.
50   Nebehay, *Klimt, Von der Zeichnung zum Bild*, pp. 264–270. Marie Zimmermann sat as model for the frontal standing girl in *Schubert at the Piano II*, 1899 (Novotny-Dobai, No.101); Strobl, Vol. 4, p. 56–57. Klimt's relationship with Marie Zimmermann lasted until around 1903, a second son, Otto, died on 11 September 1902, two and a half months after his birth. There is no evidence to support the frequently cited claim that Klimt had fourteen illegitimate children, as there was no probate procedure after his death; an obituary at WStLA; Strobl, Vol. 4, pp. 221 and p. 222, Note 2.
51   *Glück ohne Ruh'*, p. 475, Klimt's letter to Moll. The saying "eilenden heilenden Zeit" ("fleeting, healing time") is echoed on a New Year card from Klimt: "Prosit / Neujahr / Gus / Die Zeit eilt / Die Zeit heilt / Glück" ("Cheers / New Year / Time is fleeting / Time is healing / Happiness"); Strobl, Vol. 1, No. 281, dated 1 January 1897.
52   *Diaries*, p. 463.
53   *Diaries*, p. 421

Gustav Klimt and Women's Fashion

ANGELA VÖLKER

Gustav Klimt's interest in fashion and in the clothes and fabrics worn by his models or surrounding them is driven primarily by his interest in the sitter he is painting or in the theme he is addressing. Though this is particularly evident in the portraits, it is also true of the allegories. It is occasionally claimed that Klimt had a specific artistic interest in fashion as a creative discipline—a claim based on the fact that photos of his partner Emilie Flöge were published in his name—but this is neither documented nor even plausible.[1] Klimt's portrayal of robes and textiles is, for the most part, realistic and true to detail within the scope of his stylistic development. After 1900, he was inspired by the stylisation of the time, which developed into the more stringent ornamentation of his so-called golden period. The late phase is informed by vividly coloured patterning.

As for decorative details, apart from the neo-classicist forms of his early period, Klimt shows a distinct and unbroken interest in the art of Japan, later of China, Ancient Egypt, and in such simple ornamental forms as the spiral and the square, complemented by the fashionable details of the day. For the robes, fabrics and backgrounds of his portraits, he uses all-over patterns drawn from these wellsprings, generally replacing one another in chronological sequence, but also used in parallel. In this light, the 1897 drawing *Tragedy*[2] which unites all the above components in a single picture appears to be a programmatic summary of Klimt's use of ornament. Here, antiquity represents the personification itself, in type, dress and attributes. *Tragedy* wears a fashionably broad collar or choker, known as a 'collier de chien' and worked in the style of ancient jewellery. It features again in a number of in Klimt's later female personifications and portraits, adapted to suit the respective theme.[3] The background shows, to the right and left, women in long, empire-style flowing dresses, surrounded by spiral ornaments. Spiral forms also decorate the narrow margin around the central picture. At the top, between the two female figures in the surround, there is a dragon reminiscent of those that often adorn Chinese robes. Finally, the background forms a dense pattern of leaves based on the Japanese style.[4]

Klimt's drawings indicate that his sitters sometimes tried on different dresses before deciding on the one in which they were was to be painted.[5] Klimt's repertoire of accessories, to be seen repeatedly in the sketches of his models, include the *ball-entrée*—a short cape with long decorative trims—fur collars, shawls and stoles. Photographs of Klimt's partner Emilie Flöge, show interesting parallels to the dresses and accessories in his female portraits. As a fashion designer described by Klimt himself as innovative and willing to take risks,[6] and whose regular visits to Paris kept her well informed of the latest developments, she very probably advised Klimt in these matters,

1   E. g. Hanel Koeck, "Moda e Società intorno al 1900. La moda a Vienna", in Le Arti a Vienna, exhib. cat. Venice 1984, pp. 503–517, here p. 507; Wolfgang Georg Fischer, *Gustav Klimt und Emilie Flöge. Genie and Talent, Freundschaft and Besessenheit*, Vienna 1987, pp. 93ff.; photographs in *Deutsche Kunst und Dekoration XIX*, Oct. 1906—March 1907, pp. 63–73.
2   Gottfried Fliedl, *Gustav Klimt, 1862–1918. Die Welt in weiblicher Gestalt*, Cologne 1989, p. 45. The frame is also illustrated in 1898 as a decoration of Klimt's biography in the March edition of *Ver Sacrum* and in Martin Gerlach's *Allegorien* (N.F. no. 66).
3   Cf. a photograph by Madame d'Ora of Alma Maler-Werfel, 1909 in Werner J. Schweiger, *Die Wiener Werkstätte*, Vienna 1995, fig. p. 72; cf. also auction catalogue of Sotheby's Geneva, *Important Jewellery by René Lalique*, 20. 11. 1996, cat. no. 6 or 24.
4   Similar to the wall ornaments and golden laurel dome of the Secession building of 1897–98, cf. Fliedl 1989, p. 98 f.; In 1899 the same pattern inspired Kolo Moser to create his "Schweigen des Abends"/"Silence of Evening" fabric, cf. Peter Panzer, Johannes Viennaeinger, *Verborgene Impressionen/Hidden Impressions*, exhib. cat. Vienna 1990, p. 310; Japonisme catalogue Kamm, Moserstoff, Secession.

and perhaps even influenced him. She may even have provided accessories or helped him to obtain them.

The photo series of 1906–07, mentioned above, shows Emilie Flöge wearing one of the loose-fitting dresses, known as *Reformkleid*, that she probably designed herself, similar to those worn by Magda Mautner-Markhof[7] and Adele Bloch Bauer (ill. p. 116) in Klimt's portraits of them. In a photograph taken in 1908 by the famous fashion and society photographer Madame d'Ora (Dora Kallmus), Flöge can be seen wearing a *ball-entrée*[8] of the kind that can also be seen in the portrait of Marie Henneberg (ill. p. 94) and Hermine Gallias (ill. p. 104) as well as a number of sketches by Klimt.[9] Flöge can also be seen in other photographs by the same Viennese photographer wearing fashionable neo-empire dresses similar to that worn by Adele Bloch-Bauer in another Klimt portrait of 1912 (ill. p. 125).[10] Finally, there is a coloured photograph of her, probably taken in 1913, wearing a Chinese dragon robe.[11] Details similar to these motifs can be found in Klimt's portraits of women from 1912 onwards.

Gustav Klimt, Final drawing for *Tragedy,* 1897. Black chalk, stomped; washed pencil; heightened with white and gold, 42 x 31 cm, Vienna, Historisches Museum

Unfortunately, with the exception of his own blue painter's smock in which he was frequently photographed,[12] none of the dresses or accessories in Klimt's possession have survived. It was not until 1983 that the remains of Emilie Flöge 's estate were discovered, including a large number of textiles which may well have played a role in Klimt's female portraits.[13] Klimt certainly knew this collection and may even have owned similar items himself, as other Viennese artists did. It includes two Chinese robes, a North African caftan, Eastern European embroidery and the front panel of an Indian robe, the rest of which was owned by Josef Hoffmann, who also collected Eastern European embroidery.[14] A colleague of Emilie Flöge describes the Eastern European and Chinese embroideries in the reception room of Flöge's salon designed by the Wiener Werkstätte: "On one side there was a fireplace, above which there was a beautifully embroidered dragon, and at the side there were display cases full of beautiful embroideries, Hungarian costumes, Slovakian embroideries, which were something very special."[15] In his early phase, Klimt used not only neo-classical dress, but also contemporary fashion for his allegories, as in his 1895 allegory of *Love* (ill. p. 227).[16] The woman is wearing a close-fitting standing collar trimmed with a frill, and a top with voluminously puffed leg o' mutton sleeves that narrow just above the elbow. The same details can be found in 1898 in portraits of Helene Klimt (ill. p. 83) and Sonja Knips (ill. p. 85).

5   E.g., Adele Bloch-Bauer I (Strobl, Vol. 1, 1054–1057, 1096–1114), Paula Zuckerkandl (Strobl, Vol. 2, 2053–2072), Eugenia Primavesi (Strobl, vol. 2, 2141–2154) or Friederike Beer-Monti (Strobl, Vol. 3, 2524–2541).
6   Klimt writes to Emilie in 1909 from Paris: "...hier kann man alles wagen an Tracht—and fällt nicht auf. Hier gieng's Dir gut." ("...here one can dare to wear anything without causing a stir. You would be happy here.") Hans Bisanz et al (eds.), *Emilie Flöge and Gustav Klimt. Doppelporträt in Idealland-schaft,* exhib. cat., Vienna 1988/89, cat. no. 6.148.
7   Strobl, Vol. 1, 1209–1225.
8   The photograph probably shows her in the dress she wore to the opening of the 1908 Kunst-schau.

Klimt uses these large leg o' mutton sleeves again in 1899, modified somewhat, in *Schubert at the Piano.*[17] In *Music I* of 1895[18] we find a more freely adapted version of this voluminous sleeve form integrated into an antique style robe. Fashion details also occur in later pictures of biblical and allegorical themes by Klimt. One example is the broad and close-fitting choker that was evidently highly fashionable around 1900, which can be seen in both his portrayals of *Judith,* in 1901 (ill. p. 221) and 1909 (ill. p. 225) and which is also worn by a number of figures in the faculty paintings created between 1901 and 1907.[19]

Whereas Klimt's allegories and portraits of his early period look to the art of classical antiquity, by the turn of the century his main inspiration seems to be Japanese and Ancient Egyptian ornament, and, following a journey undertaken in 1903, the magnificent and sumptuous mosaics of Ravenna.[20] From around 1909 until his death, he became increasingly interested in Chinese art. A visit to the Musée Guimet, housing the largest collection of Far Eastern art in Paris, made a lasting impression on him in 1909.[21] Historical or exotic ornaments are invariably blended with the contemporary flair of the sitters themselves. Thoroughly up-to-date fashion aspects are strongly expressed in a series of portraits in which Klimt painted women with huge hats, such as the *Woman with Hat and Feather Boa* (ill. p. 210), which may possibly have been influenced by Henri de Toulouse Lautrec's treatment of similar subject matter.

Gustav Klimt clearly had a preference for pale-coloured dresses. A number of the women he painted are wearing white or pastel shades. This did not necessarily comply with current fashion trends. The softly fluid fabrics, often transparent, of the classical-style robes in his early allegories are echoed in the thoroughly different pink and white dresses in his portraits of Sonja Knips (ill. p. 85), Serena Lederer (ill. p. 89) and Gertrud Loews (ill. p. 99). Knips's highly fashionable frilled dress underlines the wearer's girlishness, while Serena Lederer's empire-style *Reformkleid* designed for a body unrestricted by whalebone corsets, emphasises the clearly sensual aspect of the wearer. Gertha Felsövanyis wears a close-fitting white dress with broad sleeve flounces and a transparent shawl with a pale blue border. Together with the unusual vertical format of the portrait, the dress underlines the petite stature and fragile complexion of this red-headed woman.

In the portraits of Marie Henneberg of 1901 (ill. p. 94), Hermine Gallia of 1903 (ill. p. 104) Margarethe Stonborough-Wittgenstein, completed in 1905 (ill. p. 109) and Fritza Riedler in 1906 (ill. p. 113), all created after 1900, but before the golden period, white dresses and accessories and the overall mood and pose of the women convey an air of cool detachment. Fritza Riedler's flounced dress has a

Emilie Flöge, photograph by Madame d'Ora, 1909. Vienna, Private collection

material lightness and voluminous softness that deliberately contrast with the geometry of its surroundings. The same tendency can be found in the portrait of Margarethe Stonborough-Wittgenstein with her upright pose, head held high, in an off-the-shoulder evening dress, surrounded by cool colours. Hermine Gallia is wearing a magnificent white dress with a train and a white *ball-entrée* of richly pleated, thin fabric that echoes the smocked sleeves.[22] The flounces of the skirt, sleeves and *ball-entrée* make her appear soft and feminine even in this representative and rather stiff portrait. In Marie Henneberg's portrait (ill. p. 94) a similar *ball-entrée* flatteringly frames the face that is gazing out of the picture so seriously and even dominates the rest of her attire.

Ball-entrée, Vienna, Historisches Museum

For the planned portrait of Magda Mautner-Markhof that Klimt started in 1904, we have only some drawings showing her in a dress with voluminous flounces on the sleeves, bodice and skirt. Like the dresses mentioned above, it was probably also made of a pale, light fabric. The loose-fitting cut, the many flounces and the fabric recall the *Reformkleid* worn by Emilie Flöge in a 1909 photograph by Madame d'Ora.[23] A pale and richly pleated dress is also worn by Adele Bloch-Bauer in the golden portrait of her created in 1907 (ill. p. 117). White dresses can also be found in Klimt's later period—in the 1912 portrait of Paula Zuckerkandl,[24] in the second portrait of Adele Bloch-Bauer (ill. p. 125) and in the 1914 portrait of Elisabeth Bachofen-Echt.[25]

Even in the highly stylised attire worn by Adele Bloch-Bauer in the first golden portrait of 1907 (ill. p. 117), the cut and quality of the fabric are clearly rendered. The many surviving drawings indicate that she or Klimt had made a conscious decision to feature this spectacularly sumptuous *Reformkleid* made of yards and yards of softly draped fabric,[26] with a short, bolero-style jacket that she has taken off in the picture. Adele Bloch-Bauer is also wearing a broad, close-fitting choker or 'collier de chien' and a highly fashionable hairstyle. A comparison of the drawings with the finished portrait of Bloch-Bauer shows that, for the final version, Klimt has abandoned the character and original effect of the dress, which is so clearly worked in the sketches, in favour of the overall pictorial concept.[27] The light, pale fabric has completely lost its material quality, and the original texture of the fabric can only be seen in the gentle, parallel lines of folds. The front panel of the dress, covered with abstract Japanese and Ancient Egyptian motifs, creates a patterned area reminiscent of a metal carapace. In principle, if not in detail, however, the portrayal of the dress does correspond to the drawings.

Gustav Klimt's studio in Hietzing, before 1918

9   Cf. e.g., Strobl, Vol. 2, 1182a–1184.
10 Exhib. cat. Vienna 1988/89, cat. nos. 5.1.11 and 5.1.12.
11 Cf. Fischer 1987, fig. 68, p. 68.
12 H. Bisanz, "Arbeitskittel und Priestergewand", in exhib. cat. Vienna 1988/89, p. 15 and cat. no. 2.1.
13 Fischer 1987; exhib. cat. Vienna 1988/89, pp. 83 ff.
14 H. Egger, "Josef Hoffmann und das Ornament", in *Josef Hoffmann and neues internationales Möbeldesign aus Österreich*, exhib. cat. Prague 1998, p. 29. There is a 1908 photograph of Mileva Roller, Alfred Roller's wife, wearing an Indian robe. Cf. Monika Faber, *Madame d'Ora. Vienna-Paris. Portraits aus Kunst und Gesellschaft 1907–1957*, Vienna 1983, Fig. 103. A fashion design created by Josef Wimmer-Wisgrill around 1910 has survived from the fashion department of the Wiener Werkstätte, featuring "Slovakian Embroidery" as a decorative element. Cf. Angela Völker, *Wiener Mode und Modefotografie. Die Modeabteilung der Viennaer Werkstätte 1911–1932*, Munich, Paris 1984, p. 16, Fig. 9; cf. in general terms H. Bisanz, "Kunst und Folklore", in exhib. cat. Vienna 1988/89, p. 82.

One interesting exception is Emilie Flöge's dress in the 1902 portrait of her, which, in spite of such fashionable details as the close-fitting cloth choker and the long puffed sleeves, defies classification in the fashionable trends of the day. It already foreshadows the plainer, more stylised portrayals of dresses of the so-called golden period. Emilie Flöge's straight-cut dress with its pattern of spirals and squares and a bodice with Japanese motifs appears like an abstract, incorporeal ornamental shell. In common with the *Beethoven frieze* and the university pictures, it reflects his intensive study of Japanese art in terms of stylised ornament, the importance of the plane, and the degree of abstraction this entails.[28] Emilie Flöge as fashion designer is, herself, like an allegory or personification, and so it is understandable that Klimt did not go in for a detailed portrayal of fashion details in her portrait. As Hans Bisanz writes, Emilie Flöge 's dress is in itself "a fantasy creation that was really designed by Klimt".[29] Flöge did not like the portrait and it was sold in 1908 to the Niederösterreichisches Landesmuseum.[30] Perhaps she found it difficult, as a fashion designer, to accept the abstract portrayal of her dress.

The portraits of Flöge and, in particular, of Adele Bloch-Bauer, clearly reflect Klimt's approach to fashion. As a precise observer of his clientele and their clothing, he examined the cut and detail of any dress with a realistic eye, only to place it entirely in the service of his compositional idea.

Klimt intensified his tendency towards ornamentalization and flat patterning, especially in his allegorical figures. The portrayal of *Immoderation* in the *Beethoven frieze*[31], the personifications in the university pictures,[32] *Hope I* (ill. p. 245), *The Three Stages of Life* (ill. p. 242), *Water Snakes I* (ill. p. 236), *The Kiss* (ill. p. 231), *Danae* (ill. p. 240) and *Expectation* and *Fulfilment* (ill. p. 233) in the *Stoclet frieze*[33] may all be seen as examples of this. He was inspired above all by Japanese and ancient Egyptian motifs, and by the mosaics of Ravenna, to create his specifically planar patterned abstractions. The robes, fabrics and bodies all seem to freeze in what is, for Klimt, a suitable form of portrayal in which clothing can be used to point towards the universal validity of the allegory as distinct from everyday life. Japanese art led Klimt to study the way different patterns can be juxtaposed, which he may have noted in Hokusai's woodcuts, and which is so characteristic of Klimt's later work, albeit using Chinese motifs.

Japonisme and an interest in East Asian art were aroused at the turn of the century by illustrated publications, exhibitions, museums and private collections. The vivid colours and, for all its stylisation, the vitality of expression inherent in Chinese art, encouraged Klimt to adopt a new style of portraiture around 1910 that abandons all "Japanese" stylisation and rigidity. As photographs of his study show, Klimt himself owned Japanese and Chinese prints and displayed them prominently.[34] More important still for Klimt may have been his encounter with the work of the Fauves, especially Henri Matisse, to whom an entire section of the second Kunstschau of 1909 was dedicated[35] and whose paintings he may well have studied at first hand in Paris that same year. Klimt was not the only artist to be influenced by their handling of colour, the intensity of their palette and the boldness of their brushwork.

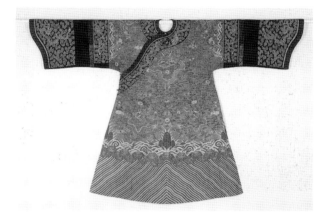

His interests in all things Chinese was consolidated by the commission received in 1912 for a portrait of Paula Zuckerkandl.[36] Her husband and her brother-in-law—the industrialist Victor Zuckerkandl and the famous anatomist Emil Zuckerkandl—owned important East Asian collections.[37] It is probably for this reason that Klimt included Chinese motifs in this portrait for the first time. The background is made up of juxtaposed Chinese cloud band motifs, and the large rectangular cloth draped over the sitter's shoulders, a fashionable accessory of the early twentieth century, might also have come from China, where it was embroidered for export to Europe and imported through Spain. The narrow-cut, white dress, on the other hand, is made of light, transparent fabric. The head is surrounded by an aureole of Chinese motifs, including a phoenix, set apart from the rest of the background.

In almost all of Klimt's portraits, we find traces of East Asian art. The bands of clouds, the fabulous creatures, the bright stripes suggesting air or rippling water, are all among the motifs that adorn the Chinese dragon robes,[38] from which Klimt may have taken some inspiration (there is a photograph of Flöge wearing just such a robe). In the background of the portraits, we find Chinese theatre figures, which Klimt may have seen on vases or in woodcuts. Klimt succeeds in integrating his elegant and fashionably dressed sitters almost casually within a framework of Asiatic and European motifs.

In the second portrait of Adele Bloch-Bauer (ill. p. 125) the harmonious juxtaposition of bands of clouds on the floor, stylised European flowers on the wall, and a background scene of Chinese figures, horseback riders and a house, is quite impressive. Bloch-Bauer stands in front of this background enclosed in a narrow cut, white dress with black ornaments, high waisted in the Parisian neo-empire style and wearing a broad choker that seems to set her head apart, lending her facial expression even more aloofness. The broad, black brim of her hat seems to shield her from the temperamental Chinese horsemen behind her.

Elisabeth Bachofen-Echt[39] is also wearing a highly fashionable dress with a hooped skirt and a flora-embroidered stole of transparent chiffon in the 1914 portrait of her.[40] She is standing on a contemporary rug such as those designed by Joseph Hoff-

Dragon robe, silk, painted and broidered, late 19th century. Vienna, MAK—Museum für angewandte Kunst

15 Exhib. cat. Vienna 1988/89, p. 34.
16 Fliedl 1989, p. 34.
17 Fliedl 1989, p. 47.
18 Fliedl 1989, p. 13. In 1901 Klimt used the personification in modified form in *Ver Sacrum*, issue 13, p. 214. Cf. Strobl, Vol. 1, 715
19 Hgyeia in Medicine, cf. Fliedl 1989, p. 85, and Justitia in Jurisprudence, cf. Fritz Novotny/Johannes Dobai, *Gustav Klimt*, Salzburg 1967, plate 16.
20 Klimt in a postcard from Ravenna to E. Flöge: "...die Mosaiken von unerhörter Pracht...", ("...the magnificent mosaics") in exhib. cat. Vienna 1988/89, cat. nos. 6.9.
21 He writes laconically to Emilie Flöge that the museum is "sehr interessant" ("very interesting"), cf. exhib. cat. Vienna 1988/89, cat. nos. 6.154.
22 Cf. Anm. 7.
23 Cat. Vienna 1988/89, Cat. nos. 5.1.10, fig. p. 44.
24 Novotny-Dobai 1967, Nr. 178, plate. 76.
25 Novotny-Dobai 1967, Nr. 188, plate 92.
26 Cf. on this type of reform fashion see K. Moser's 1902 design in exhib. cat. Vienna 1988/89, cat. nos. 1.2.3.2, or the photo of E. Flöge in Christian Brandstätter, *Klimt & die Mode*, Vienna 1998, unpaginated (15th double page).

mann for clients of the Wiener Werkstätte.[41] The Chinese figures in the background surrounding her keep at a respectable distance, and the body of the young woman is framed by the triangular symmetrical pattern of a Chinese dragon robe.

Eugenia Primavesi (ill. p. 129), whose portrait Klimt painted in 1913–14, was a co-owner of the Wiener Werkstätte and was actively involved in its programme.[42] It may

Flora, fabric design by Leopold Blonder, Wiener Werkstätte, 1911–14

either have been through her or through his work for the Palais Stoclet that he got to know the fabrics produced by the Wiener Werkstätte from 1910 onwards. The motifs and colours of Primvesi's dress recall Eastern European embroideries and the Wiener Werkstätte fabrics they inspired, without actually displaying any specifically certain recognisable pattern. Eugenia 'Mäda' Primavesi is wearing a straight white caftan of the kind offered to guests at their country house in Moldavia, built by Joseph Hoffmann.[43] These are the comfortable *Reformkleid* dresses that were popular among Viennese artist circles. Similar dresses can be found in the fashion department of the Wiener Werkstätte,[44] including Klimt's own painting smock. Photographs of Emilie Flöge also show her wearing similar dresses.[45] In the portrait of Eugenia Primavesi, Klimt begins to mix Chinese elements such as the phoenix on the top right with folkloristic European motifs.[46] Inspired by the diversity and colours of East Asian patterns, Klimt appears to have taken an interest in the expressive textiles of his own surroundings. A late allegory in which the combination of fabrics and patterns plays an important role, is his painting *The Bride* (ill. p. 248), left unfinished in 1918, indicating that Klimt was also beginning to address this genre with more vitality and intensive colouring, through the juxtaposition of different patterns.

Klimt's virtuoso handling of combinations of patterns from different sources is at its most compelling in his 1916 portrait of Friederike Beer-Monti.[47] She is wearing a dress made of *Marina* fabric designed by Dagobert Peche for the Wiener Werkstätte and a fur jacket with the lining turned out to reveal the Wiener Werkstätte's *Flora* fabric designed by Leo Blonder. In the background are Chinese battle scenes, featuring figures that are proportionally larger than in the other portraits, intertwined to create a sculptural pattern. The model is standing on a rug that bears the typically stylised blossom forms of the day. A surviving preparatory sketch for this portrait shows a rare example of Klimt's painstaking study of the fabric pattern for the jacket lining.[48] More often than not, he designed his elaborate patterns directly on the canvas. Not even the portrait of Johanna Staude (ill. p. 143), which remained unfinished in 1918, has such a study to accompany it, showing how he worked the fabric pattern for her blouse. Yet it is painted with such precision that it is quite evidently the Wiener Werkstätte fabric *Blätter* (Leaves) designed by Martha Alber. Klimt has used it as a vibrant contrast to the orange background and the head of the sitter. Most of Klimt's clientele came from the wealthy Jewish bourgeoisie. As his portraits clearly show, it was in the fashion interests of these Viennese ladies not to be committed to a single fashion trend. They chose between Parisian or London haute couture, like Serena Lederer, or Wiener Werkstätte fashion like Friederike Beer-Monti, and the specifically Viennese *Reformkleid* fashion worn by Adele Bloch-Bauer or Eugenia Primavesi. Emilie Flöge may be regarded as the model for this. A

27 No preliminary studies for the portrait of Emilie Flöge have survived.
28 Cf. K. Koshi, "Japanisches bei Klimt" and A. Mabuchi, "Die japanischen Muster and Motive bei Klimt", beides in Exhib. cat. Vienna 1990, p. 94ff./p. 109 ff.
29 Exhib. cat. Vienna 1988/89, p. 27.
30 Exhib. cat. Vienna 1988/89, cat. nos. 4.1.1.
31 Fliedl 1989, pp. 104, 1902.
32 See note 20.
33 Fliedl 1989, pp. 152, 153.
34 Exhib. cat. Vienna 1990, p. 158.
35 Catalogue of the 1909 international Kunstschau in Vienna, pp. 25 f. (Room 13); pp. 33 f. (Room 18).
36 Novotny-Dobai 1967, No. 178, plate 76.
37 See the auction catalogue of the Dorotheum Vienna pertaining to the estate of Prof. Emil Zuckerkandl, 5. and 6. 6. 1916. The Eastern Asian collection of Victor Zuckerkandls is discussed by Alice Strobl in Strobl, Vol. 2, 259.

number of photographs show her wearing Parisian style neo-empire dresses and a variety of *Reformkleid* dresses, sometimes with fashionable flounces and standing collar, sometimes in simple and casual, caftan-style dresses that completely negate the body. Klimt's sketches show that he was interested in tailoring details and fashion details only where these were important to the overall visual effect of the portrait. Nevertheless, he had a preference for certain fabrics and accessories such as *ball-entrées*, fur collars, stoles or shawls, because they flatter the sitter. When Klimt was looking for a suitable dress for his sitter, he did not pander unquestioningly to the taste of his client. He wanted to characterise her through her dress, with the fabric and cut emphasising the personality of the person whose portrait he was painting. The surroundings and backgrounds, which had a similar function, were clearly added without consultation. He was particularly interested in the impact of the portrait. It was his intention that the personality and aura of the woman he painted should be conveyed and emphasised by means of her clothing as well.

38 By way of example: *Wally*, 1916 (Novotny-Dobai 1967, No. 200, plate 99), *Pelzkragen/Fur Collar*, c.1916 (Novotny-Dobai 1967, No. 197), *Dame mit Muff/Lady with Muff* 1916/17 (Novotny-Dobai 1967, Nr. 207, Strobl), *Freundinnen/Friends*, 1916/17 (Fliedl 1992, fig. p. 224), *Tänzerin/Dancer* (Ria Munk) 1916/18 (Fliedl 1989, Fig. p. 206), *Dame mit Fächer/Lady with Fan* 1917/18, (Novotny-Dobai 1967, No. 203, plate 98), *Iltispelz/Fur* 1916/18 (Toni Stooss/ Christoph Doswald, Gustav Klimt, exhib. cat. Zürich 1992, cat. nos. G 55).
39 See note 27.
40 Cf. Angela Völker, *Moda Wiener Werkstätte*, Florence 1990, figs. 57, 59.
41 E.g., the Gallia family apartment at Wohllebengasse in Vienna, cf. Terence Lane, *Vienna 1913. Josef Hoffmann's Gallia Apartment*, Victoria (Australia) 1984, pp. 37, 45.
42 Since 1914 the Primavesis had owned shares in the Wiener Werkstätte. Cf. A. Völker, *Die Stoffe der Viennaer Werkstätte, 1910–1930*, Vienna 1990.
43 Cf. Völker 1990, pp. 52–58; Klimt was also a guest here and there is a photograph of him wearing such a kaftan, cf. ibid., fig. 81.
44 Cf. Angela Völker, *Wiener Mode und Modefotografie. Die Modeabteilung der Wiener Werkstätte*, Munich/Paris 1984, p. 9, fig. 1.
45 Exhib. cat. Vienna 1988/89, Cat. nos. 7.1, 7.2.
46 See H. Bisanz, "Kunst und Folklore", in exhib. cat. Vienna 1988/89, p. 82.
47 Novotny-Dobai 1967, no. 196, plate 83; Völker 1984, frontispiece.
48 Strobl, Vol. 3, 2550.

Gustav Klimt and Photography

FRANZ EDER

Studies from photographs (c. 1880)

Christian M. Nebehay[1] makes mention of hand-written memories by Hermine Klimt probably dating form 1928.[2] These contain references to Gustav Klimt's use of photographs as visual aids: "... Then came the day of admission to the Österreichische Museum's preparatory school [1876] two years later my brother Ernst left the Bürgerschule and was also admitted as a regular pupil. They began to work diligently, and in their free time at home drew portraits from photographs. My sister's girlfriend was the first test person ... In this way, he did countless enlarged drawings from photographs in order to earn some money and make it easier for father to support the family. At that time [1880–1884] we lived in the attic flat of Mariahilferstrasse 75, a former monastery. Many an artistic piece saw the light of day there, including some for the work Art [allegories] and Emblems ...".[3]

Photographs for the Künstler-Compagnie (1886–88)

In 1886, the Viennese silverware manufacturer A. Markowitsch provided premises where the Künstler-Compagnie,[4] founded jointly by the student friends Gustav and Ernst Klimt and Franz Matsch in 1879, could carry out preparatory studies for the ceiling paintings they had been commissioned to create for one of the two main staircases in the new Burgtheater. In the course of that work, photographs were taken and utilised as intermediary studies.

The photographs of individual models or groups that have survived from that time betray a high degree of professionalism. However, as with similar photographs

Costume photograph of Georg Klimt as Romeo (with beard)

Gustav Klimt, Portrait study for Romeo and a man in the auditorium (Strobl No. 143)

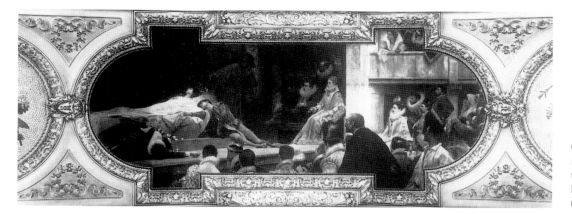

Gustav Klimt, *The Globe Theatre in London*, ceiling painting on the south staircase of the Burgtheater in Vienna—1886 (Novotny-Dobai No. 39)

Gustav Klimt, *The Globe Theatre in London*, original sized preliminary drawing for the ceiling painting on the staircase of the Burgtheater. Found in the attic of the Burgtheater in 1996.

from the estate of Hans Makart, auctioned in 1885, the photographer is unknown.[5] Makart's "costume studies" differ significantly from those of the Künstler-Compagnie, which were taken about ten years later. Initially, the artists themselves stood as models, though other family members were also photographed in various costumes and poses, for example, as studies for the ceiling painting *Theater Shakespeares* (The Globe Theatre in London), showing the death scene from Shakespeare's *Romeo and Juliet* (act 5, scene 3), for the main staircase in the new Burgtheater. In the surviving costume photograph, Georg Klimt represents Romeo with a beard, whereas the pencil studies[6] by Gustav Klimt and the painting[7] were done using a model who was clean-shaven. Klimt noted an address, "Matzleinsdorferstraße N 34", on the drawing of the head of the dead Juliet[8], just in case he should require that model again.

Two other photographs show not only Klimt's brother Ernst and his student friend Franz Matsch, but also his sister Hermine Klimt dressed up as courtly spectators at the play. Unlike the Makart photographs, these costumed figures are already sitting in the poses selected for the final version of the painting. It can be assumed that Gustav Klimt was fully involved in "positioning" the models for the photographs, as he himself does not appear in this part of the painting, although the painting has definitely been attributed to him. It is extremely interesting to note that, behind the seated female model (Hermine Klimt), we can actually see the head of the dead Romeo, sketched on paper in the original size, plus the sketch of the head of the onlooker from the left-hand side of the auditorium. The oil sketch (Novotny-Dobai No. 34) does not include this latter figure. The cartoons or transfer sketches for the ceiling paintings in the Burgtheater discovered in the attic of the Burgtheater in 1996[9] will surely shed more light on this once they have been preserved and restored. The photograph of the two male spectators is of enormous documentary value because in it one of them (Franz Matsch) is resting his arm on an oil sketch of the ceiling painting *The Globe Theatre in London*.[10]

1   Christian M. Nebehay, *Gustav Klimt Dokumentation*, Vienna 1969.
2   There are several copies and fragments in private ownership, but a final version is impossible to compile.
3   *Allegorien und Embleme*, ed. by Martin Gerlach, with explanatory texts by Albert Ilg, Vienna 1882.
4   The Künstler-Compagnie was founded in 1879 by Franz Matsch (1861–1942), Gustav Klimt (1862–1918) and Ernst Klimt (1864–1892) and existed until the death of Ernst Klimt in 1892.
5   Catalogue of the art and antiquities from the estate of Hans Makart, ed. by the guardian of the Makart children, A. Streit, publishing house R. v. Waldheim, Vienna 1885. Public auction by H. O. Miethke, Vienna, Neuer Markt 13, 26 March 1885.
6   Alice Strobl, *Gustav Klimt, Die Zeichnungen I, 1878–1903*, Salzburg 1980. Cf. Strobl p. 143
7   Fritz Novotny und Johannes Dobai, *Gustav Klimt* (with list of paintings), Salzburg 1967 (Novotny-Dobai), 39.
8   Strobl, vol 1, 142
9   Reference was made in *Art* 3/99, *Format* 9/99, *Profil* 9/99 to the preliminary drawings discovered by Angelina Pötschner in the attic of the Burgtheater in 1996.
10   Novotny-Dobai nos. 34, 39, 32.

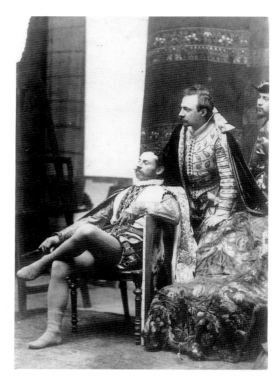

Hermine Klimt in a costume photograph, in the background an original drawing for the ceiling painting with a head of Romeo.

Costume photograph for *The Globe Theatre in London* with Ernst Klimt and Franz Matsch

11 Novotny-Dobai no. 44 and in Nebehay 1969, p. 98
12 Reproduced in the contribution by Susanna Partsch, "Gustav Klimt—'Als Person nicht extra interessant'. Von der Ringstraße zur Secesion" in *Gegenwelten, Gustav Klimt—Künstlerleben im Fin de Siècle*, ed. by Christoph Hölz, commissioned by the Bayerische Vereinsbank, Munich 1996.
13 Nebehay 1969, c. 1906
14 Wolfgang Georg Fischer, *Klimt und Emilie Flöge, Genie und Talent, Freundschaft und Besessenheit*, Vienna 1987. Cf. 159 D.
15 The compilation is based on various original documents, catalogues, journals and publications.
16 Privately owned prints and prints in the Klimt-Archiv at the Albertina.
17 Nebehay 1969, p. 14.
18 *Gegenwelten*, 1996, especially the contribution by Alfred Weidinger, "Von Blumen und blühenden Frauen—Symbolismus in den Landschaftsbildern Gustav Klimts".
19 Privately owned print, inscribed "Teschner" on the back. It shows a detail from a photograph that is reproduced in full in *Inselräume, Teschner, Klimt & Flöge am Attersee*, exhib. cat., Seewalchen 1988.
20 The privately owned print is from a series of similar photographs.
21 Rhyme and photograh were first published in the catalogue *Inselräume* 1988.

The many portraits contained in the painting *The Auditorium of the Old Burgtheater* (ill. p. 63), commissioned by the Viennese local government and housed today in the Historisches Museum der Stadt Wien, were also done after photographs.[11] For this work, which was shown at the XIX Annual Künstlerhaus Exhibition in 1890, Gustav Klimt was awarded a major state prize, the Golden Cross and Crown.

Moriz Nähr and his photographs for Gustav Klimt (1892–1909)

After the death of Ernst Klimt (1892) and the break-up of the Künstler-Compagnie, the photographer Moriz Nähr, a friend of Gustav Klimt's for many years, photographed the latter several times in the front garden of his new studio on Josefstädterstraße 21.[12] We now know that Nähr made prints of such photographs for collectors of Klimt's works, for example, the photographs owned by the Primavesi family (ill. p. 61), or the signed photographs that turned up at an auction at Villa Grisebach (Berlin) in 1999. Moriz Nähr took not only the photographs of Klimt in his studio garden, but most of those of the paintings reproduced in the Secession catalogues as well.[13] On a postcard to Emilie Flöge dated 8. 7. 1909 Klimt wrote: "Nähr took a photograph of me this morning at the Kunstschau—I'm curious."[14]

As early as 1898, the Secession magazine *Ver Sacrum* carried an article on photography with colour reproductions by members of the Viennese Camera Club. The jubilee exhibition of the Photographische Gesellschaft, marking its fortieth anniversary, took place in Vienna in 1901. Within the scope of the XIII Secession Exhibition in 1902, photographs by Heinrich Kühn, Hans Watzek, Hugo Henneberg and Friedrich Viktor Spitzer were also shown; originally these were to have been exhibited at Galerie Pisko in 1901, but were then included in the Secession programme at the intervention of Carl Moll, who was president of the Secession at the time. In 1904, Peter Altenberg included a supplement on the role of the gum-bichromate printing process in modern art photography in the magazine *Kunst*, of which he was the editor. The Viennese Secession too, dealt with the theme of art photography in its 1902 and 1904 exhibitions. In 1904, the Photographische Gesellschaft also mounted a major exhibition at the Museum für Kunst und Industrie. The Viennese Camera Club organised an "International Exhibition of Selected Art Photographs" in 1905 and the Viennese Amateur Photographers' Club held its own "Internal Exhibition" in February 1909. Art photography became socially accepted thanks, among other things, to these assiduous "club activities", to various publications, and to technical advances. It also gained admission to exhibitions in private Viennese galleries, such as Galerie Miethke (1901, 1905), Kunstsalon Heller (1909, 1912) and Galerie Pisko (1909, 1912).[15]

Photograph and sketch (1906)

Anna Klimt on her seventieth birthday on 27 January 1906

Given its parallels with a drawing by Klimt (Strobl No. 1323) and the specific occasion on which it was taken, an amateur photograph[16] that has survived for posterity points to a painting that Klimt may have planned. The photograph in question shows Klimt's mother, Anna Klimt (1836–1915) and was taken on 27 January 1906, the occasion of her seventieth birthday, which she celebrated with her family. According to the family, she received a gift of an armchair from the Wiener Werkstätte.[17] She was photographed and sketched sitting in that same armchair. This particular mode of depicting a person seated and in profile, can be found very much earlier in Klimt's oeuvre, inspired by James McNeill-Whistler. The photograph is closely related to the drawing, which also bears the outlines of a sketch portrait, upside down, which was also done from a photograph or else directly of the person sitting for the photograph.

Klimt at his summer retreat (1909–17)

Gustav Klimt, portrait drawing of his mother on 27 January 1906 (Strobl No. 1323)

It is not necessary here to go into detail on the "view-finder" included in Gustav Klimt's last sketch book, dated 1917, which he used to define the square frames for a number of his landscapes and other paintings. Needless to say, this view-finder system is similar to that used in photography, as has often been pointed out in much of the literature on Klimt.[18] The present catalogue also includes an essay that specifically addresses Klimt's interest in fashion and fashion photography and his close collaboration with the Wiener Werkstätte, the Flöge fashion salon, and, of course, with Emilie Flöge herself.

Klimt at his summer retreat, in a rowing boat[19] with Emilie Flöge[20], is one of a series of private amateur photographs in which Klimt is already surrounded by an aura of the artist. Whether his attire is a painter's smock or a kimono, for Klimt it was the male version of the loose-fitting *Reformkleid* which he only donned in his studio or in the freer, though conservative, surroundings of his lakeside retreat on the Attersee. A number of such amateur photographs were taken at the Attersee, all them snapshots of private scenes. They were taken by different people, including Richard Teschner and his wife Emma Bacher. A page in an album for Gertrude Flöge, Emilie Flöge's niece, provides yet another pointer of Klimt's attitude to photography at the time. The rhyme on the bottom dated 1913 makes direct reference to a photograph of Emilie Flöge[21]: "Kein Objektiv kann wiedergeben / Die Seele und das Innenleben, / Das sich auf diesem Antlitz zeigt / Da steht man still, das Haupt geneigt; / Es ist das Bild ein Abglanz nur / Des Meisterwerkes der Natur ..." (No lens can reproduce / the soul and inner life / that show in this

Anna Klimt, c. 1906

Dora Kallmus (d'Ora),
Gustav Klimt, 1908/09, bromide
print, 18,5 x 14,5 cm, signature
stamp on the back, private collection

Dora Kallmus (d'Ora),
Gustav Klimt, 1908/09, bromide
print, 18,5 x 13 cm, embossed
stamp, private collection

Dora Kallmus (d'Ora),
Gustav Klimt, 1908/09, bromide
print, 20,3 x 15 cm, signature
stamp on the back, private collection

22 The two colour photographs
of Emilie Flöge by Walker were first
published in the catalogue *Inselräume* in 1988. The Klimt photograph was published later.
23 On Dora Kallmus (1881–1963)
and the d'Ora studio (Wien I,
Wipplingerstraße 24) see Monika
Faber, *Madame d'Ora, Wien—Paris,
Portraits aus Kunst und Gesellschaft 1907–1957*, Vienna/Munich,
1983.
24 On Pauline Hamilton: The few
essential points are mentioned in
the text. Various sources are not
yet accessible and so have not
been exhausted. Much of what we
already know is thanks to the support of Georg Fritsch, Vienna, who
generously contributed the knowl-
edg he gained from his longer-term
investigations. A number of sug-
gestions based on his research will
be useful for finding sources in the
future.

face / Standing still, with head inclined; / The picture is but a pale reflection / of nature's masterpiece ...").

The only known colour photographs taken of Klimt are the Lumière autochromes by Friedrich G. Walker[22], which Alfred Weidinger dates as 13/14 September 1913, although Friedrich G. Walker was first invited to the Villa Paulick on the Attersee on 28 July 1912. The photographs show Gustav Klimt and Emilie Flöge, both in kimonos. In one of these colour photographs Emilie is wearing the same dress that she has on in the black-and-white photograph in the album with the rhyme. A number of different photographers took series of photographs of Gustav Klimt over the course of his life. Most of these already appeared in Christian M. Nebehay's Klimt documentation, and several of them have been reproduced since in the secondary literature on Klimt.

Two rival photographers: Dora Kallmus[23]—Pauline Hamilton[24]

Three photographs from a series by Dora Kallmus (1881–1963) are reproduced here.[25] They were taken in 1908/09 at the photographer's studio (Dora Kallmus opened her d'Ora studio in Vienna in 1907) and show Gustav Klimt in different poses but with the same lighting, wearing a normal suit rather than a bohemian kimono. There can be no question as to the high quality of the d'Ora photographs in terms of plasticity, tonality and balance. The photographer was clearly capable of masterfully catching the liveli-ness in Klimt's eyes, his mischievous expression and the occasional heaviness of his hands, and in this she obviously had the full approval of the sitter. The composition as a whole is in the style of her Berlin teacher Nicola Perscheid.

The January 1909 issue of the journal *Erdgeist*[26] was devoted to portrait photo-graphs from the d'Ora studio, with an accompanying text by the editor Gustav Eugen Diehl: "And therefore we very much welcome the fact that, once again, someone has attempted to create an effect with artistic understanding and taste, but with photo-graphic means only—and we particularly welcome the fact that this attempt has been made here by a young Viennese woman". This article was probably an announcement of

the first "Kollektivausstellung d'Ora" (d'Ora Collective Exhibition) at the Kunstsalon Heller in October 1909[27].

More than two years later, on 1 February 1912, invitations were issued to a preview of the second Kollektivausstellung d'Ora at the Kunstsalon Heller. On 8 February 1912, Adalbert Franz Seligmann, art critic for the *Neue Freie Presse*, reports on both the d'Ora exhibition at the Kunstsalon Heller and one by Pauline Krüger-Hamilton at the Kunstsalon Pisko: "Gradually it has become common to show photography exhibitions at our Kunstsalons too, and when one sees what our photographers have already achieved in this field, then there is every justification for this custom. Two such exhibitions have just been opened in Vienna. At Heller one can see a series of really splendid portrait photographs by d'Ora, very aesthetic, but without, as is often the case, being affected, extraordinarily peaceful and apposite in tonal effect, highly tasteful in every sense; the photographs by Mme. Krüger-Hamilton on show at Pisko are unequal in quality, but more diverse in terms of the problems confronted and solved, often surprisingly."

We know who Dora Kallmus was. The publication by Monika Faber provides a full description of her life and work, and even if in future isolated details emerge that further highlight this multifaceted oeuvre, it has already been secured for posterity. The same cannot be said of Pauline Hamilton. It is quite extraordinary that there should be such a discrepancy in the amount of biographical data available on two photographers who both worked in Vienna at the same time and who are both known to have exhibited in the same years.

Pauline Hamilton had two exhibitions of photographs at the Gustav Pisko Kunstsalon. Both exhibitions were reviewed in the press. On 6 March 1909, issue no. 6 of *Erdgeist* carried a review of an exhibition "Englische Maler im Salon Pisko"[28], probably also written by Gustav Eugen Diehl: "The anteroom contains photographs by Pauline Kruger-Hamilton (from Minneapolis, USA), which are more modern than the paintings discussed. The said lady is now working in Vienna and her speciality is portrait photo-

25 Two prints have a stamp on the back, the third has an embossed stamp.
26 On the art journal *Erdgeist* cf. Maria Rennhofer, *Kunstzeitschriften der Jahrhundertwende in Deutschland und Österreich 1895–1914*, Vienna/Munich 1987. *Erdgeist* was published as of 1908, as a sequel to *Moderne Revue* (from 1906); the journal was discontinued in 1909.
27 The Kunstsalon Heller, Wien I, Bauernmarkt 3 developed from the bookshop founded by Hugo Heller (1870–1923) in 1905 which included a ticket office, an artists' agency, a reading circle and an events agency. A number of publishers' products were also edited or taken over by Heller.
28 The Kunstsalon Pisko was originally opened in 1897 on Schwindgasse in Vienna, then mounted exhibitions at Parkring 7, and in 1906 moved to premises on

graphs, which she takes at the homes of the sitters and without the use of artificial light, so that an atmosphere of intimacy is preserved; one scarcely ever notices that a pose has been taken up, and one senses that the apparatus has been set and otherwise handled with artistry and patience."

On the occasion of the second exhibition in 1912, the reference in the press is to Miss Hamilton. Viennese address books for the year 1914 list a Pauline Hamilton (photographer) and a Pauline Hamilton Krüger (painter) under the same studio address, Wien I, Wiesingerstraße 3. She signed her prints, if at all, then with "Pauline Hamilton Vienna", either on the picture side or on the cardboard frame. It is a known fact that she specialised in portrait photographs taken at the homes of the sitters. The photographs of Gustav Klimt are an exception. The Historisches Museum in Vienna purchased four portrait photographs from the estate of the art critic Arthur Roessler[29], including one of Gustav Klimt (Inv. No. 75.253/2). The remarkable thing about this photograph is that, contrary to her supposed custom, it was taken outdoors. The other portraits show *Arthur Roessler*, *Ida Roessler*[30] and *Anton Faistauer*[31]. These were most probably taken around 1914 in connection with the presentation to Faistauer of the Reininghaus Prize[32] and the concomitant exhibition at Salon Pisko of the works entered for the competition, on which Arthur Roessler also reported. A note from Roessler to Schiele dated 1916 also mentions a Mrs Hamilton, who wanted to photograph Schiele's paintings.[33]

Prints of two other portrait photographs of Gustav Klimt are owned privately and have never been published until now (figs. p. 55). Both are by Pauline Hamilton and must have been taken before or around 1909. They show Klimt in a state of artistic ecstasy, almost as if hovering above the ground. It would appear here that for Klimt the kimono had become a kind of priestly robe; this was how he liked to present himself, this was how he wanted to be seen. To judge by a portrait photograph dated 1914, Anton Trcka (1893–1940) saw Gustav Klimt similarly, in an artistic priestly robe (ill. p. 55), the date, title and signature interwoven to create a picturesque ornament.

In an obituary by Albert P. Gütersloh dated 1918, and first published in the Albertina exhibition catalogue of 1968, we read: "He has entered into the centre of the earth in the Orient, this man with the high forehead of Rodin's L'homme au nez cassé and the mysterious features of Pan under the beard and hair of the ageing Saint Peter".

the corner of Lothringerstrasse 14 and Schwarzenbergplatz, where Pauline Hamilton and the Neukunstgruppe exhibited in 1909. Gustav Pisko died 1911 at the age of 44. The Salon continued to exist. In 1914 the Reininghaus Competition took place on the premises. The premises were later taken over by the Kunsthandlung Wawra.

29 The city of Vienna had a contract with Arthur Roessler and his wife Ida for a life annuity. Because of this contract part of his collection became the property of the museum after his death, the rest in 1961, after the death of Ida Roessler.

30 Ida Roessler (1877–1961), wife of the art commentator Arthur Roessler.

31 Arthur Roessler (1877–1955) was very sympathetic towards the artist Anton Faistauer, alongside Schiele. One can assume, therefore, that the portrait photograph of Faistauer was taken by Pauline Hamilton at the same time as those of Arthur and Ida Roessler. The concrete occasion was most likely the presentation of the Reininghaus Prize in 1914.

32 The works entered for the Reininghaus Prize were exhibited at Salon Pisko in January/February 1914. According to A. F. Seligmann, art critic for the *Neue Freie Presse*, only two "modern" artists were on exhibition, Faistauer and Schiele. The jury awarded the prize to Anton Faistauer.

33 Egon Schiele (1890–1918); according to a note by Christian M. Nebehay, *Egon Schiele, 1890–1918, Leben, Briefe, Gedichte*, Salzburg 1979, p. 372, Pauline Hamilton wanted to photograph paintings for Schiele (E.S. A.554/1916)

Princesses without a History?
Gustav Klimt and "The Community of All who Create and all who Enjoy"

TOBIAS G. NATTER

Never before had an exhibition in Vienna been given better advance publicity than the Kunstschau in 1908. Contemporaries called it "a festive robe for Klimt".[1]

The curiosity already aroused before the event went far beyond discussions in cafés, for there were not only innovations among the artists. Encouraged by Klimt, their paternal mentor, the young generation of Expressionists entered the arena for the first time with Oskar Kokoschka and Max Oppenheimer as their leaders. The relationship of the artists to their public was also being redefined, and it was not by chance that the organisers of the exhibition showed marketing sense, appointing their own observer service to collect all the Austrian and foreign press reports.

The centre room was reserved for Gustav Klimt, and he opened the show with a speech that received much attention. The photographs of the private view show the ladies elegantly robed and wearing the huge hats that Klimt used to such effect in his portraits of women; the gentlemen were without exception in tails and top hats. But what do we really know about the guests at the private view and the part they played in the development of the élitist art of a painter like Gustav Klimt—what do we know about their position and their view of themselves in the relationship between production and distribution? Or about their commitment to the Secession and their part in the success of the Wiener Werkstätte? To what extent did they share the vision that art and life should mingle and become one, a dream whose harmony and refinement the forceful young Expressionists who were now coming on to the scene were already rejecting?

The Opening of the Kunstschau in 1908. Photographed and inscribed by Emma Teschner Vienna, Private collection

What the pictures do not tell us

Klimt's Beethoven frieze speaks of the "longing for happiness".[2] Unlike the Expressionists—and so entirely the opposite of Kokoschka, Schiele and Gerstl—the artist who held out this hope of happiness never pursued the inner dialogue through self-portrait. Those who wanted to know something about him as an artist (and that was the only aspect that mattered), he said, "should study my paintings and try to see from them what I am and what I am aiming for".[3]

This terse statement about himself and his art fell on fertile ground for art historians. It was not coincidence that Heinrich Wölfflin published his standard work, *Kunstgeschichte ohne Namen* (Art History without Names) at almost the same time.[4] The history of the reception of Wölfflin's work documents the many shifts in approach and attitudes since that time. His considerations still stand as a brilliant attempt to write a history of seeing. But the approach usual in the humanities today, the orientation to cultural history, the inter-disciplinary approach and the awareness of conditions in the art world as an operating system, have stimulated interest in the contents of pictures that points beyond their function as pure artefacts.

1   Josef Anton Lux, "Kunstschau – Wien 1908", in *Deutsche Kunst und Dekoration*, Vol. 23, 1908/09, p. 44. The exhibition which filled 54 rooms, with adjacent terrace gardens, café and summer theatre designed by Josef Hoffmann was held on the empty site next to the Vienna Konzerthaus from May to August 1908.
2   Cf. the commentary at the time in the catalogue for the "Beethoven Exhibition", i.e. the XIVth exhibition by the Vienna Secession, from April to June 1902.
3   Quoted from Nebehay 1969, p. 32.
4   First edition Munich 1917.

So it is astonishing that although portraits of women play a dominant role in Gustav Klimt's work, we know very little about the women who sat for him. Until recently virtually nothing was known about some of them, like Fritza Riedler (ill. p. 113). Her portrait has been reproduced all over the world, but despite the proliferating literature on Klimt until recently we did not even have basic data like the dates of her birth and death. The catalogue of Klimt's work by Novotny-Dobai simply gives the provenance, "Riedler Collection, Berlin", and "Emilie Langer Collection, Vienna". An initial enquiry at the Vienna City registry office drew a blank. There were too many women of this name; without any further information, an address, for example, it was pointless to look. Berlin reported that the registration archives had been hit during the air raids in the Second World War and all the records were lost. Only in the course of further research did it become clear that Emilie Langer, who sold the portrait to the Österreichische Galerie in 1937, was the subject's sister. Then the mist lifted and it was evident that Fritza Riedler was the wife of Alois Riedler, the German pioneer of mechanical engineering.[5]

The search for information on many of the other subjects proved similarly complex. In some cases it did prove possible to find their descendants, and we owe valuable material to them, including hitherto unpublished information; in some cases we even obtained an old photograph.

The portrait of Mäda Primavesi (ill. p. 127), painted by Klimt in 1912 when she was nine, was a very special case. During the research it suddenly emerged that she was still alive, but for a long time it was impossible to learn more. Then she was traced to Montreal, where she was spending the last years of her life. But it took time to establish her address and telephone number, and when the first contact was made her son informed us with regret that his mother had died three weeks before. The death of the old lady at the age of 97 lost us the last eye witness to an era that had already come to an end, mentally and physically, in 1918, the last eye witness who had known the artist personally and seen him working at the easel.

The biographical information it has been possible to assemble on the women portrayed by Klimt is given in the comments on each painting and reference is repeatedly made to these here. This Introduction aims to give an overall view, indicating identities and collective patterns; it also aims to give some insight into structural elements in the complex relations between the painter and his sitters and clients.[6]

"... He has recently started an affair with her ..."

The client and the sitter were not always the same. The portrait of Mäda Primavesi (ill. p. 127) was commissioned by her parents, as were those of the young Elisabeth Bachofen-Echt (ill. p. 132) and Gertrud Loew at the age of twenty-one (ill. p. 99). Friederike Beer-Monti's portrait (ill. p. 137) was paid for by her friend as a gift to her. In most cases the portrait was commissioned by the sitter's husband, and where records of the financial arrangements have survived the negotiations were conducted with the male head of the family. This information is available for the portraits of Margarethe Stonborough-Wittgenstein (ill. p. 109) and Eugenia Primavesi (ill. p. 129). The financial arrangements with the men are expressive testimony to the role assigned to men by society; on the other hand it was the women and the sitters themselves who sought and maintained the personal contact with Klimt.

5 I gratefully acknowledge the help given by the Vienna registration archive, who were always willing to provide information. My particular thanks go to Herbert Koch, a senior official in the office.
6 Among the few publications on the subject Thomas Zaunschirm deserves special mention. In a book published more than ten years ago, *Gustav Klimt. Margarethe Stonborough-Wittgenstein. Ein österreichisches Schicksal*, Frankfurt/M. 1987, he has shown how stimulating it can be to consider Klimt's portraits of women in regard to the social realities as well. On those who financed the Vienna Secession and their business environment see Michel, Bernard, "Les mécènes de la Sécession", in exhib. Cat. *Vienne 1880–1938. L'Apocalypse Joyeuse*, Centre Georges Pompidou, Paris, 1986, pp. 180–189. Christian Brandstätter and Susanna Partsch have so far dealt in most detail with the subject in the narrower sense: Ch. Brandstätter, *Gustav Klimt und die Frauen*, Vienna 1994; S. Partsch, *Gustav Klimt. Painter of Women*, Munich/New York 1994. Hannes Stekl has given a more recent survey on the subject of patronage, with a detailed bibliography: "Wiener Mäzene im 19. Jahrhundert", in Jürgen Kocka and Manuel Frey (ed.), *Bürgerkultur und Mäzenatentum im 19. Jahrhundert*, Zwickau 1998, pp. 164–191. See also the exhib. Cat. *Zu Gast bei Beer-Hofmann. Eine Ausstellung über das jüdische Wien der Jahrhundertwende*, Jüdisches Museum, Vienna and Joods Historisch Museum, Amsterdam, ed. Heimann-Jelinek, Felicitas, Vienna, 1998. In the context of the public debate on the restitution of the two portraits of Adele Bloch-Bauer (ill. pp. 117, 125) demanded by her heirs Hubertus Czernin has made the first in-depth evaluation of the biographical sources on the sitter: Hubertus Czernin, *Die Fälschung. Der Fall Bloch-Bauer*, Vienna 1999, and Hubertus Czernin, *Die Fälschung. Der Fall Bloch-Bauer und das Werk Gustav Klimts*, Vienna 1999.

Serena Lederer (ill. p. 89) is only one example of this, though her active support reached outstanding proportions. In the course of a personal friendship that lasted twenty years she and her family built up the most important collection of Klimt's works ever to be privately owned.

This enthusiasm for art on the part of the women was a continuance of the salon culture that was so marked a feature of Vienna in the nineteenth century, and which William Johnston has vaguely called "feminisation": Vienna feminised culture in the nineteenth century at least as evidently as Paris had done in the eighteenth, he said. Johnston quotes Lou Andreas-Salomé, who said that "Vienna intellectuals derived their genius from their constant intercourse with women."[7] The salon culture was always dependent on the hostess's personality, and Isabella Ackerl has drawn attention to one aspect that influenced future developments: women were "allowed to practise emancipation, at least in the private sphere".[8]

Gustav Klimt with Editha Freiin Sustenau von Schützenthal and her daughter Hertha von Mautner-Markhof. Vienna, Österreichische Nationalbibliothek, picture archive

Another fact is striking in the context of Klimt and his (male) source of finance and (female) sitters: However the two stood to each other as representatives of the rigid asymmetrical social relationship between the sexes, they both had to exercise patience in dealing with the artist. Klimt worked slowly, he was a cautious artist, making thorough and detailed preparatory drawings for the paintings, which progressed only gradually. Perhaps his attitude to the time factor was one of the reasons why the "Malercompagnie" (Company of Painters) in his early years collapsed. At the time he decorated one theatre after another in rapid succession, but he soon ceased to be able to maintain this momentum. As his maturity grew he demanded time and quiet. After 1900 he painted only one female portrait a year on average. His fascination with women is underlined by the fact that after the turn of the century he never painted another portrait of a man. By then he had long since bidden farewell to his earlier career with the Ringstrasse architects. He had left the less productive phase of the early 1890s behind him, and as his work on the faculty paintings progressed he was increasingly becoming the centre of scandals. The Secession had been founded in 1897 and he was bearing its banner.

As a result of his very slow method of working many of Klimt's portraits of women went straight from his studio to their first public exhibition—quite often still unfinished. Klimt's clients willingly agreed to lend for the show, no doubt not averse to the publicity. Klimt on the other hand was a perfectionist, and he went on searching for the effect he wanted, often long after the client and sitter would have been satisfied. More than once it is recorded that the painting had to be almost torn from his hands. Both Beer-Monti (ill. p. 137) and the mother of Baronin Bachofen-Echt (ill. p. 132) went to his studio in an automobile, still a rarity in those days, and loaded the painting into the car, while the artist was still saying he would not exclude the possibility of further work on it.

He did indeed work for months on his paintings, and several years were spent on the portrait of Adele Bloch-Bauer I (ill. p. 117), for which he prepared more intensively than any other. He made hundreds of drawings and studies, the earliest of which dates from almost four years before the painting was finished. The portrait of Elisabeth Bachofen-Echt (ill. p. 132) was similarly slow to mature, and it is known that the artist worked on it for three years.

Faced with the proposal to show the three daughters of a German prince, who lived in different cities, in a group portrait, Klimt declared himself willing to undertake

7   William M. Johnston, Österreichische Kultur- und Geistesgeschichte, Gesellschaft und Ideen im Donauraum 1848 bis 1938, Vienna/Cologne/Weimar, 3rd edition, 1992, p. 130.
8   Isabella Ackerl, "Wiener Salonkultur um die Jahrhundertwende. Ein Versuch", in Jürgen Nautz und Richard Vahrenkamp (ed.), Die Wiener Jahrhundertwende, Einflüsse—Umwelt—Wirkungen, Vienna/Cologne/Graz, 2nd edition, 1996, pp. 694–709, quoted from p. 694.

the commission only on condition that the princesses came to Vienna for the sitting. The commission ultimately failed to materialise for this reason. The incident illustrates his loyalty to Vienna and his deep roots in the city.[9] But it also shows that he was selective and particular about his subjects.

We know of several cases where he turned down a commission, and not only princesses waited in vain for a portrait. Another that failed to materialise was that of the daughter of Max Liebermann, president of the Berlin Secession, and an artist whose standing in Berlin was comparable to Klimt's in Vienna.[10] Marianne Löw-Beer, née Wittmann, of Vienna, whose granddaughter Daniela Hammer-Tugendhat has contributed an article to this catalogue on the changing views of the image of Judith, was also turned down. Apparently her grandmother, who was "soft and rather plump" in appearance, was not Klimt's type.[11]

However, it was not "without risk" for society ladies and their reputation to sit for Klimt. They were quickly suspected of having an affair with the artist, who was notorious for his *amours*. Adele Bloch-Bauer, wife of Ferdinand Bloch-Bauer, is now generally assumed to have been Klimt's mistress,[12] and some believe that his painting of *Judith* (ill. p. 221) bears some resemblance to her.[13] Although it is no longer possible to confirm the rumours of their relationship, Adele's niece at least is convinced they are true. When she questioned her mother (Adele's sister) about it she was sharply rebuked: "How dare you ask such a thing! It was a purely intellectual relationship"[14]. The child was sure from the tone of voice that there had been more but it was not proper to speak of it.

Alma Mahler had fewer scruples. Her recently published diaries are a treasure trove of more than Vienna gossip. Among other things they give us Alma's own version of the erotic nature of her relationship with Gustav Klimt. They also helped to spread the rumour of his "success" with Rose von Rosthorn-Friedmann (ill. p. 93). "For the rest, he has recently started an affair with Rose Friedmann, that old hag! He takes it wherever he can get it."[15] Alma's choice of words leaves open which she despised more, her "rival" or Klimt's unbridled eroticism.

Christian Brandstätter actually suspects a *liaison dangereuse* with Sonja Knips (ill. p. 85),[16] but this must remain conjecture, and any interpretation must be seen as speculative. Certainly Klimt was known as a ladies' man, and he acknowledged three illegitimate children[17]. But it is characteristic of the social hierarchy of the time that they were the fruits of intimate relationships with "women of the people" as they were called. These women earned money in his studio as models, and clearly they offered more than the purely literary topos of the "sweet maid from the Vienna suburbs".

Among the women from the wealthy bourgeoisie who were close to Klimt only for Serena Lederer are official records available stating not only that she had an intimate relationship with Gustav Klimt but also that her daughter Elisabeth (ill. p. 132) was their love child. But there are special reasons for this; it was an attempt during the Nazi regime to protect the child by claiming a so-called "aryan" father instead of her real father.[18]

The studio: *hortus conclusus* or a harem of models?

Klimt's effect on women has repeatedly been described as extraordinary. His appearance, with his impressive Apostle's head, his powerful build and floating artist's smock, so evidently in defiance of the dress code of the time, was intoxicating. Hans Tietze comes

9   N.N., "Gustav Klimts Persönlichkeit. Nach Mitteilungen seiner Freunde", in *Die Bildenden Künste*. Wiener Monatshefte, Vol. 2, 1918, No. 1/2, Vienna, p. 4.
10   On Liebermann and Klimt see exhib. cat. *Max Liebermann und die französischen Impressionisten*, Jüdisches Museum Wien, ed. G. Tobias Natter and Julius H. Schoeps, Vienna, 1997, pp. 73–76. Carl Moll records Liebermann's desire for the portrait in "Meine Erinnerungen an Gustav Klimt", in *Neues Wiener Tagblatt*, 24 January 1943.
11   See also Daniela Hammer-Tugendhat and Wolf Tegethoff (ed.), *Ludwig Mies van der Rohe. Das Haus Tugendhat*, Vienna i. a., 1998.
12   In particular Salomon Grinberg, "Adele, Private Love and Public Betrayal", in *Art & Antiques*, New York, Summer 1986, pp. 70ff. and Jean Clair, "The Eye of Disorder and Desire", in *Art International*, No. 3, Summer 1988, p. 15.
13   A similar resemblance was thought to be recognisable between Emilie Flöge and the woman in Klimt's cult painting *The Kiss*, for example Strobl, esp. Vol. 3, pp. 8 and 241, where he assumes the identity is proven.
14   I am grateful to Maria Altmann for this information on 7 March 1999.
15   Mahler 1997, p. 431. On Alma Mahler and Gustav Klimt see the article by Hansjörg Krug in this catalogue.
16   Christian Brandstätter 1994, as Note 5, p. 50.
17   Cf. Christian M. Nebehay, *Gustav Klimt, Von der Zeichnung zum Bild*, Vienna, Edition Brandstätter, 1992, esp. the chapters "Gustav Klimt und Marie Zimmermann", pp. 264ff. and "Gustav Klimts Sohn Gustav Ucicky", pp. 272ff.
18   For more details see the comments on the painting, pp. 88-91.

close to one of the main sources of his charisma when he describes the artist as a combination of opposites: "A refined man of nature, a mixture of satyr and ascetic".[19] Klimt cultivated that aura, combining sexual attraction with the image of the genius as libertine.

Friederike Beer-Monti (ill. p. 137) found strong words for her emotions on visiting Klimt's studio in Hietzing to sit for her portrait even years later: He had an extraordinary animal magnetism, she said, he exuded a strange odour, a woman might well be afraid of him.[20]

The studio, that mysterious place arranged utterly differently from Makart's legendary studio thirty years earlier, was, for all the differences, as essential to Klimt as it had been for the "Prince of the Ringstrasse" and his art productions. In Klimt's retreat, from which the public was entirely excluded, the "divine activity" went on, the creation of art. The salvation of "mankind in their weakness" through art and love—as the Beethoven frieze programmatically proclaimed—began here.[21]

Rudolf von Alt: Makart's Studio
Vienna, Historisches Museum

Klimt's studio became a sanctuary from which the general public were excluded, where, in a world that was hostile to the body, the presence and nudity of women were natural. "Here he was surrounded by mysterious, nude women who, while he stood silent before his easel, wandered up and down in his workshop, stretched, lazed and blossomed like flowers—always ready to stay obediently still at a gesture from the master, as soon as he perceived a movement or a pose that aroused his sense of beauty and was rapidly noted down in a quick drawing."[22]

To Klimt and to his public the studio was a central place where the bourgeois order was suspended. Perhaps it was also (only) a Utopia of narcissistic regression which appeared to Klimt's female supporters as paradise regained in the midst of a neglected garden landscape. Certainly Klimt was not only part of this world, he was its creator, and this more than anything made him the authentic prophet of a personal reality. Did not the Secession's demand for the marriage of art and life appear limitless here in the seeming harmony of sexual drive and beauty?

It still arouses male fantasies. Christian Brandstätter talks of a "harem of models", in which Klimt "held sway like a pasha in his seraglio over a host of models who were paid generously to be there all the time, whether he happened to need them just then or not; they worshipped him, but not only for that."[23]

Klimt's studio in Josefstädterstrasse, around 1910. Photo by
Moritz Nähr, Vienna, Österreichische Nationalbibliothek,
picture archive

Klimt's devotion to this room was certainly comparable to his devotion to Vienna, the city in which he lived—"protected" by his immediate surroundings. Carl E. Schorske has pointed out the illuminating parallel between Sigmund Freud and Gustav Klimt. Both faced massive hostility and withdrew "from the public arena into the protection of a small but faithful following in order to secure the newly conquered terrain."[24]

One of Klimt's most powerful formulations of his attitude and the ideology of the Secession was his painting *Nuda Veritas* (ill. p. 239). He explained his withdrawal from public life in the inscription, which was certainly aggressive: "If you cannot please them all with your achievements and your art—please a few. Pleasing many is bad."

In proclaiming that "Pleasing many is bad" Klimt knew he could rely on followers who would not only cushion the attacks during public controversies but who also blindly trusted his artistic sense and would increase his influence. Alma Mahler's diary entries in particular show that Klimt's circle was small and very exclusive, all closely acquainted with each other.

The painter Carl Moll was only one of the figures in this well functioning system of multipliers, although as "the impresario of Vienna"[25] he was one of the most important. Sophisticated salon hostesses, women journalists like Berta Zuckerkandl[26] and wealthy women collectors played an equally important part, for without their sympathy and support Klimt's influence and impact could never have been what they were.

Klimt's Female Clients: Industry versus Aristocracy

When Klimt was commissioned by the City of Vienna in 1888 to paint the interior of the old Burgtheater before it was demolished he not only "portrayed" the architectural framework, he also painted the audience. In his fusion of architectural painting and group portrait he documented an impressive variety of benefactors and patrons, theatre-lovers, habitués and hangers-on. The celebrated young painter, who had already been awarded the Golden Cross of Merit with Crown, was to win the coveted Kaiser Award with his painting of the Burgtheater in 1890. To many he was the "new" Makart, with the ability effortlessly to fulfil all society's expectations to complete satisfaction. He had given manifold proof of his gift for portraiture. However, these miniatures differ in every respect from the great portraits of women he was to paint after 1900, in their approach, their function and their execution.

Klimt's painting of the Burgtheater is a key testimony to Viennese society, artistically and sociologically. All the figures are united in their desire "to play a part as spectators as well"[27], as one might say before the fall from grace: bearers of the highest offices at court, members of the Imperial government, members of the Archduke's family, actors and actresses, and in the tiers the "nouveaux riches". Even Serena Lederer (ill. p. 89), then still bearing her maiden name Pultizer, is immortalised here.

Before handing the painting over to the City Council who had commissioned it Klimt had hastily to correct an omission that had only just been noticed: he had forgotten to include the Lord Mayor—"Lueger has to go in".[28] But fifteen years later the harmony was gone. The faculty paintings for the University of Vienna that caused so much scandal were still a commission from the official establishment, but their execution went against the clients' formal intentions and the fundamental philosophy of their fields, and the controversy, which became increasingly public, separated the wheat from the chaff, sociologically as well.

Lord Mayor Karl Lueger was not the only to take sides against Klimt in the controversy over the faculty paintings. The question Lueger and his party friends asked in parliament raised the political pressure and made it appear advisable to the civic art administration to keep a low profile and maintain their distance from Klimt. This cost him his official clientele, but he was more than compensated by the commissions he received and the eagerness to collect on the part of the wealthy bourgeoisie.

They not only ensured that Klimt never needed to scrape and save, they wrapped him in cotton wool. The collector Fritz Waerndorfer had the artist's studio repainted while he was away as a surprise, and there was seemingly never any dispute over the fee for his portraits.[29] On several occasions his clients paid high sums as advances. Evidently Klimt was Hans Makart's successor in the literal sense, for it was Makart, the "painter prince", who had "taught" his public to pay high prices.

19   Quoted from Christian Brandstätter, 1994, as note 6, p. 46.
20   Christian M. Nebehay, as note 17, pp. 219ff.
21   From the description of the frieze in the catalogue, 1902: "First long wall...The longing for happiness. The sufferings of mankind in their weakness. Their pleas to the strong and powerful man as the external driving forces, pity and ambition as the inner, impelling man to take up the struggle for happiness."
22   Franz Servaes, "Gustav Klimt", in Velhagen und Klassings Monatsheften, Vol 1918/19, p. 23/24.
23   Christian Brandstätter, as Note 6, p. 116.
24   Carl E. Schorske, Wien, Geist und Gesellschaft im Fin de Siècle, Frankfurt a. M. 1982, p. 195.
25   Cf. G. Tobias Natter, "Carl Moll und die Galerie Miethke. Konturen einer europäischen Avantgarde-Galerie", in exhib. cat. Carl Moll (1861–1945), Österreichische Galerie Belvedere, ed. G. Tobias Natter and Gerbert Frodl, Salzburg 1998, pp. 129–149.
26   Cf. Olaf Herling, "Berta Zuckerkandl oder die Kunst weiblicher Diplomatie", in Frauke Severit (ed.), Das alles war ich, Politikerinnen, Künstlerinnen, Exzentrikerinnen der Wiener Moderne, Vienna/Cologne/Weimar 1998, pp. 53–74.
27   Werner Hofmann, Gustav Klimt und die Wiener Jahrhundertwende, Salzburg 1970, p. 20.
28   The Lueger episode is from L. W. Rochowanski, "Intimes von Gustav Klimt", in Neues Wiener Journal, 13 January 1929.
29   Peter Vergo, "Fritz Waerndorfer as Collector", in alte und moderne Kunst, Vienna, 1981, Vol. 26, No. 77, pp. 33/38.

Commissions to Gustav Klimt were not cheap. We have details of some of his prices. He sold the portrait of Emilie Flöge (ill. p. 101) in 1908 for 12,000 crowns to the Niederösterreichisches Landesmuseum, after offering it to the Ministry of Education for 10,000. Klimt commented: "That is what I get now for a commissioned portrait"[30]. But the department responsible in the museum thought the price "exorbitant" (and underlined the word). Klimt's private collectors were less easily shocked. In a letter written in 1905 to the industrialist Karl Wittgenstein Klimt said he received about 5,000 guilders, that is about 10,000 crowns, for "a lifesize portrait". We are even better informed on his portrait prices after 1914, although of course these were affected by inflation, as the sums paid for the portraits of Eugenia Primavesi (ill. p. 129), Elisabeth Bachofen-Echt (ill. p. 132) and Friederike Beer-Monti (ill. p. 137) show.

Gustav Klimt: The Auditorium in the Old Burgtheater, 1899 Vienna, Historisches Museum

It is difficult to relate these sums to modern prices, and their relation to companies' accounts at the time may tell us more, as may the following comparison.[31] In 1908 Moriz Gallia, whose wife Klimt painted in 1903/4, purchased a villa in Altaussee which cost around 40,000 crowns with full furniture and fittings.[32] There can be no doubt that Klimt had a very high income. These comparisons may also serve to remind us that Klimt apparently never thought of dealing with money in the way his patrons had mastered almost to perfection, that is, investing it "profitably" and making it work for him.

Only by way of exception, however, did Klimt receive a portrait commission from the nobility, and never from the aristocracy by birth, whose social lives were largely governed by their descendancy and forbears. Stefan Zweig's remark "they prefer racing stables and hunting to promoting art" was an ironic comment on their exclusivity.[33]

Of the women portrayed by Klimt only Sonja Knips (ill. p. 85), née Baroness Potier des Echelles and daughter of a Lieutenant Field Marshall, was a member of the upper aristocracy. But she too was the wife of a bourgeois industrialist when her portrait was painted. Frau von Rosthorn (ill. p. 93) was also of the nobility, for her family had been ennobled in the eighteenth century. But again there was a commercial background: her English forbear, Matthew Rawsthorne, was invited to Vienna to build up a button industry to make Austria independent of imports from England, and the Emperor Josef II ennobled the businessman in 1790 for his services.[34] Elisabeth Bachofen-Echt (ill. p. 132), daughter of August and Serena Lederer, was an even more recent entrant to the nobility. She had married into a familiy of successful beer barons who had only received a title in 1906.

The Kunstschau exhibition in 1908 mentioned at the beginning of this article brought together three of the master's finest portraits of women in the room devoted to Klimt: Fritza Riedler (ill. p. 113), Adele Bloch-Bauer I (ill. p. 117) and Margarethe Stonborough-Wittgenstein (ill. p. 109). The magnificent display caused Joseph A. Lux to suggest that the reason why Klimt's women loved to be painted by him was "They have a great longing to rise above the ordinary, everyday world, like princesses and madonnas, in a beauty that can never be ravaged and devastated by the clutching hands of life."[35] As well as their desire to become unattainable or mysterious, and to be shown as such, Lux added with double significance, Klimt had discovered the nobility in the women he painted, "the nobility which they are longing for".

30 Österreichisches Staatsarchiv, Allgemeines Verwaltungsarchiv, Ministerium für Kultus und Unterricht (Austrian State Archives, General Administration Archive, Ministry of Culture and Education), Facs. 15, Art, Acquisitions, File 21.
31 The figures are given in detail each year in *Compass. Finanzielles Jahrbuch für Österreich-Ungarn*, ed. S. Heller.
32 See Moriz Gallia's will, codicil of 15/04/1917; WStLA, Verlassenschaftsakt, BC Margarethen, Death Certificate A 158/18 with Moriz Gallia's will of 16 December 1912 with two later codicils attached.
33 Stefan Zweig, *Die Welt von gestern. Erinnerungen eines Europäers*, Frankfurt/M. 1998, p. 38.
34 H.W. Höfflinger, *Genealogisches Taschenbuch der adeligen Häuser Österreichs*, Vol. 4, 1910/11, Vienna, undated, pp. 389–395.
35 J. A. Lux, as note 1, pp. 44/46.

The fact remains that Klimt's women were self-confident enough to copy neither the attitude nor the formal artistic language of aristocratic society. Formally Klimt's portraits of women are representative portraits. But they show women who present themselves to the viewer as "sovereign and cool, but sensuous and enticing at the same time". Much in this effect is also mysteriously natural, both seductive and threatening. Klimt's portraits of women are always dangerously close to his allegories. The women "are presented to us as costly works of art in an ornamental aura, and as human beings they are removed from us."[36]

"Beautiful Rooms ...

Klimt's collectors all showed a high degree of loyalty to him. Many owned more than one of his paintings and some collected his works for years or decades, foremost among them Serena and August Lederer. But Eugenia and Otto Primavesi also ultimately owned six paintings by Klimt, a balanced selection covering all his main genres, portrait, landscape and allegory. Moreover, most of his clients also acquired a number of the preliminary drawings for the portrait they had commissioned, and this throws a significant light on the special position which drawings occupied in his oeuvre.[37]

Klimt found himself in a situation that was not dissimilar to that of the architect Josef Hoffmann, who designed many of the interiors for Klimt's female clients. Both artists were living exponents of one of the basic concepts of the Secession as expressed in the catalogue for the Kunstschau exhibition of 1908: "Imbuing life with art is not the same as adorning it with art products".[38]

In his arrangement and design of these interiors Hoffmann repeatedly took account of Klimt's paintings. We have impressive examples of this synthesis in contemporary photos, particularly those of the apartments of Hermine Gallia (ill. p. 104) and Sonja Knips (ill. p. 85). Every guest who paid a visit became part of the arrangement. The regard for Klimt is particularly evident in the placing of the portrait of Marie Henneberg (ill. p. 94), which occupied a dominant position in the reception hall of the house, elevated like an altarpiece above the chimney (ill. p. 97).

Most of Klimt's collectors concentrated on the modern movement. Some also bought historical paintings, like the Lederers, who accumulated a celebrated collection of Italian Renaissance works, both bronzes and paintings by old masters like Jacopo and Gentile Bellini; they also bought antique furniture.[39] Adele and Ferdinand Bloch-Bauer frequently invited guests to admire the collection of Old Viennese porcelain by the master of the house, which was exquisite and unique of its kind. Ferdinand Bloch-Bauer was also interested in nineteenth-century painting and his collection included works by Rudolf Alt, August Pettenkofen and Ferdinand Waldmüller.[40]

Hermine (ill. p. 104) and Moriz Gallia are a good example of the affinity which Klimt's clientele felt with the Secession artists. They not only owned numerous works by Carl Moll but also commissioned a portrait of the husband by Ernst Stöhr as counterpart to Klimt's portrait of the wife. It was also characteristic of Klimt's collectors to be blind to the very young generation of artists in Vienna. In the perspective of art history it is striking that they had little time for Schiele, for example.

In the Lederer family it was characteristically the son, Erich Lederer, whose interest in Schiele was aroused, so appropriately the contact came from the next generation. Jane Kallir said of Serena Lederer that although she supported Schiele, she could never

36 Werner Hofmann, as note 27, p. 18.
37 See the data on provenance in Strobl, esp. For Adele Bloch-Bauer, Hermine Gallia and Eugenia Primavesi.
38 Catalogue of the Vienna Kunstschau 1908, Vienna 1908, p. 59.
39 Many of the works are documented as loans to the exhibition "Meisterwerke italienischer Renaissance aus Privatbesitz" (Masterpieces of the Italian Renaissance in Private Collections) in the Künstlerhaus in Vienna in 1924, cf. the catalogue of the same title, Vienna, 1924.
40 On the collection see Hubertus Czernin, Die Fälschung. Der Fall Bloch-Bauer, Vienna 1999, esp. pp. 160–162 and ibid, Die Fälschung. Der Fall Bloch-Bauer und das Werk Gustav Klimts, Vienna 1999.

really become accustomed to him, either as an individual or as an artist.[41] The many Schiele drawings in the Lederer home were carefully stored in portfolios, they were not hung on display. Nebehay was probably right in saying that "they did not want the balance and beauty of the rooms in Bartensteingasse 8 disrupted by all-too modern works."[42] So in the Lederer home as well Schiele created a case of the classic conflict between the generations.

There was even less affinity between Klimt's patrons and Oskar Kokoschka. When Ferdinand Bloch-Bauer had his portrait painted by Kokoschka in 1936 the artist had long ceased to be an *enfant terrible*, and he had acquired considerable renown, especially in Germany.

Only the young Friederike Beer-Monti showed a broader, unprejudiced taste. She was the only one to be painted by Schiele and a short time later by Klimt as well, and then she set her heart on being painted by Oskar Kokoschka. But after 1914 the war made this impossible. How fascinating it would have been had Klimt, Schiele and Kokoschka—now recognised as the magical triumvirate of painting in Vienna around the turn of the century—tackled one and the same model at almost the same time.

"...The richest man after Rothschild ..."

But where did the wealth come from which enabled the women who adored Klimt's art to play their material part in his intoxicating colours and extreme aestheticism? Most of Klimt's patrons were major industrialists, members of the liberal (commercial) upper middle class, entrepreneurs in other words, to whom money was no object. Professor Riedler, husband of Fritza Riedler, who had a career as a university professor, was the exception who, with Otto Zuckerkandl, a doctor of medicine and his wife Amalie (ill. p. 147), confirms the rule. The Riedlers, who belonged to the classical educated bourgeoisie, differed from the other collectors of Klimt's works in another way as well, for they lived in Berlin and not in Vienna, although it is certain that the Riedler portrait (ill. p. 113) was painted in Vienna.

Klimt's collectors were enormously powerful businessmen. Ferdinand Bloch-Bauer, for instance, had a virtual monopoly of the Austro-Czech sugar industry. Karl Wittgenstein has often been called the Austrian Krupp; he had created a steel cartel and had almost unrestricted control of the monarchy's iron industry. August Lederer was in a similarly dominant position in central European spirits production.[43] In the twenties he was said to be "the richest man in Austria after Rothschild".[44]

Max Weber analysed the attitude that preached "ceaseless activity at work" instead of "humble sinning". In his study of the Protestant ethic and the spirit of capitalism Weber identifies interconnections in an attempt to understand men like Karl Wittgenstein, who seemed to be the ideal type, and whose deepest conviction was that everything could be done.[45] But to critics of capitalism all Klimt's patrons were deadly enemies. Karl Wittgenstein, for example, with his secret transactions was the target of heated social attacks, in which Karl Kraus also joined. His opposition to Klimt's painting was no doubt ultimately not unaffected by his aversion to the patrons of that art.

A chance find in the library of the Vienna Arbeiterkammer (Labour Chamber) is characteristic: August Lederer is the subject of a collection of newspaper cuttings from the interwar years, not as the supporter of the art that some commentators were already attempting to defame as "arrogant high culture".[46] On the contrary, it is Lederer's appar-

41 Jane Kallir, *Egon Schiele. The Complete Works*, New York 1990, p. 144.
42 Christian M. Nebehay, *Gustav Klimt, Egon Schiele und die Familie Lederer*, Bern 1987, p. 29.
43 Bernard Michel had already pointed this out: "Au total, les mécènes de la Sécession se recrutent donc dans la grande bourgeoisie industrielle, avec une nette prédominance du cartel de l'acier et des industries alimentaires: sucreries, alcool, brasseries. C'étaient des industries moderne, organisées en cartel depuis les années 1880, sans être véritablement des industries de pointe à la veille de 1914." Bernard Michel, as note 6, p. 189.
44 Quoted from the magazine *Freiheit*, Vienna, 12/12/1928. That the Vienna Rothschilds did not belong to the Klimt circle is further confirmation of the newcomer. Their "court painter" was Heinrich von Angeli, a member of the Academy and recently ennobled, who also worked for the royal courts in Vienna, London and St Petersburg.
45 Max Weber, "Die protestantische Ethik und der Geist des Kapitalismus", in *Gesammelte Aufsätze zur Religionssoziologie*, Vol. 1, Tübingen 1920, pp. 1–206.
46 Cf. Emil Kläger, *Durch die Wiener Quartiere des Elends und Verbrechens*, Vienna 1908, quoted from Werner Hofmann, as note 27. Hofmann also accuses Klimt of sharing this attitude in "affirmative and consonant behaviour". Unlike Adolf Loos or Oskar Kokoschka he played his part in the "danse macabre" of a late feudal oligarchy thirsting for war.

ent business speculations that are the target. The Vienna stock exchange gazette "Börse" called it "the Lederer case" in 1923.[47] Later headlines were "From the secrets of high finance. Proceedings over profit shares of 120 billion."[48] or "August Lederer and his Sons. The biggest spirits concern immobilised. A good businessman as father and his enterprising sons."[49]

Twice a bomb was placed at Lederer's door; one was defused before it went off, the second slightly injured Lederer senior. They were both laid because swindled creditors would not accept August Lederer's refusal to meet the exorbitant debts his extravagant son had amassed. Carl E. Schorske's axiom of the fathers and the revolt of their liberal sons was outdone by real life.

Very different forces demanded entry in 1938. Serena Lederer, now a widow, had to leave her house and her money, property and collections were confiscated. Huge assets were lost. The apparent greed of those who were supposed to be "different", and whose systematic persecution now began, was used by the Nazi power holders on large and small scale to legitimate their own unscrupulous and criminal enrichment.

Changes in Religion—The Search for New Identities

The business success and social advancement of Klimt's patrons, who were among the great profiteers from the industrialisation and modernisation of the economy in the nineteenth century, corresponded to a high degree of mobility in religious and denominational questions. An above-average percentage in relation to the population as a whole of Klimt's clientele—the women he portrayed and/or their husbands and partners, who are discussed in the following comments on the paintings—came from the Israelite community. Equally characteristic is the fact that almost without exception they had all left that community sometime in their lives. To give only one example, Adele Bloch-Bauer was of Jewish descent, but she died belonging to no religious denomination.[50] Clearly, it would be insufficient to see this as only pressure to assimilate and not also the desire to seize an opportunity. In some cases the parents had already entered the Christian church, generally the evangelical denomination. But Amalie Zuckerkandl (ill. p. 147) is one case of a women who joined the Jewish faith for her husband's sake.

All these changing conditions can probably be seen as the signs of a new society and the search for a new identity by some groups. The people around Klimt would probably have been surprised to learn that one day they would be cited as evidence of a Jewish identity.[51] They would have had little interest in the discussion that started around the turn of the century on whether there was a "Jewish art" or a "Jewish national style"; probably they would have thought this referred to Klimt's contemporary Isidor Kaufmann (1853–1921). His explorations in paint of the world of the East European Jews, which he studied on expeditions every year, were alien in several respects to the world of Klimt's collectors. Firstly, Kaufmann's paintings had a nostalgic element and all-too often looked back through rose-coloured spectacles to the "shtetl" from which their grandparents and forbears may well have come. Then, Kaufmann was a classical representative of Biedermeier genre painting, it was his aim to take the finished painting of the old masters to a late triumph.[52]

But Klimt's collectors wanted to identify with the avant-garde. Their temple (of art) was the Secession building on Karlsplatz with its white walls, devotional atmosphere and golden dome.[53] Their goal was a new, liberal society, in which they would find

47 Die Börse, Vienna, 18 October 1923.
48 Der Abend, Vienna, 8 June 1924, and Die Stunde, Vienna, 6 December 1924.
49 Wiener Sonn- und Montagszeitung, Vienna, 15 June 1931.
50 WStLA, post mortem report of 24 January 1925.
51 For example see Steven Beller, Wien und die Juden 1867–1938, Vienna/Cologne/Weimar 1993, Leon Botstein, Judentum und Modernität. Essays zur Rolle der Juden in der deutschen und österreichischen Kultur 1843–1938, Vienna/Cologne/Graz 1991.
52 Cf. exhib. cat. Rabbiner—Bocher—Talmudschüler, Bilder des Wiener Malers Isidor Kaufmann. 1853–1921, Jüdisches Museum Vienna, ed. G. Tobias Natter, Vienna, 1995.
53 For example see Gottfried Fliedl, Gustav Klimt. 1862–1918. Die Welt in weiblicher Gestalt, Cologne 1998, esp. pp. 96–103.

a place precisely through their commitment to modern art. It was not coincidence that the building had ardent admirers in the ranks of the feminist movement as well. Marie Lang, for instance, celebrated it as provocation of the lower classes; she saw it as a temple "basically earnest, severe, bare and demanding like the task we face". To her it was a parable on the feminist movement.[54] All this was reinforced by the efforts on the part of the government to strengthen the Austrian identity in face of the ever more forceful German Kaiserreich.

Since the Austrian monarchy had lost its political hegemony within the German-speaking countries through the war with Prussia and the defeat at Konigsgrätz in 1863, the question of an "Austrian nation" had been crucial. The writers of the "Jung-Wien" (Young Vienna) movement were especially eager to affirm this. Hermann Bahr, for example, played a particularly aggressive part in the discussion. A passionate supporter of Klimt's art, he himself admitted that he could not answer the question of what is truly "Austrian", but thanks to Gustav Klimt and his painting *Schubert at the Piano*[55] there was a demonstrable example of it and one only needed to describe the painting. "I only know that I get cross if people ask me if I am German. No, I say, I am not German, I am Austrian. But that isn't a nationality, they say. Austria has become a nation, I say, we are different from the Germans, we have our own identity. Define it! Well, how can one 'define' it? But you can see it in Klimt's painting of Schubert! That quiet, mild gaze, the radiance combined with bourgeois modesty—that is the very essence of our Austrian nationality."[56]

The Vienna Secession

In a time of social mix, that has been interpreted as a crisis of the liberal identity since Carl E. Schorske's *Fin-de-Siècle Vienna*, support for Gustav Klimt and participation in the Vienna avant-garde had the effect of creating an identity, and for the wealthy upper middle class of Vienna in particular this increasingly overlaid and compensated for religious traditions and the patterns of identity derived from these. In the Bloch-Bauer family, for instance, only one Jewish festival, Yom Kippur, was still celebrated and Ferdinand Bloch-Bauer went to the synagogue only then. But the family recalled with pride that they had a seat next to the Rothschilds.[57]

The conflict in these social transformation processes of acculturation and assimilation is evident in Hermine Gallia and her husband Moriz, both of whom had left the Jewish community, like many others. The ageing Moriz Gallia changed his will three times and only in the last one did he remember his Jewish background and leave funds to "the poor of the IVth district of Vienna, the poor of the City of Vienna with no distinction to be made according to religious denomination, to the Israelite community in Vienna, the Israelite community in Bisenz and the political community in Bisenz-Stadt."[58] The sum of 1,000 crowns which he apportioned for this purpose in his will was not large compared with his fortune (the will mentions more than a million crowns in industrial shares, real estate and so on); the fact that he remembered his roots only at the very end of his life and then assigned only a modest sum for this indicates how ambivalent his feelings were.

We should also mention Gertrud Loew (ill. p. 99). She was born in 1883, the year her parents left the Jewish community and converted to Catholicism.[59] Her second husband, Elémer von Felsővány, was also Jewish. His father Samuel had achieved financial advancement, the most evident expression of which was his ennoblement in 1897, enti-

54   Marie Lang, "Das Secessionsgebäude", in *Wiener Rundschau*, Vol. 2, 1897/98, pp. 939f.; quoted from Harriet Anderson, *Vision und Leidenschaft. Die Frauenbewegung im Fin de Siècle Wien*, Vienna 1994, pp. 359f.
55   Novotny-Dobai No. 101, painted 1899, oil on canvas, 150 x 200 cm.
56   Hermann Bahr, *Secession (Wien 1900)*, p. 122f. See also Günter Metken, "Mit der Weltbewegung Schritt halten", in exhib. cat. *Sehnsucht nach Glück, Wiens Aufbruch in die Moderne, Klimt, Kokoschka, Schiele*, exhib. Schirn Kunsthalle Frankfurt a.M., ed. Sabine Schulze, Ostfildern-Ruit 1995, pp. 145–150.
57   I am grateful to Maria Altmann, niece of Ferdinand Bloch-Bauer, for this information of 7 March 1999.
58   WStLA, file on the estate, later entry of 15 April 1917.
59   See the records of leavers kept by the Israelite church, Vienna.
60   Zoltán Barcsay-Amant, Adeliges Jahrbuch 1936/43, Vol. 14/21, Lucerne 1969, p. 237.

tling him to change his name to "von Felsóvány". But this was not enough. His son converted to Christianity, became a member of the evangelical church A.B. and in 1913 successfully applied to change the paternal name Baruch von Felsóvány, which
he no doubt thought sounded too Jewish, to Felsóványi von Felsóványi,
which seemed more elegant.[60]

Gustav Klimt,
Schubert at the Piano, 1899
Burned in 1945

Against the background of these social, religious and economic
processes the present overhasty tendency to label Klimt's clientele "Jewish"
and speak of his "Jewish patrons" is highly questionable. Christian
Brandstätter, for instance, says of Klimt's portraits of women: "Three quarters of his clients came from the Jewish bourgeoisie" but one looks in vain
for an exact and historical explanation of what is meant by the "Jewish"
bourgeoisie; it would be more accurate to speak of the search for identity
and the transformation processes of a wealthy liberal middle class of Jewish descent.[61]
Certainly the controversial and complex theme of the "Jewish identity" in Vienna at the
turn of the century appears in quite a different and very much more complex light in
view of the National Socialist "Anschluss" in 1938 and its consequences. The descriptions of Klimt's portraits and the biographical data they contain will provide much more
information on this.

It was only the National Socialists who "turned" many of Klimt's patrons and clients, men and women, back into Jews—and then persecuted them. Gertrud Loew (ill. p.
99) had been a member of the Roman Catholic church all her life, but after 1938 she was
declared a "full Jew". Serena Lederer (ill. p. 89) and her daughter Elisabeth Bachofen-Echt
(ill. p. 132) were also victimised and persecuted by the Nazis, but they both succeded in
escaping the Nazi death machine. But Amalie Zuckerkandl (ill. p. 147), whose portrait
Klimt did not finish, was deported and murdered in a concentration camp. A greater contrast between these events and the world Klimt created and inhabited, with its utopian
aesthetic and harmony, can hardly be imagined.

"La belle juive"

We do not know whether his sitters' Jewish descent was of any concern to Klimt, but he
was certainly reminded of it by the outside world again and again. Anti-Semitism quickly
formed a dark undertone in the criticism of the revolutionary element in his art and as
early as 1900—in the heat of the philosophical conflict over the faculty paintings—the
nationalistic German paper *Deutsches Volksblatt* started an anti-Semitistic campaign.
Objecting to the immoral elements in the paintings, the paper wrote accusingly: "...for
we know Jewish effrontery. To feed their poison into the people they have made it their
principle to proclaim the lowest and meanest."[62] This was to perpetuate the argument
that the Jews and liberalism were to blame for everything because of their apparent
"lack of values".

To his contemporaries Klimt's work touched on three aspects of the Jewish question. It was manifest visually in the choice of "la belle juive" as motif and in her depiction; then it was evident in his form and style as "le gout juif" and sociologically it found
expression in the wealthy Jewish businessmen who bought his works.

In this context "la belle juive" was a topos rather than anti-semitic sentiment, the
classification of a stereotype and a type of beauty—the beautiful mysterious woman
with a pale skin and dark brows, all the primary charms that play so central a role in

Klimt's faces, hung with gold and jewels like an oriental princess.[63] "La belle juive" displays exotic charms of this kind, as does the "femme fatale". Klimt said of the Venetian women once that they were "too beautiful and too healthy" for his taste, a remark that can hardly be called objective but which reveals a great deal about his perception and his aesthetic ideals.[64] It also shows how far he had moved away from Makart's ideal, Paolo Veronese's women.

The spiteful phrase "gout juif" was coined by none other than Karl Kraus. While the Ministry of Education, that had organised the Austrian pavilion at the World Exhibition in Paris in 1900 was talking of a great success, Karl Kraus sneered: " The great success of Herr Klimt and the Secession is that the Parisians have nicknamed the imported art "le gout juif".[65] Later Felix Salten took up the phrase and spoke of the "Jewish jour-dame".[66]

The stereotype of the wealthy Jewish businessman has proved most persistent. The celebrated painter Anton Faistauer from Salzburg echoed the infamous voices. He was an outstanding painter of Schiele's generation, and after Schiele's death he felt he was the leader of the Austrian artists. In 1923 he published a book *Neue Malerei in Österreich* (New Painting in Austria) and even at this early date the resentment inherent in the blood and soil ideology is frighteningly evident. Faistauer attacked Egon Schiele and Gustav Klimt for, as he thought, abandoning "bourgeois values" and for their "eccentric, perverse" deviation which he maintained was evident up and down the social scale. Both Klimt and Schiele, he argues, were products of the big city, but while Klimt was the painter of high finance Schiele was his social opposite, the "painter of the proletariat", as befitted his roots in the lower middle class. Faistauer condemned both. "Klimt attracted the shallow and superficial moneyed Jewish business class of the inner city and became their painter; while the outlying districts with their tragic faces, hunger, hatred and ill-temper weighed upon Schiele. Their depictions of women also differ in accordance with their social backgrounds. They both seek a demi-monde, Schiele in the outlying districts, Klimt inside the Ring."[67]

Klimt's portraits of women were seen as the ultimate in decadence, a stereotypical condemnation that was becoming increasingly widespread during the twenties.[68] But it is also interesting to see that the Lederer family do not appear to have taken lasting offence at Faistauer's analysis, which he published in 1923. At any rate in 1929 they gave the artist a commission for a huge ceiling fresco to decorate the vestibule of their summer residence, Schloss Weidlingau near Vienna, a commission which Faistauer accepted with thanks.[68]

After the collapse of the monarchy Klimt's portraits were not highly regarded, but this was a reflection of a general phenomenon in the reception of his art in which anti-Semitism was not always involved. This is also evident from the opinion expressed by Max Eisler, who was actually a supporter of Klimt's art, to which he devoted the first general account in book form in 1920. But in discussing the portraits of women Eisler comes back again and again to the decadent element, seeing these paintings as evidence of a "spoilt, cultured society in a metropolis... Generally it is the lady who is mocking or blasé, intellectually indifferent or maybe even dull, who wants to appear important and brilliant." Eisler's remark was particularly bold as most of these women were still alive in 1920. Finally he accused Klimt of being the "historian of this languid, lukewarm and empty social class."[70]

61 Christian Brandstätter, "Schöne jüdische Jour-Damen", in exib. cat. *Gustav Kimt*, Kunsthaus Zürich, Toni Stooss and Christoph Doswald (eds.), Zürich 1992, p. 334.
62 *Deutsches Volksblatt*, Vienna, May 1900. For more information on the subject of anti-Semitism, Klimt and state promotion of the Secessionists see Carl E. Schorske, as note 24, esp. pp. 226ff.
63 On the correspondence between "la belle juive" and the "femme fatale", both stereotypes resulting from a combination of racism with sexism, see the essay "La belle juive und die schöne Schickse" by Gabriele Kohlbauer-Fritz in exhib. cat. *Der schejne Jid. Das Bild des jüdischen Körpers in Mythos und Ritual*, exhib. in the Jüdisches Museum Vienna, ed. Sander L. Gilman, Robert Jütte and Gabriele Kohlbauer-Fritz, Vienna 1998, pp. 109ff.
64 From the memoirs of the sculptor and courier Maximilian Lenz, quoted from Nebehay, 1959, p. 496.
65 Karl Kraus, *Die Fackel*, Vol. 2, No. 41, mid-May 1900, p. 22. Kraus repeated his verdict in No. 44, Vienna, mid-June 1900, p. 15.
66 Nebehay 1969, pp. 254f.
67 Anton Faistauer, *Neue Malerei in Österreich, Betrachtungen eines Malers*, Zurich/Leipzig/Vienna, 1923, p. 18.
68 For example see Albin Egger-Lienz, who set up against the sophistication of the metropolis the image of simplicity and greatness that was "deeply felt and entirely part of his homeland". Quoted from Wilfried Kirschl, Albin Egger-Lienz, 1868–1926, Vienna 1996, Vol. 1, p. 212.
69 Cf. Fuhrmann, Franz, *Anton Faistauer*, Salzburg 1972, p. 27 and WV No. 372.
70 Max Eisler, *Gustav Klimt*, Vienna 1920, pp. 22/23.

Gerbert Frodl, writing seventy years later, saw the portraits quite differently, and he is only one of many we could cite who hold the opposite view to Eisler: "Apart from very few exceptions in his early work, Klimt has only painted portraits of women and there is no doubt that it was Klimt who gave the female portaiture of his time its most convincing expression." [71]

Pioneers of the Emancipation of Women?

Interior of Schloss Weidlingau
with the Faistauer fresco

Sociologically Klimt's society is easy to define. But the biographical data published here for the first time show that the group of Klimt's women was extremely heterogeneous, both in their nature and their personalities. Adele Bloch-Bauer (ill. p. 117), for instance, is described by her niece as "suffering; she always had a headache, she smoked like a chimney and was frightfully delicate; she was dark, with a transparent skin, slim and elegant, always in search of mental stimulus."[72], while Rose Rosthorn (ill. p. 93), whom Klimt has shown as a vamp in glittering sequins, was one of the few women Alpine climbers of her day; she rose with the dawn and could proudly list the many peaks she was the first to climb—"one of the most highly profiled women mountaineers".[73]

Looking back at the start of a new century to a hundred years that are often called "the women's century" one inevitably faces the question of how these women saw their lives. That Klimt's women could have their portraits painted by one of the most expensive painters in Europe but were not allowed to vote is all too often overlooked today. And it was only after 1900 that they could enter the Faculty of Arts in Vienna University; the other faculties opened their doors to women students even later.

In such circumstances the professional success which some of Klimt's women enjoyed is particularly striking. Chief among them was Emilie Flöge, who ran her own business as fashion designer (ill. p. 101). Eugenia Primavesi (ill. p. 129) also played an active part in the fortunes of the Wiener Werkstätte, and Gertrud Loew-Felsöványi (ill. p. 99) is expressly named as President in office of the Loew Sanatorium, which was the biggest and oldest in Vienna.

A strikingly large number of the women whom Klimt painted were themselves active as artists. Ability to handle brush and watercolour was part of the standard education of ladies in the upper classes and the drawing lessons which Serena Lederer was privileged to receive from Klimt for years can probably be seen in the same context. On the other hand many of the women whom Klimt portrayed abandoned social conventions and pursued serious artistic aims, chief among them Emilie Flöge. Encouraged by Klimt, Serena's daughter Elisabeth Bachofen-Echt (ill. p. 132) also embarked on an artistic career, attending sculpture classes at the Kunstgewerbeschule in Vienna. In the thirties she created works that received public recognition. And Johanna Staude and Sonja Knips also saw themselves as artists, stating this as their occupation in their registration documents. However, no works by either have so far come to light.

Much surprising information on Adele Bloch-Bauer's financial position and degree of emancipation has emerged during the current restitution debate on the two Klimt portraits in the Österreichische Galerie. Adele Bloch-Bauer appeared to be the prototype of the emancipated woman. She was thought to be rich and she continued to use her maiden name after her marriage in a double name, which was by no means usual at the time.[74] However, this was not a sign of emancipation, it was due apparently to a wish on the part of her father, for all his male descendants were dead and he wanted to see the name continue. We have also learnt now that whether or not the two portraits of Adele Bloch-Bauer painted by Klimt have been her property is a point at issue, although she had huge financial resources after the death of her father in 1905 and is known to have bought sixteen works on paper by Klimt from the Galerie Miethke the following year.[75]

In other cases the financial circumstances were clearer. Often we learn from the executor's records that all the moveable items in the house belonged to the wife even during her husband's lifetime. Sometimes the Klimt pictures were actually individually listed in this context. This form of division of the property was apparently quite usual, and it is a vivid illustration of the belief held in society that the interior was the wife's sphere, while the building and apartment were provided by her husband, they were the external framework to which she had to adapt. The Civil Code perpetuated this difference in the roles of man and wife right into the 1970s. Paragraph 1237 of the Austrian Civil Code stated that if there were a lack of clarity over questions of property "the man had acquired the property."[76]

How women were perceived (by men) in 1933 is evident from the Secession exhibition *The Life of Woman*. Like the foreword to the catalogue the concept for the exhibition was based on the idea that the wife was to be her husband's loyal companion on his path through life. "Her life derives its contents and fulfilment from her relation to her husband."[77]

But for this very reason we cannot agree with Hubertus Czernin when he sees Adele Bloch-Bauer at her husband's side as an appendix rather than an independent personality. Perhaps she and most of the other women portrayed by Klimt did not succeed in breaking out of the role expectations and the image of woman held by the society of their time. But it would be wrong to deny that they attempted to cross this barrier. To assume that Frau Bloch-Bauer was not an independent woman, as Czernin does, is seriously to misjudge her: "Adele was not a part of this, she remained a decorative adjunct—even after death. She was a lady of the salon who won much for herself, but not enough to overcome the limits of the salon. She was honoured, she was listened to, but no more than that. According to everything that can be learnt about her eight decades later, she was ultimately only one of the "salon sibyls" to whom Milan Dubrovic was referring in his characterisation of Vienna social life at that time."[74]

The proclamation by middle class society that "It is the will of God that a woman's life should be in marriage and the family" inevitably evoked the opposite, woman as whore and mistress. The two aspects belong together like two sides of the same coin and Klimt handles them with sovereign ease, allowing neither to cancel the other. He does not call in question the bourgeois institution of marriage, with its "good mother" and housewife, nor does he deny Eros and Thanatos. Perhaps it is this that gives his portraits of women their powerful attraction.

Berta Zuckerkandl saw Klimt as the creator of the modern woman with her gamin slenderness: "The term 'vamp' had not been coined then, but Klimt created the type of a Greta Garbo, a Marlene Dietrich, long before it was a reality."[79]

We can look again at the comparison of Klimt's portrait of Fritza Riedler (ill. p. 113) with Velasquez's portrait of the Infanta (ill. p. 153) which inspired him here, for it will thematise another contradiction. The two paintings are closely related in motif, technique and in their claim to representation; they are even closer in their handling of

71 Gerbert Frodl, *Gustav Klimt in der Österreichischen Galerie in Wien*, Salzburg 1992, S. 41.
72 Information gratefully received from Maria Altmann on 7 March 1999.
73 Eduard Pichl, *Wiens Bergsteigertum*, Vienna, Österr. Staatsdruckerei, 1927, p. 16 and esp. p. 134: "She was the first woman to climb the Ortler over the Marltgrat and through the Minnigeroder gulley, the Thurwieser and the Trafoier ice wall...".
74 Christian Brandstätter expressly draws attention to the use of the double name in this context: cf. Brandstätter, as note 61, p. 330.
75 See Strobl, Vol. 4, p. 224.
76 This clause was only annulled by the Law to Amend the Marriage Legislation, Federal Gazette 1978/280. Since then the principle of separation of assets has applied. I am grateful to Mag. Dr. Franz Smola for the information on the legislation.
77 Heinrich Leporini, *Das Leben der Frau*, exhib. cat. and reprinted in a special issue of the magazine *Österreichische Kunst*, Vol. 4, Vienna 1933, March 1933, p. 1.
78 Hubertus Czernin, *Die Fälschung. Der Fall Bloch-Bauer*, Vienna 1999, p. 75.
79 Berta Zuckerkandl-Szeps, "Erinnerungen an Gustav Klimt. Zu seinem sechzehnten Todestag", in *Neues Wiener Journal*, 4 February 1934.

the body and their rendering of physical quality. But precisely this reveals a deep contradiction in the aesthetic (formed by men) of turn of the century Vienna. Where the domestication of the bodies in Velazquez is a result of the rigid ceremonial at the court of Spain, the geometrisation of the image of the woman in Klimt's painting is a deliberate choice by the artist. In his portraits of women Klimt negates the physical quality in the two-dimensional surface. By overlaying with gold and ornamentation he is making a gesture that is contrary to the efforts of the reform movement in women's fashions. For their ideal was the unrestricted waist, clothes that flowed freely along the body; they were rebelling against corsets and tight garments that restricted the body.[80]

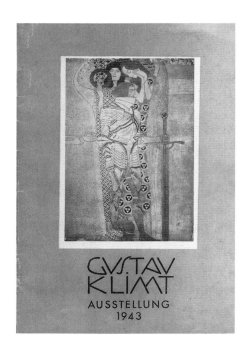

Catalogue of the Gustav
Klimt exhibition, Vienna,
1943

How Adele Bloch-Bauer became the "Woman in Gold"

The history of the reception of Gustav Klimt's work right through the twentieth century, with all its many supporters and critics, has not been fully written even today. It is often assumed that he was persecuted in the Third Reich like Kokoschka and Schiele, who were stigmatised by the National Socialists as "degenerate artists". But actually only Oskar Kokoschka was persecuted; Egon Schiele, who was regarded as suspect in Germany, still had his admirers in Vienna under the Nazis, while the euphoria with which Gustav Klimt had been celebrated became open admiration.

At the personal initiative of the Reichstatthalter of Vienna, Baldur von Schirach, the largest exhibition devoted to Klimt's work that was ever held in the twentieth century was mounted in the Künstlerhaus in Vienna in 1943. The response was enormous. The *Völkischer Beobachter* maintained that the pictures were more apposite then than around 1900![82] and the *Frankfurter Zeitung* maintained that Gustav Klimt was enjoying a "resurrection".[83]

How could that be? So marked a reinterpretation was the result of complicated processes and events on various levels that can only be hinted at here.

Firstly, it was the result of "opposition" on the part of the Vienna National Socialists to the centralism in Berlin.[84] In the game of power politics they believed they could establish a special position for Vienna that would work to their advantage; consequently they attempted to stylise the old tradition and cultural richness of the Danube metropolis. Berlin was to be reminded that Vienna was an art centre, it was Great Vienna, a truly New Vienna that Ludwig Hevesi had seen emerging long before, under totally different circumstances, when the Secession was founded on Karlsplatz.[85]

The Vienna Klimt exhibition was held at a time when all resources of personnel and finance were being mobilised for total war. Even the supplies of paper to print the catalogue could only be obtained with special permission—a highly illuminating example of the influence the art world was able to exercise and the favours it could obtain. Klimt was reinterpreted from outside. But there were certain traits in his work and in his personality that were now brought out and emphasised, and which could be made to suit the Nazi ideology and its appropriations—his role as high priest, for instance, which brought him dangerously close to Nietzsche's "Herrenmensch".

What is decisive here, however, is the need to take Klimt out of his context, see him as an a-historical figure. In fact, massive manipulation was needed to integrate the Viennese painter into the Nazi context, and this greatly affected the portraits of women.

Only when the biographical details and the individuality of the subject were eliminated could Adele Bloch-Bauer become the highly praised "Lady in Gold".[86]

The "princesses" of the wealthy upper middle class in Vienna had become anonymous models. The tendency on the part of art historians to suppress the biographical details in any portrait had been elevated to total perversion.[87]

To feel and experience what has been created

When Klimt opened the Kunstschau of 1908 with a short speech[88] he first spoke in warm support of the total work of art and then discussed the relation between "high" and "low" art. He cited William Morris, that even the most seemingly unimportant thing will help to enhance the beauty of this earth if it is executed perfectly.[89] He then spoke about applied and fine art.

Klimt took a wide (and modern) view of the concept of art, but he was even more radical in his definition of the artist, propounding the equation of artist and receptor, whom he described in a characteristically hedonistic formulation as the person "enjoying" art. He proclaimed: "We define the term 'artist' as broadly as we define the term 'work of art'. Not only those who create, those who enjoy are also artists to us, because they are capable of experiencing and feeling what has been created and of honouring it. For us 'artists' are the ideal community of all who create and all who enjoy".

In the catalogue for the Klimt exhibition in Zurich in 1992 Philip Ursprung speaks of "heralds", in a retrogressive image.[90] But these were not fanfares sounding for the entry of crowned heads. The Klimt group, when they moved away from the art of the nineteenth century, were a group of artists who stressed their international outlook. They did not shy away from the comparison with the European avant-garde and they evolved new ways of hanging and presenting exhibitions. They originated the variable, open location that enjoyed a vogue in the later twentieth century as the "white cube". They pioneered methods of selling art, with modern galleries, press relations work, market cultivation, international contacts and so on, all of which have remained characteristic of the art world today.

Klimt's "heralds" were part of a society that was redefining itself, through innovations in business and industry. It was the utopia of a society for whom the art to which they were committed was a superior principle, and which involved standing shoulder to shoulder with the artistic avant-garde. Against the ideological background of the ennoblement of the world through art and the dominant opposites of Eros and prudery Klimt elaborated his obeisances to feminine beauty.

In his portraits he gave the women their own space within ornamentation. At the same time, he enveloped all and everything in the world of "art", he "harmonised" in his pictorial worlds long after there was nothing to harmonise. Klimt's portraits of women hover between beautiful appearance and an abyss, between naturalistic form and abstract desire, between aestheticisation and that battle over sex and identity that is at least as topical in the present gender debate as it was then, when the efforts of the feminist movement were only gradually setting it in motion. Rosa Meyreder, the Viennese pioneer feminist, recognised an immanent socio-political dilemma in her *Zur Kritik der Weiblichkeit* (A Critique of Feminity) (1905). She analysed the demand for harmony between the sexes, arguing that it would lead to a loss of more rights for women.

80 See the article by Angela Völker in this catalogue.
81 Referring to the "erotic" cf. Gottfried Fliedl, "Das Weib macht keine Kunst, aber den Künstler. Zur Klimt-Rezeption", in Renate Berger/Daniela Hammer-Tugendhat (eds.), *Der Garten der Lüste. Zur Deutung des Erotischen und Sexuellen bei Künstlern und ihren Interpreten*, Köln 1985, pp. 89–145.
82 Richard Meister, "Klimts Fakultätsbilder. Ein Nachwort zur Ausstellung", in *Völkischer Beobachter*, 2 April 1943, p. 3.
83 Ernst Benkard, "Wiedersehen mit Gustav Klimt. Zur Ausstellung in der Wiener Sezession (!)", in *Frankfurter Zeitung*, 4 April 1943.
84 On the attempt to take a separate path in cultural policy from Berlin see Oliver Rathkolb, "Die Wiener Note in der deutschen Kunst. Nationalsozialistische Kulturpolitik in Wien 1938–1945", in exhib. cat. *Kunst und Diktatur. Architektur, Bildhauerei und Malerei in Österreich, Deutschland, Italien und der Sowjetunion 1922–1956*, Jan Tabor (ed.), Künstlerhaus Wien, Baden 1994, Vol. 1, pp- 332–335.
85 Hevesi on 27 March 1897, quoted from ibid 1906, pp. 1–3.
86 The painting was exhibited with the title "Damenbildnis mit Goldhintergrund" (Portrait of a Lady with Gold Background) and this title is retained in the catalogue. Other titles were similar: "Damenbildnis mit Goldgewand und Goldhintergrund" (Portrait of a Lady in a Golden Robe and with a Gold Background). Certainly the intention was exclusively to indicate a formal characteristic. Referring to the alteration of titles see Alessandra Comini, "Titles can be troublesome. Misinterpretations in Male Art Criticism", in *Art Criticism*, Vol. 1, No. 2. New York 1979.
87 If Klimt, Schiele and Kokoschka have become the triple star that outshines all others in turn of the century Vienna, it should not be forgotten that each of the three artists experienced a completely different reception and popularity curve in the course of the twentieth century. But that is a subject in itself, as is the story of Gustav Klimt in the Third Reich, of which only the main outline can be indicated here.
88 It does not matter whether he wrote it himself or someone else wrote it for him, which is more likely as Klimt was notorious for neglecting to open letters and for his dislike of writing.
89 The speech is reprinted in the catalogue of the Kunstschau, Vienna, 1908, pp. 2–5.
90 Cf. the excellent essay by Philip Ursprung, "Wir wollen eure Herolde sein. Gustav Klimt und die secessionistische Kunstkritik", in exhib. cat. *Gustav Klimt*, as note 61, pp. 315–321.

But it would be inadequate to accuse Klimt of aesthetic flight into an unreal world, as politically committed art critics were inclined to do in the seventies. For often enough these "unreal worlds" prove to be more effective than the seemingly real worlds.

In Giacomo Puccini's opera *Tosca,* which was first performed in Rome in 1900, the heroine of the title sings "Vissi d'arte, vissi d'amor!"—"I lived for art, I lived for love!". It could hardly be applied to a more suitable exponent than Gustav Klimt. But the art of the theatre shows us more than the rude awakening when Tosca is forced to realise that politics and intrigue have torn her out of her dream.

A consideration of the portraits of women by Gustav Klimt reveals the split in the image of woman that was typical of the time, the split into a threatening manifestation and the corresponding adoration. But only a knowledge of the biographical data will reveal the closely integrated relationship between life and art, between artist and sitter, man and woman. Klimt was fully sensible of their ambivalences, their variety and contradictions. But to him this was "the ideal community of all who create and all who enjoy".

Catalogue

Portrait of the seventeen-year-old Emilie Flöge

GUSTAV KLIMT

1891
Pastel on cardboard,
67 x 41.5 cm
Marked on the lower right:
"Gustav Klimt–/1891"
Private collection, courtesy of
Galerie Welz, Salzburg
(Strobl, Vol. 1, No. 247)

Gustav Klimt
Portrait of Emilie Flöge, 1893
Oil on cardboard
Private collection

"Send for Emilie" was the dying Klimt's request when he came out of his coma again, longing to see the woman who had lived for thirty years at his side as his confidante and companion, yet had to share him with many others. "Fräulein Flöge" and Klimt first met in 1891. Emilie was a seventeen-year-old girl at that time, while Klimt, twelve years her senior, had brilliantly accomplished his first furnishing and decoration commissions and was on the verge of becoming an established painter. Their closeness was strengthened by a marriage between close relatives, Gustav Klimt's younger brother Ernst and Emilie's sister Helene, which took place in 1891.

Emilie's features are highlighted by the three-quarter profile. The face has been drawn with a precision that, together with the brown tone of the picture, is reminiscent of a photograph, a painting technique the public would appreciate, as the artist knew. The sharp nose has been modelled with slight touches of white. While the face and particularly the eyes have been carefully developed the white dress appears to be rather sketchy, blending easily into the monochrome background. The painting is enclosed by a gilt frame, which Klimt decorated with cherry blossom and grasses. This is the first sign of the Japonisme that will become particularly evident in Klimt's late works.

A second portrait of Emilie Flöge dates from 1893. This time, the whole figure is shown in a red-green costume decorated with ruches and bows. It is quite different from the typical Klimt portraits after 1900 both stylistically and in its nature, since it was intended for the Burgtheater in Vienna, rather than a bourgeois salon: it was actually a detail from *The buffoon on the Rothenburg extempore stage*. There, she appears in the crowd beside Klimt's sisters Hermine and Klara, who had likewise been asked to pose as supernumeraries for the buffoon painting.[1]

Ernst and Gustav Klimt
Buffoon on the Rothenburg
extempore stage, 1893/94
Easel painting after the Burg-
theater decorations (Detail).
Private collection

1   For Details about the buffoon painting, see Alice Strobl, "Hanswurst auf der Stegreifbühne zu Rothenburg. Das Burgtheater- und das Staffeleibild—Aufklärung eines Missverständnisses der Klimtliteratur", in Christian Beutler, Peter-Klaus Schuster and Martin Warnke, (eds.), *Kunst um 1800 und die Folgen—Werner Hofman zu Ehren*, Munich 1988, pp. 337–345, and Strobl, Vol. 4, p. 35.

Portrait of a lady

c. 1894
Oil on canvas, 155 x 75 cm
Marked on the upper right:
"Gustav. Klimt."
Private property
(Novotny-Dobai No. 66)

The subject was a friend of Emilie Flöge's with whom she stayed in contact even after the "Schwestern Flöge" fashion house had closed down. Though the portrait has been known to Klimt literature, it has been practically inaccessible since the owners have been keen to maintain their anonymity. This reticence, however, contributed to the fact that this painting is the only Klimt portrait still in family ownership and hanging in its original position.

Standing erect, the woman is depicted life-size. For his composition, Klimt uses the effect of pairs of opposites. He turns the woman's shoulders into the picture space, but shows the face in strong profile. The second eyebrow is only partly visible. The white complexion of the face and the décolletage shine brightly, impressively contrasting with the black colour of the silk evening dress. Klimt pays much attention to the details of the garment, underlining the fashionableness of the wide puff sleeves, the large décolletage, the slim waist. The shades of black are amply modelled. The flesh-tones, however, shimmer coldly with admixtures of a greenish tone. The lively composition is balanced by strong pictorial architecture, in which the thirty-one-year-old woman's erect posture is paralleled by a bright streak of wall. The chaise longue whose back supports the woman's hand mitigates the severely orthogonal quality. In its composition, the painting is reminiscent of the Leopold Collection's sitting girl in a white, but similarly fashionable dress, which, however, is painted on wood and is unusually small.

The undated picture, reproduced in colour here for the first time, is an important preliminary stage for the portrait of Sonja Knips (ill. p. 85). For the first time among Klimt's portraits of women, we encounter a life-sized representation almost in full length. What will be critical for the Knips portrait is not only the changed square format, but also the use of deliberately obscured perspective.

Gustav Klimt
Sitting young girl, c. 1894,
Oil on wood, Vienna, Museum
Leopold Privatstiftung

Portrait of a woman
(Portrait of Frau Heymann?)

GUSTAV KLIMT

c. 1894
Oil on wood, 39 x 23 cm
Marked on the upper left:
"Gustav . Klimt ."
Vienna, Historisches Museum,
Inv. No. 61.061
(Novotny-Dobai No. 65)

Gustav Klimt
Portrait of a lady, c. 1898/99
Oil on cardboard
Vienna, Österreichische Galerie
Belvedere

Purchased from the collector Dr. August Heymann's bequest, this painting had been inventoried at the Historisches Museum in Vienna as "portrait of an unknown woman".[1] Attempts have subsequently been made to interpret it as a portrait of Frau Heymann, working on the basis of the collection context, but this remains questionable, as the provenance is the only iconographic indication.

The face of the woman who meets the spectator's glance without hesitation is faithfully rendered. Seen from close up, but apparently distant as it is so unwrinkled, it almost seems to be waxen. The curly hair suits the painter's artistic taste and forms together with the high-necked, sketchily rendered garment a counterpoint to the precision of the face, which stands out in relief. The profile and the darker background form a clear contrast. In the background, simple stereotyped floral patterns presage the "Holy Spring" of the Wiener Secession that will be founded under Klimt's leadership three years later. Falling from above, the light has no clear function, except that it provides the composition with a stage-like atmosphere.

The portrait of an unknown lady belonging to the Österreichische Galerie Belvedere seems to be even more deliberately arranged. Seen from an extremely low angle, the face is modelled by a shaft of light coming from below. Although her identity is unknown, this is clearly a new type of woman: the alleged Frau Heymann's formality is gone and a mondaine beauty steps out of the darkness. Behind the palisade-like brushstrokes, she enigmatically announces the new nature of the femme fatale.

1   Vienna, Historisches Museum, inventory, entry to Inv. No. 61.061. For details about August Heymann, see Czeike, Vol. 3, 1994, p. 180.

Portrait of Helene Klimt

GUSTAV KLIMT

1898
Oil on cardboard, 60 x 40 cm
Unmarked
Bern, Kunstmuseum, loan from a
private collection
(Novotny-Dobai No. 92)

Helene Klimt with her grandparents Hermann and Barbara Flöge, Photograph c. 1907/08, Salzburg, private collection

Despite its intimate character, this painting has been shown repeatedly, first in 1898, and also in the Secession's Klimt exhibition in 1903.[1] We see the six-year-old Helen, a niece of Gustav Klimt's. The full hair has been cut into a pageboy bob. The front bangs are touching the brows. All that is left for the eyes, the nose, and the mouth is a small, silhouetted stripe. The hair's chestnut colour reflects the warm red of the flesh tones. The background is markedly simple, the blouse is white, enriched with blue tones. The contrast achieved by Klimt is as delicate as the interplay is well balanced. On the one hand, the effect of the picture is dominated by the clear-cut coiffure, the strong profile, the high-necked blouse, on the other hand, it is complemented and given a new interpretation by Klimt's generosity in rendering the fabric with few strokes and ennobling it in an impressionistic manner. Though, at a first glance, the picture may seem unpretentious, it already displays what would later become Klimt's characteristic dualism of mimesis and dissolution, faithfulness and artistic freedom. There is also already a sense here of the preference for detail in a spiritualised environment, as well as of the Viennese quality of the Secession.

The subject, Helene Luise Klimt, was the pride of the family, the only child of her parents Ernst and Helene Klimt, née Flöge, who had married in 1891. The young family met with a hard reverse of fate when the father died unexpectedly on 9 December 1892.[2] Born in the same year on 28 July, little Helene was then only a few months old. Gustav Klimt took over the girl's guardianship.[3] Ernst Klimt's sudden death put also an end to the "Malercompagnie", in which the Klimt brothers and Franz Matsch had joined. Mother and daughter, however, found refuge in the extended family.

The young widow found a job in her elder sister Pauline's sewing school and became co-owner of the "Schwestern Flöge" fashion house, which developed from the school. Later, her daughter Helene also joined the business, becoming co-owner after her mother's death in 1936. She worked as a receptionist and advised customers, frequented social gatherings and bridge afternoons, and often brought home valuable ideas that could be used in the fashion house.[4] She also worked on administration and orders, but especially on bookkeeping. After the fashion house closed in 1938, Helene Klimt, married name Donner, lived with her two aunts at 39 Ungargasse, where she died on 5 January 1980.

1   Catalogue of the Wiener Secession's second exhibition, November/December 1898, Cat. No. 33 ("Kinderporträt"), and the catalogue of the Wiener Secession's collective Klimt exhibition, November/December 1903, Cat. No. 48 ("Bildnis eines Kindes—Privatbesitz").
2   Ernst Klimt (1864–1892), and Helene Flöge (1871–1936). See WStLA, biographical collection; Nebehay 1992, p. 23f; Czeike, Vol. 3, 1994, p. 533.
3   Nebehay 1969, p. 18, esp. note 23.
4   Report by Herta Wanke who as an apprentice joined the salon in 1932. See Fischer 1987, p. 16, passim.

Portrait of Sonja Knips

GUSTAV KLIMT

1898

Oil on canvas, 145 x 145 cm
Marked on the lower right, with
gold colour: "Gustav–/Klimt."
Vienna, Österreichische Galerie
Belvedere, Inv. No. 4403
(Novotny-Dobai No. 91)

Sonja Knips, née Baroness Potier
des Echelles, c. 1895

The portrait of Sonja Knips is regarded as the first among Klimt's portraits to be painted in a new manner, a fact that has already been pointed out by Hevesi.[1] Also new, however, is the natural size and the square format, henceforth preferred by Klimt for its poise. The portrait found early international recognition, for example, when shown at the world exhibition in Paris 1900.[2] The Viennese public—it first saw the picture in 1898—also shared this appreciation.[3] There was talk about female portraits "that are raised from the realm of the individual into the eternally typical".[4] Berta Zuckerkandl mentioned the "sublimated essence of the modern type of woman".[5]

The preliminary studies that have survived document Klimt's vacillation between horizontal and vertical formats until he found an adequate means of expression by blending both into a square, which matches the woman's sitting position as well as her upright posture. The portraitist frequently returned to this characteristic format that became the trademark of the Wiener Jugendstil and owed its success to no less an extent to Josef Hoffmann.[6] In his landscape paintings, Klimt uses it almost exclusively. In the portrait of Sonja Knips, he divided the square into halves with the corresponding contrast between light and dark, foreground and background, full and empty.

Frau Knips is sitting on the foremost edge of an easy chair that is shifted from the centre of the composition and appears only as a vague impression. The scenery is reminiscent of a garden whose details vanish into the twilight. Some observers claim to detect elements of garden architecture and even human shapes.[7] It is crucial for his further development that Klimt will place all subsequent portraits of women indoors.

Frau Knips is looking straight out of the picture. With her left hand, she clasps the armrest as if she were about to rise to her feet. Through her bent arms, body energy is flowing to her girlish face. This, however, is completely calm—without shunning the observer's gaze and proximity. Much of the magic of the picture is concentrated in this direct visual contact. Like many protagonists immortalised by Arthur Schnitzler in his literature, Sonja Knips seems to personify the essence of bourgeois order and, at the same time, to be harassed by constraints and subliminal eroticism. The picture's spell can hardly be put into words, but it may reasonably claim to be virtually the end point of the Austrian art of painting in the nineteenth century as it combines the best elements of its era. Though still reminiscent of symbolism, it is literally *the* work of the fin-de-siècle. At the same time, however, it points into the future, being the starting point for large-format female portraits after 1900.

Klimt masks the quiet artificial arrangement as a casual snapshot. In a highly differentiated painting technique, some areas of the picture are conceived in a cursory way while others are focussed upon with utter precision. The painter oscillates with ease between sketchy outlines and tangible precision. The tulle dress exudes painterly richness, with a flood of mostly parallel brushstrokes creating electric tension and ample movement.

The bisection of the picture area and the composition's careful balance still reveal James McNeill Whistler's influence. In analogy with Whistler and his picture title,

the portrait of Sonja Knips has also been named "Symphony in pink". According to the subject, Klimt himself had chosen the dress. The sketchbook, which she is holding in her right hand, also goes back to Klimt who gave it to her because he thought the composition lacked a colour accent.[8] It is characteristic of Klimt and his time that in solving a colour-scheme problem he still felt obliged to preserve the connection between colour and object. The next generation of expressionists would have opted for red without recourse to a sketchbook. The picture—it is no coincidence that it was created at the same time as Secession—nevertheless became a masterpiece of Austrian art approaching the "Wiener Moderne", not least for its frame design. The thin ornamental frame created by Gustav Klimt's younger brother Georg conforms to the ideal of the Gesamtkunstwerk.

The Knips apartment in the Gumpendorferstraße, Vienna, 1903: Sitting corner in the salon with Klimt composition *Fruit trees*

As daughter of a baron, Sonja, correctly Sophie Amalia Maria, Knips, née Freifrau Potier des Echelles, was one of the few noblewomen portrayed by Klimt. She was born on 2 December 1873 in the Galician town of Lvov, where her father, lieutenant general Maximilian Freiherr Potier des Echelles, was serving.[9] In 1986, she married the industrial magnate Anton Knips.[10] Two years later, Klimt painted the portrait. As Sonja Knips's niece recalls, "I know she had an unhappy marriage and a tragic life. Both her sons died, one having survived World War I only to die shortly after of the Spanish flu. My father died from liver disease before he was fifty. She lost a favourite brother early who was thrown from a horse that she had given him. She felt a great deal of guilt and as a result she kept herself aloof from personal relationships."[11]

The Knips apartment after redesigning in 1915/16: Sitting room with Klimt landscape

Sonja Knips was the sort of ideal upper-middle-class patron of art who demonstrated her commitment to modern art, and especially to Gustav Klimt and Josef Hoffmann, through repeated orders. She also was one of the best customers of the Wiener Werkstätte and participated in its refounding in 1914 by taking shares.[12]

Josef Hoffmann engaged in artistically arranging her everyday environment for the first time when he redesigned her apartment at 15 Gumpendorferstraße in 1903.[13] A contemporary photograph shows her combined living and working room with a sitting corner whose grey fabric covering and white framework took into account the Klimt landscape (*Fruit trees*) hanging there.[14] At the same time as the city apartment, he also designed the Knips family's country residence including a boathouse in the Carinthian village of Seeboden near Lake Millstatt.[15]

The city apartment acquired several neighbouring rooms and finally covered the entire first storey in its building; it was repeatedly transformed by Hoffmann.[16] Hoffmann also designed the family tomb at the cemetery of Wien-Hietzing ordered by Sonja after the death of her eldest son in 1919.[17] "At Christmas she would walk several kilometres, fasting, to and from a favourite church and she did this till she was eighty-five when she decided it was too much for her."

But the main product of the acquaintance of Josef Hoffmann and Sonja Knips was the Knips family's home at 22 Nußwaldgasse, Wien XIX.,

1 Review Hevesi of 21 November 1903, as quoted in Hevesi 1906, p. 451.
2 See Berta Zuckerkandl, "Die Klimt-Ausstellung", in *Wiener Allgemeine Zeitung*, 15 November 1903. The Paris *Figaro* published a colour reproduction in the *Figaro Illustré—Les Sections Etrangères à l'Exposition de 1900*. In the same edition, we also find a favourable review by Alexandre Arsen. A first reproduction of the portrait already appeared in 1899 in *The Studio*, Vol. 16, London, 1899, p. 37.
3 See the catalogue of the Wiener Secession's second exhibition, November/December 1898, Cat. No. 75 ("Damenportrait").
4 H. Ubell, "Die Klimtausstellung der Wiener Secession", in *Die Gegenwart*, Vol. 64, No. 52, p. 409.
5 B.(erta) Z.(uckerkandl), "Gustav Klimt", in *Wiener Allgemeine Zeitung* of 14 November 1903.
6 See Strobl, Vol. 1, Nos. 409–426.
7 E. g. Strobl, Vol. 1, p. 131 and Harald Jurcovic, "Gustav Klimt—Sonja Knips", in Edwin Becker and Sabine Grabner (eds.), *Ausstellung Wien 1900—Der Blick nach innen*, Amsterdam, 1997, p. 56.
8 Note from Sonja Knips to Johannes Dobai, see Novotny-Dobai, p. 306.
9 Nebehay 1992, p. 189, and Nebehay 1987b, p. 22.
10 See WStLA, registration office, communication of 16 August 1999, and WStLA, biographical collection. Anton Knips was born on 27 September 1865. His fortune was based on the Bohemian ironworks C.T. Petzold & Co. at Neudeck, whose owner he was.

which was constructed in 1924/25 based on preliminary drafts of 1919. Hoffmann thus created the last of a series of urban garden residences in Vienna. The Klimt portrait was given a central place in the living room where it could be seen through a glazed partition as soon as one entered the vestibule.[18] Once more, Sonja Knips demonstrated to what extent she personified the type of patron that was "demanded" by Josef Hoffmann in his uncompromising pursuit of a synthesis of the arts. She gave him a free hand and later insisted that not even the smallest detail in his arrangement of furnishings and equipment should be changed.[19] While a great deal changed inside the house after Frau Knips's death, this building in the middle of a spacious garden-plot still conveys the impression that luxury and discretion are a natural part of Sonja Knips's life, and also matches the atmosphere of the portrait Klimt created of her.

The Knips villa, 1926: The lady's salon with Klimt allegory *Adam and Eve*

We are also reminded of one of the most important Klimt collectors. Frau Knips owned the portrait painted by Klimt in 1898 and the above-mentioned *Fruit trees* from 1901. She purchased the unfinished allegorical composition *Adam and Eve* from the Klimt estate exhibition, and it was placed in the lady's salon in the Nußwaldstraße.[20]

Sonja Knips seems to have stayed in close contact with Josef Hoffmann to the very end. It was through him that her portrait as well as the *Adam and Eve* composition were bought by the Österreichische Galerie Belvedere in 1950.[21] Moreover, the museum recently even succeeded in buying a sketchbook formerly owned by Sonja Knips, which is possibly identical to the one that she was holding in her hand in the portrait.[22]

Sonja Knips died in her country residence at Seeboden on 25 June 1959.[23] It should be mentioned that, in her late registration documents, she described herself as an "artist", but no details are known about this.[24]

The Knips villa, 1926: The living room with the view into the dining room

11 Communication from Barbara Creaghan, née Knips, of 12 March 2000, whose mother had moved to Canada after the separation from her husband. Many thanks to John B. Collins, National Gallery of Ottawa, for mediating the contact.
12 Schweiger 1982, p. 251, fn. 382. See also Gmeiner/Pirhofer, 1985, p. 233.
13 Sekler 1982, entry 79.
14 Novotny-Dobai, No. 119.
15 Sekler 1982, entry 78.
16 Sekler 1982, entries 129 and 193.
17 Sekler 1982, entry 219; Cemetery of Wien-Hietzing, group 32, grave B.
18 Sekler 1982, entry 265. See also Gmeiner/Pirhofer 1985, p. 233.
19 Sekler 1982, pp. 174 and 232.
20 Novotny-Dobai, No. 220.
21 See acquisition document entry 41/1950, Österreichische Galerie Belvedere, archives.
22 See Christian M. Nebehay who was the first to publish the sketchbook: *Gustav Klimt—Das Skizzenbuch aus dem Besitz der Sonja Knips*, Vienna 1987. For the acquisition see *Neuerwerbungen—Österreichische Galerie Belvedere–1992–1999*, exhib. cat. of the 224th changing exhibition at the Österreichische Galerie Belvedere, Vienna, 1999, pp. 86–87.
23 She was buried according to the Catholic rite at the cemetery of Hietzing, group 32, mausoleum B. Her husband who had been laid to rest at the same place had died on 18 May 1946. A copy of the obituary in the *Adler*, Vienna.
24 WStLA, biographical collection.

Portrait of Serena Lederer

GUSTAV KLIMT

1899

Oil on canvas, 188 x 83 cm
Marked on the lower right:
"Gustav–/Klimt"
New York, The Metropolitan
Museum of Art. Purchase Catha-
rine Lorillard Wolfe Collection,
Bequest of Catharine Lorillard
Wolfe, by exchange, and Wolfe
Fund; and Gift of Henry Walters,
Bequest of Collis P. Huntington,
Munsey and Rogers Funds, by
exchange, 1980
(Novotny-Dobai No. 103)

The contemporary press liked this picture. What most attracted attention was the contrast between the white garment of the figure and the head with the heavy eyebrows and the dark hair. Hevesi, for instance, was reminded of "an upright flower, long-stalked, without leaves, like a tulip or something".[1] The vertical picture format accentuates the subject's slim stature. Serena Lederer's elegance is further underlined by the garment's seemingly infinite flow, and the fineness of the brushstrokes that compose it. Its momentum seems to sweep over the picture's edge.

Allegedly the portrait was painted in 1899.[2] It was first exhibited in spring 1901.[3] Right from the outset, Klimt must have decided to portray Serena Lederer standing upright since no other studies are known.[4] It was also his decision to choose a loosely falling garment for his portraits for the first time, leaving the waist almost unmarked and thus reminiscent of the Empire style. When, in the same year, Klimt was looking for similarly valuable robes for the women who were to be portrayed in his composition *Schubert at the piano* Serena Lederer's wardrobe was again at his disposal.[5]

Serena (alias Sérena, Szerena or Sidonie) Lederer, née Pulitzer, of Hungarian-Jewish extraction, was born to wealthy parents in Budapest on 20 May 1867.[6] In her youth she was a radiant beauty, reportedly the best-dressed lady of the Viennese society.[7] At any rate, she was always a "grande dame", and certainly didn't hesitate to cultivate the appropriate airs and graces.

On 5 June 1892, she married, before the rabbinate of the Israelite community in Pest, the industrial magnate August Lederer who was born on 3 May 1857 at Leipa in Bohemia.[8] He started his financial career by taking over the state-owned, loss-making spirit factory in Györ, a town halfway between Vienna and Budapest, and successfully refurbishing it.[9] The plant included a lordly mansion dating back to the baroque period, where the Lederers often spent time. Their main domicile, however, was an apartment at 8 Bartensteingasse. It was near Vienna town hall, and only a few minutes away from Klimt's studio in Josefstädter Straße.[10]

It was in Bartensteingasse that the Lederers put their art treasures together for the first time. Unfortunately, there

1   Review Hevesi of 16 March 1901, as quoted in Hevesi 1906, p. 318.
2   According to the recollections of Erich Lederer, as quoted in Strobl, Vol. 1, p. 143.
3   See the catalogue of the Wiener Secession's tenth exhibition, March-May 1901, Cat. No. 66. A photograph of the exhibition hall shows the picture on a wall reserved exclusively for portraits.
4   Strobl, Vol. 1, p. 143.
5   Communication from Erich Lederer, as quoted in Nebehay 1969, pp. 176 and 178, note 6. For the picture, see Novotny-Dobai Nos. 100/101.
6   WStLA, registration archives, communication of 22 October 1999. Among her relatives, the editor, journalist, and prize donor Joseph Pulitzer has won great fame in the United States.
7   At least, such is confirmed by Josef Hoffmann, see Nebehay 1969, p. 176.
8   WStLA, registration archives, communication of 22 November 1999. The wedding date is mentioned in the "certificate of extraction" of Elisabeth Bachofen-Echt, issued on 18 March 1940, Vienna, private property.
9   Nebehay 1992, p. 194, and Nebehay 1987, p. 11.
10 Bartensteingasse is also the office address, see S. Heller (ed.), *Compass — Finanzielles Jahrbuch für Österreich-Ungarn*, year 32, Vienna, 1899, p. 871.

are no photographs—neither of the Györ mansion nor of the Vienna apartment—allegedly because the lady of the house refused to admit photographers.[11] In the Lederer apartment, a whole room was dedicated to Gustav Klimt's art. The portrait of Serena Lederer was only the beginning. In 1905, Josef Hoffmann was asked to combine two rooms in order to make enough room for the newly purchased faculty picture *Philosophy* measuring three by four metres.[12] Its counterpart, *Jurisprudence*, however, which August Lederer purchased in 1918, was left rolled up and thus kept in store.

With Klimt they were on friendly terms. Reportedly, he dined with them every Thursday.[13] According to Egon Schiele, Serena Lederer even took drawing lessons with Klimt for many years "and thus has acquired considerable though, of course, unoriginal and uncreative skills".[14]

Portrait of the young Serena Lederer with her uncle Sigmund and his wife Tinka Politzer, 1888. Detail from Gustav Klimt's *Auditorium in the old Burgtheater*, Vienna, Historisches Museum

Egon Schiele owed his position with the Lederers to Gustav Klimt who had unselfishly introduced him to his patrons at a time when Schiele needed financial support more than ever before.[15] A close relationship developed with Erich Lederer in particular, the Lederers' second son, who was nine years younger than Schiele. This included not only drawing lessons with Schiele, but also a common interest in young women. The anxious mother's concerns didn't escape Schiele, so he said to Erich: "Let your mama know that I'm quite harmless to you."[16]

Over a period of years, with enormous financial commitment and driven by undiminishing enthusiasm the Lederers created what would become the most important Klimt collection that ever has existed in private hands. There is a detailed description in Christian M. Nebehay's *Gustav Klimt, Egon Schiele und die Familie Lederer*.[17] The collection's spectacular pieces include the two faculty pictures *Jurisprudence* and *Philosophy*, *Schubert at the piano*, and *The music II*, as well as numerous landscapes, several female portraits, and the Beethoven frieze that August Lederer purchased from Carl Reininghaus in 1915, leaving Schiele with an agent's commission.[18]

It is most likely that the driving force behind the purchases was Serena Lederer. Long before her marriage to August Lederer she had been introduced to Gustav Klimt by her uncle, Dr. Politzer. This is why Klimt inserted the portrait of the then still unmarried Serena among the numerous miniature portraits of his composition "Auditorium in the old Burgtheater".[19] She is probably also responsible for the fact that three generations of her family were painted by Klimt: Her own portrait was painted in 1899, followed by the portrait of her daughter Elisabeth (ill. p. 132), and finally the remarkably simple representation of her mother Charlotte Pulitzer, née Politzer.[20] What a gallery of ancestors! Moreover, each of these three pictures represents a completely different stage in the painter's stylistic development.

But Serena also carefully built up the most important collection of Klimt's graphic works. Here again, the result was unequalled. The collection consisted of several hundreds of drawings, including such important works as the twenty-five, purchased directly from Klimt, that were repro-

Serena and August Lederer in front of their country residence Schloß Weidlingau at Hadersdorf, c. 1930, Vienna, private collection

11 At least, such is reported by Nehehay in Christian M. Nebehay, *Gustav Klimt, Egon Schiele und die Familie Lederer*, prefaced by Ottokar von Jacobs, Bern 1987, p. 11.
12 Sekler 1982, p. 94 or entry 94; Nebehay 1987, pp. 11–13.
13 Interview Erich Lederer, see Nebehay 1986a, p. 8.
14 Schiele in two letters to Arthur Roessler of 22/24 December 1912, see Nebehay, 1979, Nos. 428/429.
15 Heinrich Benesch, *Mein Weg mit Egon Schiele*, New York 1965, pp. 19–20.
16 Egon Schiele in a letter to Erich Lederer of 12 January 1915, as quoted in Nebehay 1987, p. 94.
17 Nebehay 1987.
18 See Nebehay 1979, esp. No. 1377. During the 1930s, Lederer suggested to show the Beethoven frieze provisionally for a period of two or three years in the Theseus temple, Volksgarten, Vienna. See Österreichische Galerie Belvedere, archives, Akt entry 78/1933.
19 The picture (Novotny-Dobai No. 44) is in the Historisches Museum, Vienna, where there exists also a heliogravure after the picture including an explanatory mirror.
20 For the portrait of Charlotte Pulitzer, see Novotny-Dobai No. 190, there dated 1915. For the dating 1917, see Strobl, Vol. 3, p. 129. For the biographical dates, born in October 1833, death on 14 November 1920, see IKG Wien, register of deaths, entry 2512/1920.

Egon Schiele, Portrait of Serena Lederer. One of three known drawings from the year 1917. Private collection

duced by the Viennese editor Gilhofer & Ranschburg in a separate folder in 1919. The collection was continually expanded. Some of the snobbishness that seems to have accompanied Frau Lederer's every appearance in public is reported by the art dealer Gustav Nebehay. When immediately after Klimt's death he offered for sale 200 drawings from the estate, Frau Lederer—as the bewildered witness reports—rushed into the shop, inspected the exhibition, and immediately asked for the total price, adding that she wanted to buy everything. Uttering the word "bought!" she left the stunned dealer.[21] Later, the collection was complemented by about 150 drawings and studies that Carl Reininghaus handed over when the Beethoven frieze was bought.[22]

After Austria's "Anschluss" in 1938, Serena Lederer fell victim to Nazi despotism. After her husband's death on 30 April 1936, devout obituaries for the late industrialist appeared in the *Neue Freie Presse*.[23] When Serena Lederer died in Budapest on 27 March 1943,[24] she had long been turned out of her home and robbed. Today, it's almost impossible to reconstruct her personal ordeal. Her withdrawal from the Israelitische Kultusgemeinde in 1939 can only be understood as just another attempt to escape from the Nazi terror, though, from today's perspective, such a step appears as absurd as it was of little help in those days.[25] Neither do we know the details of the collection's fate—compulsory expropriation in 1938, evacuation of most of its parts to Immendorf castle (Lower Austria) where, under circumstances that can't be unambiguously determined any more, it was burnt during the last days of the war as the German Wehrmacht retreated. Nevertheless, the Klimt portraits of mother and daughter reappeared in the Dorotheum in Vienna three years after the war where they were withdrawn from the auction and restored to their legitimate owners.[26] In view of its importance for cultural and collecting history, a publication about the Lederer family and the fate of their collection, already considered by the heirs, would be highly desirable.

Serena Lederer, Photograph c. 1938/39, Vienna, private collection

Gustav Klimt, Portrait of Charlotte Pulitzer, 1917 Oil on canvas. Whereabouts unknown

21   This anecdote is reported in Nebehay 1987, pp. 24–26. For the exhibition and the drawings, see Strobl, Vol. 4, pp. 221 and 227.
22   Nebehay 1969, p. 291.
23   *Neue Freie Presse,* 1 May 1936. Obituaries in the name of the family, the Jungbunzlauer Spiritus & chemische Fabrik AG, and the Raaber Spiritusfabrik & Raffinerie AG. The interment on the cemetery of Hietzing took place on 2 May 1936.
24   Being published here for the first time, this date is mentioned in an "acquisition document" of the Österreichische Galerie Belvedere, archives, dossier entry 67/1944 ("Erwerbung von 2 Gemälden von G. Klimt: 'Philosophie' und 'Jurisprudenz'"). According to another source, Frau Lederer died on 30 March 1943. See memorandum of Dr. Höberle, official liquidator of the inheritance of August Lederer, of 17 July 1946. Courtesy of Otto von Jacobs, Purbach.
25   Withdrawal on 4 June 1939, see IKG Wien, register of withdrawals, No. 675/1939.
26   See Dorotheum, Vienna, art auction on 18/19/20 March 1948, auction catalogue, Nos. 75/76. Both pictures reproduced on plate 28.

Portrait of
Rose von Rosthorn-Friedmann

GUSTAV KLIMT

1900/01

Oil on canvas, 140 x 80 cm
Private collection
(Not in Novotny-Dobai)

Frau von Rosthorn is standing upright in a dark evening robe in front of a blue background.[1] The observer sees sparkling sequins, flashing jewellery, a tight waist, a shining décolletage. The gesture of leaning with the right hand on an easy chair looks affected. Nothing can be sensed of the "other" side of the subject who, as a passionate alpinist, stood out among the "mountaineering ladies" of her time.[2] For Felix Salten, such portraits "breathe true life while, at the same time, lacking reality. They are faithful to reality, yet are almost unreal".[3] For his colleagues from the *Neue Freie Presse,* it is the picture of a woman "who has passed her prime, yet is vibrant with untamed and glowing life".[4]

Even contemporaries realised the link with Klimt's symbolic nixie picture (ill. p. 237). Hevesi talked about a "modern sphinx in the shape of the head and the accent of the radiant face, in which the teeth are gleaming".[5] Yet the nixie- and vamp-like element also suggests a special relationship between the painter and his model. Once again, our source is the best-informed witness Alma Mahler. She knew Rose von Rosthorn, but did not like her. At the time when Klimt painted the Rosthorn portrait, Alma circulated the latest gossip. In an entry dated 19 January 1900, she mentions a new liaison of Klimt's: "By the way, since very recently he has been having an affair with that old hag Rose Friedmann. He takes what he can find."[6] Whether this assertion was true, however, remains to be proved.

Born in Vienna on 12 February 1864, Rose von Rosthorn was first married to Dr. Bruno Wagner von Freynsheim, a legal advisor to the Österreichische Staatsbahnen.[7] In 1886, she married her second husband, the industrialist Ludwig (Louis) Friedmann, who was born in Paris on 29 June 1861.[8] While nursing wounded soldiers Frau Rosthorn-Friedmann contracted a fatal typhoid infection. Her early death on 13 January 1919[9] induced Hugo von Hofmannsthal to write a long letter to her husband, emphasising not only the impressive beauty, but also the intelligence and warmth of this exceptional woman.[10] The deceased's stable living conditions were also subject to probate procedure. As the heirs of her fortune, which included, besides her jewellery, an estate in the district of Lilienfeld, Lower Austria, she nominated her husband and her two "well-married" children, her daughter by first marriage Dora von Wagner-Freynsheim (b. 1885), Köhler by marriage, wife of a consul in Bern, and Marie Alexandrine Friedmann (b. 1887), by marriage Satzger von Balvanyos, wife of an estate owner in Hungary.

1   After the Second World War the portrait was long forgotten. It was first shown at the tenth Secession exhibition in 1901, and again at the collective Klimt exhibition in 1903 as "Lady in black". See Sotheby's London, exhib. cat., 31 March 1987, No. 24A.
2   Pichl, Eduard, *Wiens Bergsteigertum*, Vienna: Österreichische Staatsdruckerei, 1927, p. 16 and esp. p. 134. Many thanks to Peter Sándor, Vienna, for the bibliographical hint.
3   Felix Salten, "Secession (Der Fall Klimt)", in *Wiener Allgemeine Zeitung*, 14 April 1901.
4   Franz Servaes, "Secession", in *Neue Freie Presse*, morning edition, 19 March 1901.
5   Review Hevesi of 16 March 1901, as quoted in Hevesi 1906, p. 318, see also p. 451.
6   Mahler 1997, p. 431. (See also pp. 413, 416, and 417, 458).
7   WStLA, register of deaths, AI 60/19. For Herr von Freynsheim, see *Genealogisches Handbuch des Adels*, Vol. 7, Glücksburg a. d. Ostsee 1954, pp. 210 and 273.
8   WStLA, registration archives, communication of 29 May 2000.
9   WStLA, register of deaths, AI 60/19. Place of death Baden, Protestant denomination. The widow died on 1 April 1939.
10   The funeral service took place in the Protestant church in Dorotheergasse, the interment in the family grave at the Zentralfriedhof. An obituary in the *Adler*, Vienna. There also an obituary of her father Adolf Edler von Rosthorn in the name of the children Oscar Elder von Rosthorn, Hermine Felsen, née von Rosthorn, and Rose Friedmann, née von Rosthorn.

Portrait of Marie Henneberg

GUSTAV KLIMT

1901/02

Oil on canvas, 140 x 140 cm
Marked on the lower right:
"Gustav Klimt"
Halle an der Saale, Staatliche
Galerie Moritzburg, Landes-
kunstmuseum Sachsen-Anhalt,
Inv. No. I/1724
(Novotny-Dobai No. 123)

The portrait, which is "dissolving into pointillism", was still unfinished when it was first exhibited in 1902.[1] Nevertheless, Hevesi was fascinated by the lyrical atmosphere of the picture. For Hevesi, the unfinished condition even intensified this "ephemeral atmosphere that is over as soon as it has been sensed".[2] The unfinished part was the easy chair, in which Frau Henneberg is sitting. "The figure is sitting in a invisible easy chair (since it is not yet painted), which makes her even more artificial, she seems to hover weightlessly."[3] A German critic even used the term "astral chair".[4] In its finished condition, however, the outlines of the furniture are emphasising a depth of perspective that Klimt normally tried to suppress in the indefinite quality of the surroundings.

The delicate colouring with short brushstrokes and lilac dots makes the picture one of the most remarkable examples of the "Fleckerlmanier" that became fashionable in Vienna around 1900. This was not modelled on the founder neo-impresisonists Signac and Seurat, however, but on the Belgian Theo van Rysselberghe. The subject is in a sitting position. While the one hand is propped up the other one grasps the shawl that is cascading down her. The observer is as much enthralled by its motion as he is fascinated by the iridescence of the "trout dots". The dynamics of colour, however, culminates in Frau Henneberg's bouquet of violets that "combines with the rosy flesh tones to form a song-like pianissimo" (Hevesi).

Marie, correctly Maria Anna, Henneberg was born to her Catholic parents Julius Hinterhuber, pharmacist, and his wife Rosalia, née Baumgartner, in the parish of St. Andrä in Salzburg on 23 September 1851.[5] When her father died in 1880, she was a teacher in Amstetten, Lower Austria, according to official documents, "but currently at home" where she presumably looked after the father since the other sisters except Anna, a minor, had already left home.[6] When on 21 August 1888 the thirty-six-year-old went to the altar of the Protestant Augustan church in Vienna, the marriage was unusual not only for the advanced age of the bride. It was also noteworthy that her life companion Hugo Henneberg was twelve years younger than her.[7]

Dr. Hugo, correctly Hugo Franz Simon, Henneberg who was born in Vienna on 27 July 1863—in the marriage register Protestant, in later registration documents of no specific denomination[8]—had studied physics, chemistry, astronomy and mathematics at the universities of Vienna and Jena and had attained his doctorate in physics shortly before the marriage in 1888. Listed in the marriage register as "person of private means", he had come into the fortune of his father, factory director Bruno Henneberg, who had died in 1887. His mother, Ottilie Magdalena Henneberg, née

1   See the catalogue of the Wiener Secession's thirteenth exhibition, February/March 1902, Cat. No. 33 ("Portrait, unvollendet").
2   Review Hevesi of 1 February 1902, as quoted in Hevesi 1906, p. 363.
3   Review Hevesi of 13 February 1902, as quoted in Hevesi 1906, pp. 370f.
4   Franz Dülberg in Zeitschrift für bildende Kunst, year 15, Leipzig 1904, p. 255.
5   Communication WStLA, registration office, of 22 October 1999. However, the register of marriages of the Protestant church, Wien I., Dorotheergasse, for the year 1888, entry No. 150, misstates the date of birth as 23 September 1851. The date of 23 December is confirmed by Roswitha Preiß, Salzburger Landesarchiv, in her communication of 6 July 2000.
6   Register of marriages of the Protestant Helvetian church, Wien I., Dorotheergasse, for the year 1888, entry No. 150.
7   WStLA, registration office, communication of 22 October 1999; see also Czeike, Vol. 3, 1994, p. 142.
8   WStLA, inheritance dossier; register of marriages of the Protestant church, Wien I., Dorotheergasse, for the year 1888, entry No. 150.

Güntner, had also died in the same year.[9] Dr. Henneberg became known as an etcher and woodcutter, but mainly as a photographic artist, board member of the Vienna Camera-Club and, with Hans Watzek and Heinrich Kühn the third in the legendary Trifolium.

Hugo and Marie Henneberg's newly built home in Wien XIX., 8 Wollergasse, was part of the artists' colony on the Hohe Warte, together with the houses of the Carl Moll, Kolo Moser and Dr. Friedrich Spitzer families. Seen by the architect Josef Hoffmann as a linked group, the Henneberg house, like the other buildings, had a studio on the upper floor. The rooms were done in different colour moods, the furniture was created especially for this purpose. The Hennebergs were happy to keep open house for their numerous artist friends from all over Europe. The Swiss Ferdinand Hodler, for instance, moved in for weeks when he had a major exhibition at the Secession in 1902.[10] Every guest was greeted by the Klimt portrait of the lady of the house that hung in the central reception hall over a partly gilded marble fire-place that, flanked on both sides by open showcases, supported the picture like an altar.[11]

Garden view of the Henneberg residence, photograph 1903

The lively contact with the "impresario of the Wiener Moderne" and best friend of Klimt's, Carl Moll, and his family went far beyond neighbourly proximity. The Hennebergs are often mentioned by Alma Mahler in her diaries.[12] On 15 March 1898, she writes: "Frau Henneberg—from today aunt Marie". However attached she was to her in general, there is another entry: "I've *never* seen her laughing—*really* laughing."[13] Alma is also the first to mention a date of origin for the picture. On 22 May 1902, she noted a conversation with "aunt Mie": "She told that she had spoken to Klimt about me (he is now painting her)."[14]

Entrance hall in the Henneberg residence, view of the staircase, 1903

Later the couple moved two streets away, into Probusgasse. A difficult time began for Marie Henneberg when her husband died unexpectedly on 11 July 1918.[15] In Alma's diary we still read about endless invitations and parties with "aunt Mie", coffee-parties and champagne, soirées in the hotel Imperial, journeys etc. etc. But the carefreeness was obviously gone. In August 1888, Frau Henneberg announced her new domicile in Wien VII., 36/3/19 Kandlgasse, where she died on 23 June 1931.[16]

The fireplace in the hall, Henneberg residence, 1903

Financial bottle-necks and, probably, the inconvenience of the repeated moves also forced her to sell her Klimt portrait, which may have gone directly to the Leipzig music publisher Dr. Max Kuhn.[17] In his domicile at 10 Richterstraße, Leipzig-Gohlis, built by Bruno Paul in 1925, the picture found a stylistic environment that was in no way inferior to the residential colony on the Hohe Warte. The Klimt portrait had its place on the first floor in a room with a fireplace, richly equipped with furniture from Dresden-Hellerau and numerous objects from the Wiener Werkstätte, while to the left of it, Kokoschka's portrait of Baron von Dirsztey was hanging between the windows.[18] Other works in the house were by Erich Heckel, Franz Heckendorf, and there were drawings everywhere, especially by Lovis Corinth. After Dr. Kuhn's death in 1966, the family of his wife Luise, née Borm, lent the Klimt portrait to the Staatliche Galerie Moritzburg, which purchased it in 1979.[19]

9   Nebehay 1969, p. 336.
10   Sekler 1982, NO. 54.
11   Mahler 1997, p. 37 passim.
12   Mahler 1997, p. 703, entry of 21 August 1901.
13   Mahler 1997, p. 699.
14   WStLA, registration office, communication of 22 October 1999. From Dr. Hugo Henneberg's last will of 14 September 1918, see WStLA, it follows that Marie Henneberg owned the furniture, except for the living room, already when he was still alive.
15   WStLA, biographical collection. She was buried beside her husband at the cemetery of Penzing.
16   The following information I owe to a communication from Dr. Annegret Janda, Berlin, who as a young girl was a frequent guest at the Kuhns'.
17   Winkler-Erling No. 69. Now Sprengel Museum, Hannover.
18   Up to now, nothing had been known at Moritzburg about the picture's history before 1966. Many thanks to Wolfgang Büche, Staatliche Galerie Moritzburg, for details about the acquisition process.

Portrait of Gertrud Loew
(Gertha Felsöványi)

GUSTAV KLIMT

1902

Oil on canvas, 150 x 45.5 cm
Marked on the upper left:
"Gustav Klimt 1902"
Private collection
(Novotny-Dobai No. 125)

Johannes Dobai mistakenly included the portrait of the young woman in the complete catalogue as "Portrait of Gertha Felsöványi". When the picture was painted, however, the subject was in fact still unmarried and living with her father Dr. Anton Loew. He was the owner of the oldest and biggest sanatorium in Vienna.[1] The most famous patients included Gustav Mahler, who died there in 1911, and Gustav Klimt.[2] Gertrud, correctly Gertrud Franziska Sophie, Loew was born in Vienna on 16 November 1883.[3] It was probably the father who commissioned Klimt to paint the portrait of the nineteen-year-old. Dr. Loew was an enthusiastic supporter of the Secession and thus is repeatedly mentioned in Alma Mahler's diary.[4]

The portrait was first exhibited in the Wiener Secession's Klimt exhibition in 1903.[5] Hevesi describes the picture with its remarkably tall format: "... the most sweet-scented poetry the palette is able to create."[6] He didn't fail to notice the symphonic wallowing in white, but also Klimt's ability to give life to the counter-world of colours, as in the portrait of Frau von Rosthorn, the portrait of the "Lady in black" (ill. p. 93) shown at the same exhibition. A second review praises "the still half-closed bud of a girl's chaste soul!"[7] Given the fragmentation and dualisation of the feminine element, typical of that time, it is an interesting coincidence that Dr. Loew was also the owner of Klimt's *Judith* (ill. p. 221).[8] Here, the shy virgin, portrayed in white transparency and with a dematerialised body, and there, the "femme fatale" in an elaborated corporeality, both united under the roof of a single collector.

The above-mentioned collective Klimt exhibition took place in November/December 1903. Already on 10 February 1903, "Fräulein" Loew had married the company owner Dr. Johann Arthur Eisler von Terramare (1878–1938).[9] Since then, the picture also appears in literature as a portrait of Frau Eisler-Terramare. Later, Frau Loew married the industrialist Dr. Elemér Baruch von Felsöványi who was born in Marosvásárhely, Hungary, on 15 July 1882. This union was blessed with four children: Nikolaus (b. 1907), Anton (b. 1914), Maria (b. 1917), and Franz (b. 1921).[10]

Her father's estate made Frau Felsöványi a wealthy woman. After his death on 14 September 1907[11], she became principal shareholder and chairwoman of the Sanatorium Loew.[12] Although she had been Roman Catholic since her birth, the Nazis whose victim she became regarded her as Jewish. According to the last entry in the registration office, she resided in Reichenau, finally in Wien I., 6 Freyung. Underneath, there is only a note that she had "unregistered" to Berlin on 23 April 1939.[13] The sanatorium had been closed by order of the new rulers as early as 1938. Further details and the circumstances of her persecution are not known.

1   Concerning the Sanatorium Loew, see Czeike, Vol. 4, p. 41f.
2   Nebehay 1969, pp. 483 and 486f, suggests that after having a serious stroke in 1918, Klimt was first nursed in the Sanatorium Loew. He died in the Allgemeines Krankenhaus.
3   See WStLA, registration archives; in the documents, the year of birth is also given as 1884.
4   Mahler 1997, p. 14 passim. According to Strobl, Vol. 1, p. 321, no preliminary studies have yet appeared.
5   In the catalogue among the Klimt portraits no longer unambiguously identifiable.
6   Review of 14 November 1903, as quoted in Hevesi, 1906, p. 443f.
7   Franz Servaes, "Klimt-Ausstellung", in *Neue Freie Presse*, evening edition, 23 November 1903.
8   Nebehay 1969, p. 336, suggests that the painter Ferdinand Hodler purchased the picture from Dr. Loew. For Loew as loaner of the Klimt exhibition 1903, see Nebehay 1969, p. 329, note 10d.
9   Österreichisches Familienarchiv, Vol. 1, 1963, p. 26. Since then, the picture also appears in literature as a portrait of Frau Eisler-Terramare. A daughter, Gertrude, born on 13 March 1903, died at the age of two on 3 June 1905.
10   Zoltán von Barcsay-Amant, *Adeliges Jahrbuch 1936/43*, years 14–21, New (German-language) series, years 14–21, Lucerne 1969, p. 237.
11   See WStLA, post-mortem protocol and biographical collection.
12   Resident in Wien IX., Pelikangasse 5–7, see entries in Lehmann until 1938.
13   WStLA, registration archives, communication of 17 February 2000.

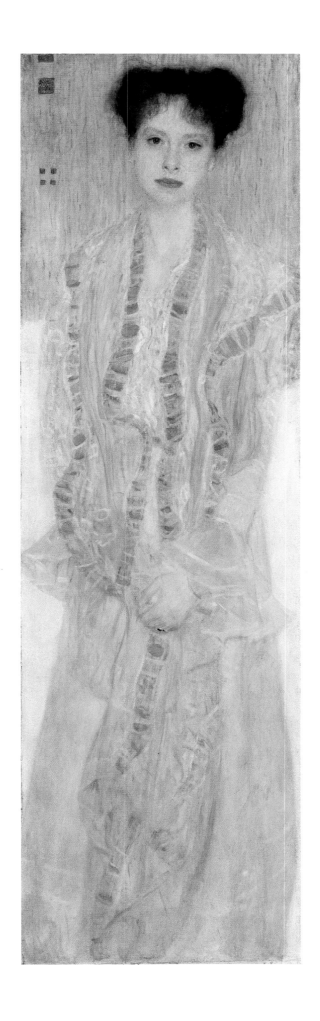

Portrait of Emilie Flöge

GUSTAV KLIMT

1902
Oil on canvas, 181 x 84 cm
Marked on the lower right:
"Gustav–/Klimt–/19 02",
thereunder: "GK" (ligated)
Vienna, Historisches Museum,
Inv. No. 45.677
(Novotny-Dobai No. 126)

Emilie Flöge, 1909, Photograph
by d'Ora Benda, Vienna,
Österreichische Nationalbibliothek, photographic archives

Since Emilie Flöge and her mother didn't like the portrait, in which she poses like a mannequin, Klimt sold it to the Niederösterreichisches Landesmuseum in 1908. On 6 July 1908, the painter informs Flöge: "Today you'll be 'sold off' or 'confiscated'—yesterday your mother chided me." Two days later, the picture had already been photographed and handed over.[1] After the constitution of Vienna and Lower Austria as separate Provinces, the picture came to the Wiener Städtische Sammlungen in accordance with the separation treaty.

From an exchange of letters not known until recently and being considered here for the first time, we learn that plans to sell the picture date back to 1904. Klimt offered the picture, which belonged to Emilie, to the government for sale: "In response to your esteemed letter (...) I have the privilege to inform you that I didn't intend to sell the portrait of Fräulein Flöge. Since the present case concerns a possible acquisition by the Staatsgalerie, I am ready, with the owner's approval, to sell the picture after its completion to the Moderne Galerie."[2] Because of Klimt's refusal to reduce the price of 10,000 crowns the sale did not take place until 1908. At that time, Klimt received the proud sum of 12,000 crowns. That was more than the total budget the Niederösterreichische Kunstsammlungen had at their disposal in most years.[3]

The painting was first exhibited in the Wiener Secession's Klimt exhibition in 1903: "Another, unfinished portrait has come to us as if from a blue-mottled world of majolica and mosaic."[4] On the occasion of the Dresden exhibition in 1912, Franz Servaes adds: "There is this pretty young Viennese in her peacock-blue silver-garnished dress (which was exhibited before, yet has now been finished) (...)."[5] These comments about the picture's unfinished condition in 1903 are also interesting because Klimt added signature and date as early as in 1902.

The male critics seemed to take for granted that the subject was pure womanliness, "pure womanliness in all its ornamental splendour". Berta Zuckerkandl, however, used more prosaic language to point out the characteristics of the composition: "The lovely face, subtly and exquisitely modelled, is even more emphasised by the unusual framing. Around the head, there is a green-blue wreath of blossoms with all the colour mysticism of Byzantine backgrounds."[6]

It is generally held that, despite early intentions to sell it, the connection between Klimt and Flöge finds a lasting expression in this picture, which is why it is considered an important document of this exceptional relationship. Flöge is standing upright, with her right hand on her hip. She is wearing a flowing reform dress, ornamented with intricate wave, ring,

1   As quoted in Fischer 1987, p. 173.
2   Österreichisches Staatsarchiv, Allgemeines Verwaltungsarchiv, Ministerium für Kultus und Unterricht, Fasz. 15, Kunstwesen, Ankauf, dossier entry 4197/1904. Klimt's letter is dated 17 January 1903, yet it ought to be 1904. It was Jeroen B. van Heerde to call my attention to this important piece of writing.
3   See Wolfgang Krug, "Die Kunstsammlung des Nieder-österreichischen Landesmuseums", in Waldmüller—Schiele—Rainer, exhib. cat., Kunsthalle Krems, Vienna—Munich, 2000, pp. 6ff., esp. pp. 7 and 10–11.
4   Review by Hevesi of 14 November 1903, as quoted in Hevesi 1906, p. 444.
5   Strobl, Vol. 1, p. 321, and Franz Servaes, "Klimt—Zu seinem 50. Geburtstag", in Merkur, Vienna, year 3, third quarter, p. 544.
6   B.(erta) Z.(uckerkandl), "Die Klimt-Ausstellung", in Wiener Allgemeine Zeitung, 15 November 1903.

and spiral patterns. The two square signatures, reminiscent of Japanese stamps, are part of the composition in terms of their colour and position. Angela Völker suggests that the fashion-designer subject's disapproval came from the nature of the garment, which didn't match the fashion trends of the time, while Klimt saw it as an ornamental masterpiece, but also as an abstract, incorporeal covering.[7] Hans Bisanz, who dismisses the frequent references to Gustav Klimt as a fashion designer as being in the realm of fantasy, observes that this dress was the only garment the alleged "fashion stylist" had ever "designed".[8]

There is a clear contrast between the bizarre, minutely executed fantasy dress and the open context.[9] Never before in his portraits has Klimt placed a woman in such an empty, unspecific environment.

Emilie, correctly Emilie Louise, Flöge was born in Vienna on 30 August 1874. Wolfgang Fischer has concerned himself more than anybody else with her character and personality. His book *Gustav Klimt und Emilie Flöge—Genie und Talent, Freundschaft und Besessenheit* (Vienna, 1987) is based on the Flöge estate that Fischer gained access to in 1983. Besides jewellery and objects from the Wiener Werkstätten, the estate consisted of a textile collection from the Flöge atelier, Emilie Flöge's own design studies, numerous fashion photographs, and nearly 400 letters from the Klimt/Flöge correspondence between 1897 and 1917.[10]

Despite the quantity of surviving correspondence, the letters are of little help in the search for hints as to a common ground between Klimt and Flöge and leave the nature of their relationship more or less in the dark. In fact the cards tend to be ordinary and banal. But we should remember that after Klimt's death Frau Flöge burnt all writings left in his studio. Emilie's niece reports that basketfuls of post were destroyed.[11]

Between attachment, respect, love and discretion, the nature of their closeness is hard to determine. Christian M. Nebehay suggests that Klimt found with Emilie Flöge the "peace, balance, and friendship he couldn't find elsewhere".[12] Wolfgang Fischer assumes a "remarkably unerotic aspect of the relationship" and describes it as an "uncle and niece" atmosphere.[13] This judgement is strongly denied by Susanna Partsch.[14] Referring in particular to a recently surfaced love letter, Hansjörg Krug has spoken about an "intimate relationship".[15] Anna Moll, however, who was married to the painter and sociable Viennese art impresario Carl Moll, already knew that Klimt had "a flirtation with his sister-in-law".[16] Many of these interpretations, attempting to sum up the relation of Klimt and Flöge in a simple phrase, are basing their speculations too much on the standard notion of marriage with its claim to permanence. It seems much more that their relationship had developed into a crisis-proof partnership whose "extramarital" privileges were primarily for the benefit of Gustav Klimt. Be that as it may, the relationship was as permanent as it was unshakeable. The fact that the sexual element had once been "put aside" is clearly indicated by Klimt's chummy lamentations during his trip to Paris in 1909. In his frequent postal greetings he first complains that the "belle parisienne"

Emilie Flöge in a model dress, 1910, Photograph by d'Ora Benda, Vienna, Österreichische Nationalbibliothek, photographic archives

7   Hans Bisanz, "Emilie, ihr Boudoir und ihre Sammlung", in *Flöge und Gustav Klimt—Doppelportrait in Ideallandschaft,* catalogue of the 112. special exhibition of the Historisches Museum, Vienna, 1988, p. 27.
8   Strobl, Vol. 1, p. 321, points out that no preliminary studies are known.
9   See Wolfgang G. Fischer, "Emilie Flöge", in *Parnass—Sonderheft Gustav Klimt,* year 20, No. 17/2000, Vienna, 2000, pp. 94–102. Unfortunately, the bequest has been divided in an auction in 1999. See Sotheby's, London, auction catalogue of 6 October 1999.
10 Laura Arici, "Schwanengesang in Gold 'Der Kuss'—Eine Deutung", in Toni Stooss, and Christoph Doswald, (eds.), *Gustav Klimt,* exhib. cat., Kunsthaus Zürich, Zurich, 1992, note 25, p. 50f.
11 Nebehay 1969, p. 267.
12 Wolfgang G. Fischer, "Klimt—Flöge", in *alte und moderne Kunst,* Nos. 186/187, p. 9.
13 Partsch, Susanna, "Gustav Klimt—'Als Person nicht interessant'", in *Gegenwelten—Gustav Klimt—Künstlerleben im Fin de Siècle,* exhib. cat., Bayerische Vereinsbank, p. 32. See also Arici 1992, cf. note 10, p. 50, note 25, and Christian Brandstätter, *Gustav Klimt und die Frauen,* Vienna: Verlag Brandstätter, 1994, pp. 32ff.
14 Hansjörg Krug, "Liebe Midi—Ein Liebesbrief Gustav Klimts", in *Parnass—Sonderheft Gustav Klimt,* Vienna, 2000, pp. 22–23.
15 Mahler 1997, p. 95.
16 As quoted in Fischer 1987, p. 177.
17 Fischer 1987; Susanna Partsch, *Gustav Klimt—Maler der Frauen,* Munich—New York 1994, pp. 22ff; Arici 1992, cf. note above, esp. pp. 50f., note 25.
18 WStLA, biographical collection.

had still not appeared, and when finally he catches sight of some of them, he writes on the following day that having seen "some pretty women", he had glimpsed the "first young women ('cocottes' of course), but at least no 'wrecks'" etc.[17]

In 1904, Emilie Flöge, as an independent fashion designer, founded the "Schwestern Flöge" fashion salon, with her sisters Pauline and Helene. At that time, the three sisters moved their already existing atelier from Neubaugasse into the "Casa piccola" at 1b Mariahilferstraße. The exquisitely equipped fashion salon, designed by Josef Hoffmann and Kolo Moser, was completely in tune with the spirit of the Wiener Werkstätte, and it was no coincidence that the Flöge sisters dressed Klimt's protrait subjects.[18]

For more than thirty years, the salon maintained its leading position at the centre of the Viennese fashion quarter. Yet, today, one tends to underestimate the entrepreneurial feat performed by Emilie Flöge. Though in the beginning the salon may have benefited from Klimt and his wealthy clientele, she constantly had to prove herself as an entrepreneur and businesswoman. Later, economically precarious times demanded an enormous effort. All too often, Emilie Flöge is still seen as Klimt's "better half", occupying herself with reform clothes and other "esoteric" aspects of fashion. The facts speak differently: for instance the up to eighty(!) seamstresses and three cutters that Frau Flöge and her sisters provided with work and income. Moreover, the house, which even in bad times included a chauffeur, a cook, and a chambermaid, also had to be looked after. Twice a year, Frau Flöge

travelled to Paris and London in order to inform herself about current developments and trends at the international fashion houses such as Dior. As late as 1934, Clarissa Rothschild had her wardrobe for the London coronation of Edward VII prepared at the Flöge salon.

With Austria's "Anschluss" to Nazi Germany, Emilie Flöge lost most of her customers and had to close the salon. She died in Vienna on 25 May 1952.[19]

Portrait of Hermine Gallia

GUSTAV KLIMT

1903/04

Oil on canvas, 170 x 96 cm
Marked on the upper right:
"Gustav–/Klimt.–/19 04"
London, The National Gallery,
NG 6434
(Novotny-Dobai No. 138)

An interior view of the Wiener Secession shows the picture as part of the collective Klimt exhibition in the late autumn of 1903.[1] The exhibition catalogue lists the picture as unfinished, but a comparison with its present state shows that Klimt made only slight changes after this date, particularly to the coiffure and the décolletage.[2] Only then does the painter date the picture to "1904".

The subject is wearing a white dress with a sweeping train that Klimt pulls to the front. Over it, she wears a *ball entrée* (ill. p. 45), reminiscent with its richly pleated ruches and cascades of a dress designed by Eduard Wimmer-Wisgrill and worn by Emilie Flöge in a photograph taken in 1909.

Hermine Gallia, née Hamburger, was born in Freudenthal, Sleszko (Hussova Ulice) on 14 June 1870.[3] On 16 May 1893, she was married to Moriz Gallia, who was twelve years older, under the wedding baldachin of the Israelitischer Stadttempel in Vienna.[4] Her husband who was born in Bisenz (Moravia) on 15 November 1858 was the manager of the Viennese branch of Baron Carl von Auer-Welsbach's light bulb factory and later an independent entrepreneur in this industry.[5] Herr Gallia was given the title of Geheimrat for his commitment to the development of the "Moderne Galerie" in Vienna. The family seems always to have been aware of this,[6] but a source-based confirmation has now been found in the Österreichisches Staatsarchiv. Obviously, prior to ordering the portrait from Klimt, Moriz Gallia had already been an active supporter of the Secession. In order to encourage its initiative of founding a state-owned modern collection, he purchased Giovanni Segantini's masterpiece *The wicked mothers*, donating it to the government for this purpose.[7]

Emilie Flöge in a reform dress similar to the one Hermine Gallia is wearing, photograph by Madame d'Ora, 1909

The Gallias first lived at 4 Schleifmühlgasse, Wien IV.,[8] but then had an old building at 4 Wohllebengasse in the same district demolished and reconstructed by Franz von Krauss and Josef Tölk. The five main rooms on the first floor of the building were furnished by Josef Hoffmann in 1913.[9] Again, the Klimt portrait was taken into account when the architect designed the room. Numerous contemporary photographs convey an impression of the rooms. The lady's salon was equipped with low furnishings whose red silk contrasted with the white fluted pillars. On the wall behind the sofa, the portrait of Hermine Gallia hung next to a portrait of the master of the house painted by Ferdinand Andri, which cannot be made out in the photograph reproduced here.[10] The floor was covered with a carpet whose geometrically austere ornament resembles the floor pattern in Klimt's picture and even returns, slightly modified, in the wallpaper.

Herr and Frau Gallia were enthusiastic collectors of art. Klimt painted the portrait of the lady of the house, but also the landscape *Beech*

1   Reproduction in *Die Kunst*, year 10 (*Dekorative Kunst*, year 7/1904), p. 355.
2   Catalogue of the Wiener Secession's collective Klimt exhibition, November/December 1903; one of the portraits of women exhibited as "unfinished".
3   For the most important source regarding Hermine and Moriz Gallia, see WStLA, inheritance dossier, Bezirksgericht Margarethen, register of deaths A 158/18 including Moriz Gallia's last will of 16 December 1912 and two later codicils.
4   See IKG Wien, marriage certificate No. 497/171893; and WStLA, post-mortem protocol.
5   Inheritance dossier; and IKG Wien, communication of 22 Sept 1999. Moriz Gallia owned at last the third part of the company Julius Pintsch, involved in the construction and operation of oil gas plants for the Austrian railways, and was a co-founder of the Grätzinlichtgesellschaft, owning half of the shares. See the inheritance dossier.
6   See the excellent exhib. cat. *Vienna 1913—Josef Hoffmann's Gallia Apartment*, National Gallery of Victoria, Melbourne, 1984, p. 63.
7   See Österreichisches Staatsarchiv, Allgemeines Verwaltungsarchiv, Ministerium für Cultus und Unterricht, Präsidium, entry 425/1901. The Segantini picture now Österreichische Galerie Belvedere, Inv.No. 485. Many thanks to Frau Heike Eipeldauer for the investigations.
8   Lehmann 1910.
9   Sekler 1982, pp. 148f; and No. 174.
10   The picture's whereabouts is unknown.

The Gallia apartment, design
Josef Hoffmann, photograph
1916:
Salon with the portrait of
Hermine Gallia
Living hall
Music room with Klimt's *Beech
forest II*

forest II,[11] dating from the same period, which got a place of honour in the music room with its black-and-white upholstered furniture. They owned numerous works by Carl Moll, reportedly ten paintings from the time before 1910. Other works were by the landscape painter Emil Jakob Schindler and the Secessionist Ferdinand Andri as well as Ernst Stöhr, not forgetting the objects from the Wiener Werkstätte that were to be found in abundance in the apartment.[12]

The Gallias were also closely associated with the Wiener Werkstätte financially. Hermine became a partner after it was restructured in 1914.[13] Moreover, Frau Gallia and her husband were involved in the founding of the Österreichischer Werkbund in the same year and remained members until 1928.[14]

When her husband died on 17 August 1918, the funeral was very quiet—"for even alive I was no friend of formalities". The death notice was to be sent out only afterwards.[15] Moriz Gallia was buried following the Roman Catholic rite in the cemetery of Hietzing.[16] They had withdrawn from the Kultusgemeinde as early as 1910.[17]

Hermine Gallia, to whom her husband had left everything, took over the business of the factory for the duration of the inheritance procedure led by her brother-in-law Dr. Adolf Gallia. Already joint owner of the common apartment in Wohllebengasse, she now received her husband's share. The furniture and fittings, including jewellery, silver, porcelain etc. as well as all painting had already been hers when her husband was still alive.[18] Consequently, her loans to the Klimt memorial exhibition on the occasion of the tenth anniversary of Klimt's death were listed as "property of Frau Regierungsrat Hermine".[19]

Hermine Gallia died on 6 February 1936.[20] She was interred next to her husband in Hietzing.[21] The obituary appeared in the name of her chil-

The Gallia family, photograph c. 1903. Back row: Hermine and Moriz Gallia, Henrietta Hamburger, Otto Hamburger, Guido Hamburger. Middle row: Ernst Gallia, Josephine Hamburger, Robert Hamburger, Nathan Hamburger, Margarete Gallia. Front row: the twins Lene and Käthe Gallia

11 Novotny-Dobai No. 137.
12 See *Vienna 1913—Josef Hoffmann's Gallia Apartment*, exhib. cat., cf. note 6.
13 Schweiger 1982, p. 96 and fn. 382.
14 Gmeiner/Pirhofer 1985, p. 227.
15 See inheritance dossier, last will of 16 December 1912; and codicil of 15 April 1917.
16 See also the documents in the WStLA, registration office, communication of 16 August 1999
17 IKG Wien, registrar's records: record of withdrawals from Judaism, entry 511/10 of 6 December 1910.
18 See inheritance dossier.
19 See catalogue of the Wiener Secession's ninety-ninth exhibition, Klimt memorial exhibition, Vienna, 1928, Cat. Nos. 18 and 20.
20 WStLA, post-mortem protocol. The cause of death has been specified as pulmonary embolism following a gallstone operation. At the local court in Margarethen, the inheritance dossier Hermine Gallia is listed under the number 2A 193/36, yet the dossier couldn't be found.
21 Cemetery of Wien-Hietzing, group 12, grave No. 102/3. See obituary in the "Adler", Vienna.
22 All buried in the Gallia family grave at the cemetery of Hietzing.
23 All entries from the year 1901; see Mahler 1997, pp. 641, 647, 648, 728, and 732.
24 Mahler 1997, index p. 837.
24 Catherine Dean, *Klimt*, London 1996, p. 80.

dren Ernst Gallia, Margarete Herschmann-Gallia, and Dr. Käthe Gallia. The fourth daughter, Käthe's twin Dr. Helene, known as Lene, Gallia, had died in 1926.[22]

Several entries in the young Alma Mahler-Werfel's diary suggest that she was acquainted with the Gallia family.[23] However, there is no positive indication that the repeatedly mentioned "Gallias" are identical with Moriz and Hermine Gallia. If the editors of Alma's diary identify this Frau Gallia with Hermine Gallia whom they believe to be "a daughter of the industrial magnate Karl Wittgenstein" it must be said that this person is not identical with the Hermine Gallia portrayed by Klimt.[24] This mistake, however, also crept into the volume of Klimt reproductions published by the renowned Phaidon Press in 1996.[25]

Portrait of Margarethe Stonborough–Wittgenstein

GUSTAV KLIMT

1905

Oil on canvas, 180 x 90 cm
Marked on the lower left: "Gus-
tav–/Klimt."
Munich, Bayerische
Staatsgemäldesammlungen,
Neue Pinakothek
(Novotny-Dobai No. 142)

Margarethe Stonborough-
Wittgenstein,
photograph c. 1920
Vienna, private collection

Margarethe, correctly Margarethe Anna Maria, Stonborough-Wittgenstein was born on 19 September 1882. She was the youngest daughter of steel magnate Karl Wittgenstein who, though himself Protestant and from a Jewish family, for the sake of his wife Leopoldine had his children baptised and educated as Catholics. Out of the eight children, six reached adulthood, and of these three committed suicide; incidents that have been attributed to the dominant father and his attitude to life, which was characterised by superhuman demands. Margarethe was especially attached to her brother, the later world-famous philosopher Ludwig Wittgenstein, over whose life she more than once held a protective hand. When her brother's mental health was causing him difficulties, she engaged him to help to build the Wittgenstein house, so that he could help the architect Paul Engelmann to create its external form and internal character.[1]

After her marriage to the son of a New York factory owner, Jerome Stonborough, on 7 January 1905, she anglicised her first name and called herself Margaret. In the same year, she and her husband moved to Berlin. Whether the Klimt portrait travelled along with them is questionable. At the International Art Exhibition in Rome in 1911, the "portrait of Fräulein Wittgenstein" was still referred to as her father's loan.[2] Her first son was born on 9 January 1906. Around 1923, a decision was made to live separately from her husband, while maintaining contact. The husband moved to Paris while Margarethe stayed in Vienna where she died on 27 September 1958.

The portrait of the twenty-three-year-old Margarethe was commissioned by her parents. Her father, one of the most important industrialists under the Austrian-Hungarian monarchy, disposed of a seemingly inexhaustible wealth.[3] He had already proven his commitment to the Wiener Secession by contributing massively to the construction of the Secession building.[4] The choice of painter was possibly influenced by Margarethe's elder sister Hermine. Herself a painter and an enthusiastic Klimt adherent, she shaped her father's taste in questions concerning the fine arts.[5]

At the beginning of 1904, Klimt wrote to Leopoldine Wittgenstein thanking her for her confidence while asking for more time since he couldn't start before the middle of March.[6] In a second letter, Klimt asked permission to borrow the unfinished portrait, since at the Deutscher Künstlerbund's second exhibition in spring 1905 he would have to "fill a hall" and needed the picture desperately.[7] When Klimt writes a third time he refers to financial agreements, but mostly he is concerned about the problem of the portrait's likeness. "The answer is difficult for me, not because the picture isn't finished, but rather because it is not yet good—thus I only can name the current price of my life-size portraits, which is c. 5,000 gul-

den. Even less can I accept your kind offer of paying for the portrait now—for the above-mentioned reason. I hope that I shall be able to finish the picture after the end of the exhibition in autumn, and I also hope that it will finally become a good portrait."[8]

So Klimt wants to improve the picture so that it will become a good "portrait". But the subject never got to like the picture either. This disapproval, which is difficult to understand from today's perspective, led to the rumour that she herself had repainted the mouth. At least this is reported in a recent publication about Margarethe, her brother, and the Wittgenstein family. The additions were allegedly removed when the picture was sold by the family to the Bayerische Staatsgemäldesammlungen in 1963.[9] The Munich gallery is not aware of any such occurrence, however, and according to the restoration unit there it never happened.[10]

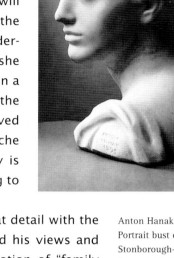

Anton Hanak
Portrait bust of Margarethe
Stonborough-Wittgenstein, 1925
Österreichische Galerie Belvedere

Thomas Zaunschirm has concerned himself in great detail with the issues of portrait likeness and societal reality.[11] He based his views and interpretations on the Wittgensteinian epistemological notion of "family similarity". Klimt himself made several changes to the picture. An old photograph shows it in its unfinished state.[12] He did not add the dark line in the lower third of the picture and the ornamental arc behind the subject's head reinforcing the surface integration into the background until afterwards. Special attention is focused on the watered-silk dress with its ample lace trimming, regarded by some as a wedding dress despite its strapless cut. Here, the well-mastered contrast between naturalism and a geometrical approach is most effective.

1   Paul Wijdeveld, *Ludwig Wittgenstein—Architekt*, s. l. 1994.
2   See catalogue of the Austrian division of the International Art Exhibition, Rome, 1911, Cat. No. 110, and fig. p. 149.
3   For Karl Wittgenstein, see Allan Janik, and Stephen Toulmin, *Wittgensteins Wien*, Vienna 1998, pp. 201–206.
4   See "Karl Wittgenstein als Kunstfreund", *Neue Freie Presse*, necrologue on Wittgenstein, Vienna, 21 January 1913.
5   Cecilia Sjögren, "Die Familie", in *Wittgenstein—Biographie, Philosophie, Praxis*, exhib. cat., Wiener Secession, Vienna 1989, pp. 99–117, esp. p. 114.
6   The undated letters were first published by Johannes Dobai: "Das Bildnis Margaret Stonborough-Wittgenstein von Gustav Klimt", in *alte und moderne Kunst*, Vienna, year 5, No. 8, 8 August 1960, pp. 8–11. Here with dates corrected as quoted in Strobl, Vol. 2, pp. 34f; and Zaunschirm, p. 16–19.
7   Cf. note above.
8   Cf. note above.
9   Wijdeveld 1994, see above.
10   Communication from the Landeskonservator B. Heimberg, Munich, 5 July 2000.
11   Thomas Zaunschirm, *Gustav Klimt—Margarethe Stonborough-Wittgenstein—Ein österreichisches Schicksal*, Frankfurt-on-Main 1987.
12   *Kunst und Künster*, Vol. 3, 1905, p. 398.

Portrait of Fritza Riedler

GUSTAV KLIMT

1906
Oil on canvas, 153 x 133 cm
Marked on the lower left:
"Gustav–/Klimt–/1906"
Vienna, Österreichische Galerie
Belvedere, Inv.No. 3379
(Novotny-Dobai No. 143)

There were only two painters, Klimt claimed: Velázquez and himself.[1] In the portrait of Fritza Riedler, some of his enthusiasm for the great Spaniard becomes apparent. He had already studied his infanta portraits in the Kunsthistorisches Museum twenty years earlier (ill. p. 153). The reference to Velázquez is especially obvious in the ornamental arc behind Fritza Riedler's head. Its form and decoration are reminiscent of the voluminous coiffures worn by the infantas. However, the ornamental field may also be read as a window. In compositional terms, the "nobility form" placed behind the head ties the figure into the pictorial plane. Klimt had already tried out this effect in the portrait of Margarethe Stonborough-Wittgenstein (ill. p. 109).

Another indication of Velázquez's popularity in the artistic circles of that time is the pantomime *The Infanta's Birthday* after Oscar Wilde (music by Franz Schreker) performed in 1908. Played in the garden theatre of the Wiener Kunstschau where Klimt's portrait of Fritza Riedler was hanging in a memorial room, the stage setting was done completely in Velázquez's style.[2] The fact that in 1907 Klimt's former companion Ernst Matsch also portrayed his daughter in an infanta costume, contributes to the overall picture.

Fritza Riedler is sitting erect, and very straight. Her clasped hands are resting in her lap. The composition consists of two halves meeting on the diagonal. Early in the preliminary studies, Klimt decided in favour of the sitting motif and the triangular arrangement. In the final elaboration, he dispensed with the high backrest of the fauteuil that appears in the studies. In its conceptualisation, the seating is drawn rather naturalistically, yet this aspect disappears behind the decoration. As if floating on the open sea, the Horus eyes borrowed from Egyptian nobility symbolism, together with the wave bands, develop a strong life of their own in their arrangement.[3]

In representing the white dress with its lavish ruches and frills, Klimt employs a variety of design tools. At the same time, the portrait of Fritza Riedler is the first to contain closed gold areas. Werner Hofmann interprets the result as a blurring of borderlines and observes "a playful interweaving of the animated and the inanimate, the plane and the body, the organic and the artificial".[4]

The portrait of the "Frau Geheimrat" was first exhibited in Mannheim in 1907, together with the portrait of Adele Bloch-Bauer I (ill. p. 117) finished shortly before.[5] In view of the two outstanding portraits, Ludwig Hevesi emphasised the "theatre director" in Klimt. Klimt, he wrote, was

The gallery room of the Kunsthalle Mannheim, 1907. The portrait of Fritza Riedler amidst the exhibits of the Wiener Werkstätte

concerned with representing fantasms, he was concentrating on things that were "beautiful to the eye", and displaying them in fabulous combinations. The women "are wearing today's dresses made from today's fabrics and styles, or nearly so. At least according to Klimt's notion of 'today'."[6]

In the context of the Mannheim exhibition, which was organised as part of a presentation of objects by the Wiener Werkstätte, the "handicraft" quality of the pictures was particularly conspicuous. Hevesi sharply analysed the incorporeal, feast for the eyes of "rummaging in precious stones that don't exist. In shine and glitter and multifarious sparkle without tangibility." An early photograph of the picture in a review of the Mannheim exhibition shows that Klimt changed it afterwards.[7] The early state is even more clearly recognisable in a reproduction published by Hugo Haberfeld in 1912.[8] Klimt did not sign the picture until after the first public exhibition. The comparison with the current state also shows differences in the ornamentation: especially the dark rectangles on the walls, which are missing.

In Vienna, the picture was first exhibited at the Kunstschau in 1908. There, it made a clear impression on the young Egon Schiele who under its fresh spell painted a portrait of his brother-in-law Anton Peschka, which with its composition, its square format, its surface organisation, its decorative insertions and its use of metal colour cannot deny its kinship with Klimt's work.[9]

Biographical details about Fritza Riedler used to be surprisingly sparse. Though her portrait had been in public hands for over sixty years, even such information as her dates of birth and death were unknown. The fact that Frau Riedler was married to a man holding a prominent place in the history of German technology had also been completely forgotten.

Fritza, correctly Friederike, Langer was born in Berlin on 9 September 1860.[10] She was married to Dr. Aloys Riedler who was born in Graz on 19 May 1850. After attaining his doctorate at the Technische Hochschule in Graz, he was an assistant at the universities of Brünn and Vienna. Further stages of his academic career prompted the couple to move to Munich in 1880, to Aachen in 1884, and to Berlin in 1889.[11]

Personally encouraged by Kaiser William II, Riedler, as "the first man at the first German institute of technology", held a chair at the Technische Hochschule in Berlin-Charlottenburg. As a practising engineer and innovative mind, Prof. Riedler got lucrative orders from German industry, but was also prominently engaged in the struggle for restructuring the study of engineering. His enthusiasm may have caused the young Ludwig Wittgenstein to take up mechanical engineering in Berlin in the same year as Klimt was completing the portrait of "Frau Professor", after finishing the portrait of Wittgenstein's sister the year before.

All public and private attempts to appoint her husband to a chair in Vienna came to nothing. In 1903/04, about the time when Klimt began the portrait sittings, the chronic failure of these efforts even provoked the *Fackel* to caustic comments: in Germany, unnoticed by Austria, Riedler had

Egon Schiele, Portrait of his brother-in-law Anton Peschka, 1909. Oil on canvas. Private collection

1   Nebehay 1969, p. 507, note 10.
2   Many thanks to Christiane Böker for directing my attention to this reproduction.
3   Strobl, Vol. 2, p. 28, assumes that this pattern had been inspired by sketches by Margarete Macdonald Mackintosh.
4   Werner Hofmann 1965, p. 36.
5   See catalogue of the international art exhibition in Mannheim, 1907, Cat. No. 497. A photograph of the hall in *Deutsche Kunst und Dekoration XX*, 1907, pp. 328–333.
6   Ludwig Hevesi, Bilder von Gustav Klimt. Galerie Miethke. Jubiläumsausstellung in Mannheim, in: *Fremdenblatt*, 21 July 1907.
7   *Deutsche Kunst und Dekoration*, year 20, 1907, fig. pp. 328 and 332. For the exhibition design see Sekler, 1982, No. 113.
8   Hugo Haberfeld, "Gustav Klimt", in *Die Kunst—Monatsheft für freie und angewandte Kunst*, year 13, No. 4, January 1912, Munich, p. 181. The old photograph can also be found in Max Eisler 1920.
9   Jane Kallir, Egon Schiele. The Complete Works, New York, 1990, No. 150.
10 WStLA, registration archives, communication of 28 April 2000.
11 The residential address was 11 Kurfürstendamm, West Berlin. See register of deaths.

Franz Matsch
Portrait of his daughter Hilde,
1907, Oil on canvas
Vienna, private collection

Scene from the pantomime
The Infanta's Birthday by Oscar
Wilde. Performance at the garden theatre of the Wiener Kunstschau in 1908, directed by Eduard Wimmer-Wisgrill, music by
Franz Schreker.

risen to be the world's leading mechanical engineer, "So what is he doing in Austria?"[12]

In Klimt's development process, the portrait of Fritza Riedler marks an important step towards an increasingly geometrical quality that reaches its peak in the portrait of Adele Bloch-Bauer. Professor Riedler hammered into his students "that one should not start out from given formulas and rules, but from ingenuous considerations and from reality in order to design a machine appropriately",[13] and his credo certainly created an interesting frictional surface for Klimt's design technique.

But how did the connection between Gustav Klimt and Fritza Riedler come about? We also do not know where the portrait was painted. It is certain that Klimt didn't travel to Berlin for this purpose. Too many anecdotes confirm his aversion to travelling. Moreover, a Klimt portrait could not be painted in a couple of weeks. Regarding the preliminary studies, Alice Strobl suggests that most of the drawings were created "not much later than in 1904, some of them, however, not earlier than in 1905".[14] To all appearances, Frau Riedler was repeatedly in Vienna for this purpose. In fact, at her husband's workplace she was regarded as a "Viennese", as was explicitly emphasised in an obituary for Prof. Riedler, which described her as having given her husband "grace, freshness, naturalness, and vivacity".[15] Their attachment to Vienna made the childless couple move there as soon as they had reached retirement age, a decision probably further encouraged by the fact that Fritza Riedler together with her sister and her brothers owned a house at 14 Hahngasse, Wien IX.

Frau Riedler died in that house on 8 April 1927. She left her share of it to her youngest brother Prof. Paul Langer, to her sister Emilie Langer and her brother Hofrat Dr. Alfons Langer, retired public prosecutor, the latter two also living in Vienna.[16] The Klimt portrait was bequeathed to the unmarried Emilie Langer, registered in Hahngasse since 1920. Whether she received the picture directly from her sister or only after the death of her brother-in-law in 1936, who made her his sole heiress, cannot be established.[17] The Österreichische Galerie Belvere bought the picture from her in 1937.[18]

12 Karl Kraus (ed.), *Die Fackel*, No. 148, 2 December 1903, pp. 15f; and No. 151, 4 January 1904, pp. 12f. See also necrologue in *Elektrotechnik und Maschinenbau*, year 54, Vienna, 1936, No. 50, p. 604. Many thanks to Erich Jiresch, archives of the Technische Universität Wien, for the quotation.
13 Otto Kammerer, *Riedler als Lehrer und Ingenieur*, Graz 1938, p. 8. Speech at the disclosure of the memorial tablet for Prof. Riedler at the Universität Graz. See also Kammerer, Otto, "Alois Riedler", in *Forschungen und Fortschritte*, year 12, Nos. 35/36, Berlin, 1936, pp. 458f. Many thanks to Gerhard v. Knobelsdorff, archives of the Technische Universität Berlin.
14 Strobl, Vol. 2, p. 27 and Nos. 1226–1246; and Vol. 4, Nos. 3542–3543b.
15 Otto Kammerer, see note 13.
16 WStLA, register of deaths, Bezirksgericht Josefstadt, entry A VIII 478/27.
17 WStLA, Aloys Riedler's last will of 9 December 1897 with two codicils of 2 April 1920 and 14 April 1920, resp. Prof. Riedler died in the Villa Deifel am Semmering on 25 October 1936. See also WStLA, register of deaths, Bezirksgericht Josefstadt, entry A 1061/36.
18 See Österreichische Galerie Belvedere, archives, acquisition dossier entry 482/1937. The acquisition coincides with the withdrawal of Friederike Beer's two Klimt loans, see ill. p. 137.

Portrait of Adele Bloch-Bauer I

GUSTAV KLIMT

1907

Oil, silver and gold plating on
canvas, 138 x 138 cm
Marked on the lower right:
"Gustav–/Klimt.–/1907"
Vienna, Österreichische Galerie
Belvedere, Inv. No. 3830
(Novotny-Dobai No. 150)

The portrait of Adele Bloch-Bauer is arguably the most famous Klimt portrait and a chief work of his so-called "golden style". Adele Bloch-Bauer was twenty-six years old when Klimt painted her, yet nothing juvenile can be detected in the portrait. The history of the picture goes back a long way. Like no other portrait, Klimt prepared it with numerous drawings and studies, which Strobl dates to 1903/04, assuming that a realisation of the picture in gold was planned even then.[1] The early date is confirmed by a letter from Adele Bloch to Julius Bauer dated 22 August 1903, in which she discusses the plans for the wedding anniversary of her parents on 15 October 1903. "Originally, we children wanted to make them a joint present, but now we have totally abandoned the idea. My husband decided to have me painted by Klimt who, however, cannot start work before winter. So my parents will just have to be patient."[2]

The picture was first exhibited as part of a presentation of objects of the Wiener Werkstätte in Mannheim in spring 1907.[3] The first encounter with the Viennese public took place on the occasion of the Kunstschau in 1908.[4] In the *Wiener Allgemeine Zeitung,* one could read about an "idol in a golden shrine",[5] while disapproving voices stated mockingly: "More *Blech* than Bloch".[6]

The subject is sitting or rather floating in front of a golden chair whose back reveals itself only to the most attentive eye. All details of the picture—especially the subject's body—seem to dissolve in the splendour of the golden shimmer. As with Byzantine idols, only the face and the hands remain visible under the gold. Still under the "revelation's" spell, Klimt reported from Ravenna in 1903: "(...) the mosaics of unprecedented splendour."[7]

For Hevesi, it was "mosaic painting", with the woman's portrait a cross between painting and handicraft, executed with the meticulousness of a goldsmith. Johannes Dobai ascribed a structural role to the gold colour: "In this case, gold symbolises body as well as space, denseness as well as lightness in a world detached from itself."[8]

Mosaic from Ravenna: Empress Theodora

Klimt used this gold in different ways: in the spirit of Japanese lacquer painting in the background, producing a diffuse lustre, or making the pattern stand out in full relief and enriching it with real gold plating. The strongest inner contradiction arises between the naturalistically conceived motifs and their ornamental stylisation. The subject's coat, opening wide at the side, is treated as a sweeping zone of texture. The garment visible underneath is strewn with Egyptian god's-eye motifs, and hangs on thin straps from the narrow shoulders. The magic of the geometry, the orches-

1   Strobl, Vol. 1, pp. 301f. and Nos. 1054–1151; and Vol. 4, Nos. 3520–3531c.
2   Österreichische Nationalbibliothek, autograph collection, Sign. 577/52–1.
3   International art exhibition, Mannheim, 1907, Cat. No. 497a.
4   See catalogue of the Kunstschau Wien, room 22, No. 4 ("Porträt der Frau A. B.").
5   *Wiener Allgemeine Zeitung,* 6 June 1908.
6   *Blech,* German for "sheet metal", "rubbish" (translator's note). Fritz Novotny attributes this dictum to the journalist Julius Bauer, see letter from Fritz Novotny to Johannes Dobai of 13 February 1960, in the artists' archives of the Österreichische Galerie Belvedere, Klimt folder No. XII. Nebehay, 1969, p. 425, note 15, suspects the Klimt opponent Eduard Pötzl of being the author of the judgement.
7   Card to Emilie Flöge of 2 December 1903, as quoted in Fischer 1987, p. 171.
8   Johannes Dobai, "Die Landschaft in der Sicht von Gustav Klimt—Ein Essay", in *Mitteilungen der Österreichischen Galerie,* years 22/23, 1978/79, Nos. 66/67, Salzburg 1978, p. 256.

tration of squares and circles and the alternation of spiral and triangular ornaments are further enhanced by the compositional ambivalence that allows us to see Adele Bloch-Bauer in a sitting as well as in a standing position, thus transforming the easy chair into something completely irrational and decorative.

The picture suggests not only Adele Bloch-Bauer's restlessness and her denial of society's expectations, but also the element of conflict within the gender role. The full lips and the red cheeks contribute little to the vividness. The ornamental stiffness conflicts with the conception of the human being; an unresolved dialogue that already characterised the majesty of the Empress Theodora in Ravenna. Gold as the colour of merciless ceremonial is reminiscent of Egyptian pretensions to eternity, the profanity of the medieval gold-ground panel painting, but also the exoticism of Japanese lacquer painting.[9]

Whether there was a liaison amoureuse between Klimt and Adele Bloch-Bauer, as has often been speculated, remains questionable. Such a relationship was suggested by the American psychiatrist Salomon Grimberg whom many others followed.[10] Hubertus Czernin, however, who has recently concerned himself with Adele Bloch-Bauer in great detail, rather doubts the possibility of a love relationship.[11]

Adele Bauer was born as the daughter of the banker Moriz Bauer and Jeannette Bauer, née Honig, in Vienna on 9 August 1881.[12] As a member of the country's economic elite, her father, in his capacity as Generaldirektor, controlled the fortunes of the seventh biggest bank in Austria-Hungary, the Wiener Bankverein, and was the Präsident of the Orientbahn.[13]

Adele Bloch-Bauer, photograph c. 1910. Österreichische Galerie Belvedere, archives

On 19 December 1899, Adele married the industrialist Ferdinand Bloch who was seventeen years her senior.[14] It was a marriage "based on mutual respect rather than love. They respected each other tremendously."[15] In the summer of 1899, the young Alma Mahler, later one of Adele's best friends, noted: "Adele Bauer, next to her hideous fiancé."[16] This marriage of convenience was matched by the marriage of Adele's sister Thedy, correctly Marie-Therese, to Ferdinand Bloch's brother, the lawyer Dr. Gustav Bloch. Since all male descendants of the Bloch family later died out, the families changed their name officially in 1917, henceforth calling themselves Bloch-Bauer.

Ferdinand Bloch, who came from Bohemia, where he attended the commercial college in Prague, was born on 16 July 1864 and developed his father's company into one of the biggest sugar factories in Central Europe. The marriage remained without issue, Adele lost two children during pregnancy, a third one died a few days after its birth. After the collapse of the monarchy in 1918, the Bloch-Bauer couple that had lived before in Wien IV., at 10 Schwindgasse,[17] opted for Czechoslovakian citizenship with a residence in Schloss Jungfer-Brezan near Prague.[18]

9   For the Viennese perception of Japonisme see *Japonisme in Vienna*, exhib. cat., Tobu Museum of Art, The Austrian Museum of Applied Arts, Vienna, et al., 1994, esp. Akiko Mabuchi, "Klimt and the Decorative—Japonisme in Viennese Painting", pp. 209–212.
10   Salomon Grimberg, "Adele—Private Love and Public Betrayal", in *Art & Antiques*, New York, summer edition 1986, pp. 70ff.
11   Hubertus Czernin, *Die Fälschung—Der Fall Bloch-Bauer*, Vienna 1999, esp. the chapter "Ménage à trois", p. 57ff.
12   See IKG Wien, register of births, entry 24/56/VI/1881. However, according to the IKG Wien's register of marriages, entry 1106/1/1899, the date of birth is 9 April 1881.
13   Brandstätter 1992, pp. 328–330; *Der Standard*, Vienna, 8 March 1999; For Adele Bloch-Bauer and her family's general history, see Hubertus Czernin, cf. above, pp. 50ff.
14   IKG Wien, register of marriages, entry 1106/1/1899. Later, Adele Bloch-Bauer withdrew from the Israelitic religious community. No exact date can be established. In the post-mortem protocol, WStLA, her profession of faith is given as "unchurched".
15   Communication from Frau Maria Altmann, 7 March 1999.
16   25 August 1899; Mahler 1997, p. 351.
17   Lehmann 1910.
18   See also Nebehay 1992, note 17, p. 225.

Maria Altmann, the only niece still alive, remembers her aunt whose principle of life demanded an exclusive orientation toward the intellectual. She describes Adele with the following attributes: "Sick, suffering, always with headache, smoking like a chimney, terribly frail, dark. A spiritual face, slim, elegant. 'Complacent, arrogant', that was the impression she made on me when I was a child. Always seeking intellectual stimulation." The niece also mentions a crippled finger that the aunt always tried to conceal. This is reportedly why Klimt chose this particular hand position in the portrait.

In December 1919, Ferdinand Bloch-Bauer bought the house at 18 Elisabethstraße, nearly opposite the Akademie in Schillerplatz. Here, Adele Bloch-Bauer practised the hospitality that had turned her house into one of the centres of the Viennese Fin de Siècle. In the 1920s, she continued to gather intellectuals, artists and Social Democratic politicians round her: Alma Mahler-Werfel and her husband, Richard Strauss, Stefan Zweig, Jakob Wassermann, Karl Renner, and Julius Tandler frequented her house. As her niece Maria Altmann remembers, "Adele was not happy at home. She wanted to study, which was not customary for a young girl at that time, so she married instead."[19] She was a disciplined woman who had intensively studied German, French and English literature.

Adele Bloch-Bauer, photograph c. 1920. Archives Christian Brandstätter, Vienna

Adele Bloch-Bauer died on 24 January 1925.[20] When two days later her corpse was cremated, which was forbidden by the Catholic church, Adele once again demonstrated her sympathy for social democracy.[21] Out of a characteristic sense of social responsibility, she left her Klimt pictures to the then "Moderne Galerie", now Österreichische Galerie Belvedere, with the charge, however, that the pictures remained at her husband's disposal while he was alive. After Adele's death, her room with a view of Schillerplatz was turned into a "commemorative room" always decorated with fresh flowers.[22] On the walls hung the two Klimt portraits flanked by four Klimt landscapes, with the master's photograph on a side table next to the chaise longue.

A little more than a decade after Adele's death, the Nazis took over. After the *Anschluß*, Ferdinand Bloch-Bauer's fortune including his valuable art and porcelain collection was Aryanised. At that time, the Klimt pictures were also confiscated. This is the basis of Ferdinand Bloch-Bauer's heirs' restitution claims, which they plan to put forward in an action against the Republic of Austria for return of the pictures. Apart from the legal argument, the way Austria is dealing with the dark sides of its past thus becomes the subject of politico-social and politico-cultural debates.[23]

Ferdinand Bloch-Bauer who successfully emigrated first to Czechoslovakia and, after its occupation, to Switzerland, died in Zurich on 13 November 1945. The fact that he was laid to rest next to his wife in the urn grove of the Wiener Zentralfriedhof, is strangely touching.

19 *Der Standard*, Vienna, 8 March 1999.
20 WStLA, post-mortem protocol. See also the necrologue in the *Neue Freie Presse*, Vienna, 25 January 1925.
21 WStLA, post-mortem protocol.
22 Statement by Maria Altmann, see note 15. See also *Der Standard*, Vienna, 11 November 1998.
23 For details, see Hubertus Czernin who in March 1999 in the Viennese daily paper *Der Standard* published a comprehensive series available also in book form. See note 11.

Lady with Hat and Boa

GUSTAV KLIMT

c. 1910

Oil on canvas, 69 x 55 cm
Marked on the middle left:
"Gustav—/Klimt"
Vienna, Österreichische Galerie
Belvedere, Inv. No. 4415
(Novotny-Dobai No. 161)

A Parisian flair surrounds this female portrait, which seems to turn the subject into the likeness of a modern cocotte. But precisely this atmosphere produces an element of strangeness in the picture in the context of Viennese art that is unusual for Klimt's work. The young woman's eyes are turned to the left, the lids lasciviously lowered. The unknown belle's cool face, which she is partly concealing, is framed by thick sandy hair. The huge hat with the blue-violet scarf has been pulled slightly aslant. It was this hat and its colour that in later years gave the picture the title "The violet hat". This picture's intense colour-scheme became fully visible only after it was restored a few years ago.[1] But, however much the blue-violet may radiate, the painting is not identical with the "violet hat" exhibited in the Wiener Kunstschau in 1906, with which it has been identified until now.

Once again, Gustav Klimt was late in delivering his pictures for the exhibition opening. When he finally sent in the "violet hat",[2] several newspapers published separate reviews that are evaluated here for the first time. The *Österreichische Volkszeitung* explicitly talks about a "wicker hat overgrown with roses" and a "glowing red coat".[3] But both are missing from the picture in the Österreichische Galerie Belvedere. The *Neues Wiener Abendblatt* also explained: "From the title, one need not conclude that the violet hat was the most prominent part of the portrait study designated thereby; this very hat's superbly painted rose decoration and the red coat stand out much more, they even drown everything else."[4]

These descriptions enable us to prove for the first time that the "violet hat" of 1909 is not identical with the picture of the *Lady with hat and boa* in the Österreichische Galerie Belvedere. The picture exhibited in 1909 is the one included in the Novotny-Dobai catalogue as No. 169 with the title *Lady with rose hat*.[5] A third description in the *Illustriertes Wiener Extrablatt* confirms this assignment: "To this violet, most fashionably tub-shaped hat decorated with little roses belongs a most lovely woman, somewhat roguish, slightly guileful, a little deceitful and jittery, herself of the most fashionable make. The little face, which is topped by a red-dyed crown of hair, is only partially visible as a dark feather boa reaches out with its shaggy ornamental work to the rosy made-up cheek. And a red coat like a trumpet fanfare (...)".[6] The description is also interesting for its perception of the subject as a "jittery woman". The same line of argument was adopted by Richard Muther who described her as a *Judith*.[7] Other critics expressed a similar view. "The new Viennese woman—a specific sort of new Viennese woman—their grandmothers are Judith and Salome—has been discovered or invented by Klimt. She is delightfully vicious, charmingly sinful, fascinatingly perverse."[8]

Gustav Klimt
The violet hat
(Lady with rose hat), 1909
Oil on canvas
Whereabouts unknown

1   See Erhard Stöbe, "Die Rückkehr eines Bildtitels—Die Restaurierung von Gustav Klimts 'Der violette Hut'", in *Belvedere—Zeitschrift für bildende Kunst*, 1/1995, Vienna, pp. 70–73.
2   In the catalogue of the Kunstschau, room 22, No. 1, listed as "The violet hat".
3   N.N., "Der violette Hut und anderes", in *Österreichische Volkszeitung*, Vienna, 19 May 1909.
4   *Neues Wiener Abendblatt*, 7 May 1909. The flashy red coat is also mentioned by the review in *Die Freistatt*, Vienna, 15 September 1909.
5   Novotny-Dobai No. 169.
6   "Neues aus der Kunstschau", in *Illustriertes Wiener Extrablatt*, 6 May 1909.
7   Richard Muther, "Die Kunstschau—Die Wiener Maler", in *Die Zeit*, Vienna, 5 May 1909.
8   "Neues aus der Kunstschau", in *Illustriertes Wiener Extrablatt*, 6 May 1909. The chronology between the pictures *Violet hat* from the Kunstschau in Vienna, 1909, and the portrait of a woman in the Österreichische Galerie Belvedere cannot be treated here.

The black Feather Hat

1910

Oil on canvas, 79 x 63 cm
Marked on the lower right:
"Gustav–/Klimt–/1910"
New York, Neue Galerie
(Novotny-Dobai No. 168)

The picture was first exhibited in Venice in 1908 where it hung next to Klimt's *Judith II* (ill. p. 225) in a special Klimt hall.[1] The Judith picture was purchased by the Italian government, but the B*lack feather hat* returned to Vienna. There, it remained only briefly in the custody of art dealer H. O. Miethke, Klimt's exclusive agent. From the scarce remnants of the gallery's business documents, which are held in private property, it can be gathered that the picture arrived at Miethke's on 2 November 1910 and was sold to Rudolf Kahler only three weeks later. Klimt received 4,000 of the sale price of 5,000 crowns.[2]

The woman sits in a waiting position, leant slightly forward. She fits Klimt's image of the ideal woman: slender, striking face, light complexion, dark eyes, prominent brows, shining red lips. She wears a white jacket with tight-fitting sleeves, and over it a stole. The bent arm, on which the subject rests her head, ties the inclined figure back into the plane, as does the huge feather hat, which is cropped by the right edge of the picture as if in a snapshot. The model's posture and facial expression give a lurking, thoughtful impression. The wilful personality, but also the markedly fashionable headgear, bring the lady with the black feather hat close to the *Woman with hat and boa* (ill. p. 121).

Stylistically, the picture is influenced by ideas from Toulouse-Lautrec's lithographs. Examples of these had been exhibited in Vienna several times since 1899, where Klimt had had the possibility to acquaint himself with them on several occasions.[3] French modern art was especially prominently represented at the Wiener Internationale Kunstschau in the summer of 1909. Subsequently, Klimt spent some time in Paris. Back in Vienna, the new ideas were heightened further by the Toulouse-Lautrec exhibition presented by the Galerie Miethke until December 1909.

Not only Klimt was impressed by his works. Public discussion questioned whether it was worth depicting the "other side of big-city life", yet some newspapers emphasized Toulouse-Lautrec's search for beauty in places "where normally we wouldn't expect it, where we haven't been taught to see it".[4] Thus they referred to a learning process that Klimt was also eager to encourage.

1   See the catalogue of the ninth International Exhibition in Venice, 1910, Klimt hall, Cat. No. 19.
2   The file is privately owned in Salzburg.
3   Cf. Strobl, Vol. 1, p. 237 and esp. Vol. 2, pp. 217, 218, and 224.
4   Cf. G. Tobias Natter, "Ausstellungen der Galerie Miethke 1904–1912", in G. Tobias Natter and Gerbert Frodl (eds.), *Carl Moll–1861–1945*, Salzburg 1998, esp. p. 180.

Portrait of Adele Bloch–Bauer II

GUSTAV KLIMT

1912

Oil on canvas, 190 x 120 cm
Marked on the lower right:
"Gustav–/Klimt"
Vienna, Österreichische Galerie
Belvedere, Inv. No. 4210
(Novotny-Dobai No. 177)

Adele Bloch-Bauer was the only woman who had enough wealth and enthusiasm for the arts to be painted twice by Klimt. Unlike the first picture (ill. p. 116) where the subject is sitting, this time Klimt shows the lady standing, a compositional decision that apparently had been clear to the painter from the outset.[1] Klimt divides the background into asymmetrically staggered areas of violet, red, pink and green. Galloping riders—motifs taken from Asian examples—enliven the topmost zone.

There is a huge difference between the two Bloch-Bauer portraits. With the standing portrait of Adele Bloch-Bauer, Klimt's development took a completely new course. In a lecture about the painter in 1912, the art historian Hugo Haberfeld talks about an "auspicious" new beginning: "(...) now the artist is going to paint a naturalistic portrait, so to speak, of the lady he has previously formed hieratically in gold and silver like an idol."[2]

Yet "naturalistic, so to speak" is only an allusion to what is new. The novelty lies primarily in the use of colour. This vividness of colour, as well as the new freedom in its application, can already be found in Klimt's landscapes, but now for the first time these factors play a role in the portraiture. It is generally believed that these tendencies were influenced by the young Henri Matisse.[3] Obviously, the Fauves' presentation at the Wiener Internationale Kunstschau in 1909 had made a vivid impression on Klimt, as had also the experience of his travels to Paris in 1909 and Brussels in 1911 where he attended the mounting of his frieze in the Palais Stoclet.

In comparison with the portrait Adele Bloch-Bauer I (ill. p. 116), a new relationship to corporeality as well as ornamentation becomes apparent. Both notions are redefined rather than abandoned. The carpet's splendid patterns run into each other. The body silhouette becomes a richly undulating, almost arabesque-like outline reminiscent of the one of Elisabeth Bachofen-Echt where it was described by Hatje as "vaselike strict form".[4]

1   Again, Alice Strobl, Vol. 2, p. 265, and Vol. 4, Nos. 3637–3638a, notes that no studies in other positions are known.
2   Hugo Haberfeld, "Gustav Klimt", in *Die Kunst—Monatsheft für freie und angewandte Kunst,* year 13, No. 4, January 1912, Munich, p. 183.
3   Novotny-Dobai, p. 391.
4   Ingomar Hatle, *Gustav Klimt. Ein Maler des Wiener Jugendstils,* Graz 1955, p. 98.

Portrait of Mäda Primavesi

GUSTAV KLIMT

c. 1912

Oil on canvas, 150 x 110 cm
Marked on the lower right:
"Gustav–/Klimt"
New York, The Metropolitan
Museum of Art. Gift of André
and Clara Mertens, in memory
of her mother, Jenny Pulitzer
Steiner, 1964.
(Novotny-Dobai No. 179)

The couple Otto and Eugenia
Primavesi with her four children,
photograph c. 1906. From left to
right: Mäda, Otto, Melitta, and
Lola. Vienna, private collection

1   See catalogue of the Roman
Secession's second exhibition,
Rome, 1914, room 4, Cat. No. 12.
With a view of the picture as part of
the total arrangement, which was
designed by Dagobert Peche.
2   See exhib. cat., Vienna 1928,
Cat. No. 63. Obviously the Primavesi family's Klimt collection has
been liquidated at that time. Many
of the Klimt works belonging to
them are not unambiguously recognisable in the catalogue, and particularly all those clearly identifiable
such as *The baby* or *The hope* were
on offer, which certainly was an immediate consequence of the Primavesi banking house's bankruptcy in
1926.
3   WStLA, registration office, communication of 22 October 1999.
4   Registered address Wien XIX.,
94 Döblinger Hauptstraße. Communication from WStLA, registration
office, of 22 October 1999; and
inquiry to the residents' registration office, Roßauer Lände, of 16
September 1999.
5   See Ruth Reif, "Last Klimt to be
sold in Auction", in The New York
Time, 9 May 1987.
6   Communication from her son
Richard Primavesi, Montreal.

Mäda grew up with the privilege of being the daughter of a family that made it possible for her to get acquainted with Klimt from an early age. In the house of the banking family Otto and Eugenia Primavesi in Olmütz (Olomouc), Moravia, enthusiasm for the painter was as natural as Klimt's visits were frequent. With great difficulty, Klimt finished the portrait of the daughter just in time for the Christmas celebrations of 1913 and he showd it publicly for the first time in Rome in 1914.[1] After the ruin of the family's fortune, the picture was probably sold in the late 1920s, since it is listed as for sale at the Klimt commemorative exhibition in 1928.[2]

In accordance with her vocation, Mäda, correctly Mäda Gertrude, Primavesi, born in Olmütz on 22 December 1903,[3] was trained as nursery-school teacher. In 1945, she emigrated to Canada, where she founded a children's convalescent home in Montreal, becoming its director. Nevertheless, she kept a *pied-à-terre* in Vienna to the end.[4] When she left Austria, she took the Klimt portrait of her mother (ill. p. 129) with her. She sold it in 1987.[5] Her death on 25 May 2000 deprived us not only of Klimt's last surviving model, but probably also of the last witness who had known Klimt personally.[6]

Klimt captured no child portrait other than the one of Mäda Primavesi on a canvas of this size. The nine-year-old is standing upright. Her eyes meet the viewer's defiantly. In hardly any other portrait does Klimt make so much use of pairs of opposites on various levels, and yet he succeeded marvellously in uniting these opposites here.

Mäda is represented as neither adult nor child. Safely anchored, she occupies the front picture plane while an imaginary space opens behind her. The merging of figure and ground remains ambivalent. Perspective motifs and two-dimensional elements meet dialectically. The secure motif of the girl standing with her feet firmly planted contrasts with the dissolution of the graphic form. The girl looks unwaveringly forward, but keeps her hands—which play such a prominent role in the other Klimt portraits—hidden behind her body.

The silk garment is also ambiguous: it is elaborately adorned with a floral belt and pleats, but has the effect of a simple little dress. Lines and colours are constantly changing their relationship. On the one hand, Klimt outlines elements of form with a turquoise contour like the one delineating the body, on the other hand he writes the flower motifs freely onto the floor, applied with broad, vibrating brushstrokes as if floating like the water lilies in Monet's pond pictures. The triple wave line in the foreground seems to be drawn with the greatest ease, the contrast between a pastose application of paint and places where the canvas is shining through seems effortless. The restlessness of the search and the weeks of preparation have disappeared behind the virtuosity of the painter's bravura.

Portrait of Eugenia (Mäda) Primavesi

GUSTAV KLIMT

1913/14

Oil on canvas, 140 x 84 cm
Marked on the lower right:
"Gustav–/Klimt"
Toyota, Municipal Museum of
Art
(Novotny-Dobai No. 187)

Otto and Eugenia Primavesi,
photograph c. 1900, Vienna,
private collection

By hiding her behind the caftan-like dress, Klimt leaves open the question of whether Eugenia Primavesi is represented in a sitting or in a standing position. The matronly appearance is backed by an arc-like form. This has been employed previously to organise the pictorial space in the portrait of Fritza Riedler (ill. p. 113). Its flower pattern can also be read as a view into a Klimt landscape. But most importantly, the background shines in a bright yellow. There, Klimt fits in a Chinese phoenix motif that he has repeatedly used in the context of other paintings.[1] Lines and colours communicate with each other in a free dialogue, with their relationship being repeatedly redefined. There is a very dominant turquoise contour line in the face and breast region in particular, while other colour areas are handled in a purely painterly way. Heavy, almost crude brushstrokes contrast with the more delicate treatment of the flesh tones. Occasionally, the thick application of paint is reminiscent of cloisonné enamel. Towards the lower edge, the formal description gets ever more generous, more structural, and the open canvas plays an ever greater role.

Details about the circumstances of the picture's creation can be learnt from surviving letters. Early in February 1913, Eugenia Primavesi writes: "On the eighteenth, I am to sit again."[2] Several months later, Klimt confirms in a letter to Otto Primavesi of 28 Juni 1913: "Dear Sir! With heartfelt thanks I confirm the receipt of 15,000 crowns (fifteen thousand), which I have correctly received as a payment on account for the two portraits. Yours faithfully, Gustav Klimt." Obviously, the two portraits of Eugenia and her daughter Mäda (ill. p. 127), for which Klimt had also received an order, were painted at the same time. Mäda remembers the sessions in Klimt's studio: "We went every few months to Vienna and stayed about ten days. I was a little girl, and Professor Klimt was awfully kind. When I became impatient, he would just say, 'Sit for a few minutes longer'."[3]

Klimt's notorious hesitancy almost prevented the picture's punctual arrival as a Christmas present. On 19 December 1913, he apologises: "Dear Miss! Only this evening (Friday) shall I get the frame—the picture will also take that time—unfortunately! Since now, during the holiday, dispatch by express is very uncertain, I shall send the picture and the frame tomorrow morning as passenger luggage, possibly on the express train, to Olmütz. I shall buy a ticket to Olmütz, check the case as passenger luggage, and send the receipt by registered post to your address. This way, I was told, the picture can be there in one day—and nobody needs to travel with it. I hope that everything will turn out all right and that you will obtain the picture in time and that you will forgive me the difficulties I am causing you.— Unfortunately, I have a very big artist's hangover. I wish you a merry Christ-

1   For instance, two years earlier in the portrait of Paula Zuckerkandl, current whereabouts unknown, see Novotny-Dobai No. 178.
2   As quoted in Hedwig Steiner, "Gustav Klimts Bindung an Familie Primavesi in Olmütz", in *Mähring-Schlesische Heimat—Vierteljahresschrift für Kultur und Wirtschaft*, year 1968, Steinheim-on-Main, 1968, No. 4, pp. 242–252.
3   Cf. Rita Reif, "Last Klimt to be sold in Auction", *The New York Times*, 9 May 1987.

mas and remain truly yours, Gustav Klimt."[4] This is generally understood as referring to the Mäda portrait.

It seems that after all, the picture finally arrived in time to be given a place of honour above the desk in Mr. Primavesi's room. At that time, the Primavesis' new country residence in Winkelsdorf (Kouty) near the Moravian town of Schönberg was under construction. Situated in the gorgeous landscape of the Altvater Mountains, the house became—similar to the Palais Stoclet—an outstanding example of its architect Josef Hoffmann's conception of the Gesamtkunstwerk.[5] Here, the unity of art and life that had so often been called for was realised up to the smallest detail of the interior decoration

Eugenia Primavesi in her house at Winkelsdorf, photograph c. 1916. Vienna, private collection

and the design of the table cutlery and bed linen. Forms of social life and festive gatherings were integrated into the total concept.[6] Even the clothes suggested an approach to life in which hospitality and festivity were integral parts. For the well-being of her guests, Frau Primavesi even kept records about their individual preferences regarding room, dishes, flowers, number of cushions etc. She was, however, less successful with her rigid health regime, which the master of the house and his guests readily circumvented.[7]

In November 1913, the first "Schweindlfest" took place, legendary domestic feasts, to which Klimt, Hoffmann and Hanak were invited, among others. More of them followed, enjoying great popularity especially during the First World War when the supply situation in Vienna was particularly bleak.

There was a special Klimt surprise at the first Christmas celebration after the family moved into the country house in summer 1914. On 1 January 1915, Eugenia reports: "And then here on Christmas Eve with a Klimt picture as a surprise, which I had liked so much in his studio on that Saturday. It is called 'Vision' and I like it very much (...)."[8] Today, the picture is known as *Hope II*.

Eugenia (also Eugenie) Primavesi, née Butschek, was born on 13 June 1874 in Langenzersdorf,[9] the birthplace of the sculptor Anton Hanak, for whom she was an important patroness. As a girl, Eugenia had drama classes at the Viennese Conservatory. Her first engagement took her to Olmütz (Olomouc), Moravia, where she performed under the stage name Mäda. There she met Otto Primavesi whom she married on 19 November 1895. The twenty-one-year-old had then to leave the stage, but she kept the name Mäda and her love for the theatre remained as well. She frequently made use of complimentary tickets for the proscenium box in the Viennese Burgtheater into her later years.[10]

The banker Otto Primavesi, owner of a prosperous private bank and, like his wife, from a Catholic family whose roots point to Upper Italy, was born in Olmütz on 27 February 1868. The union was blessed with four children: the first-born son Otto, the daughters Lola, Mäda, and Melitta, the youngest.

The name Primavesi is closely linked with the Wiener Werkstätte as an institution. After the founding director Fritz Waerndorfer's failure in 1914, the Primavesi family financed the Werkstätte's further existence. Moreover, Otto and Eugenia Primavesi were members of the supervisory board, and Otto even became managing director in 1915.[11]

When Otto separated from his wife in 1925, apparently without an official divorce, he made the company over to her. Frau Primavesi actively supervised the

4   Cf. note 2.
5   Sekler 1982, p. 127ff and No. 179; see also Strobl, Vol. 2, p. 273, and Brandstätter 1992, p 331.
6   See Hanel Koeck, "Mode und Gesellschaft um 1900. Zur Modeszene in Wien", in exhib. cat. *Wien um 1900. Kunst und Kultur*, Vienna/Munich 1985, p. 464.
7   See Josef Hoffmann's reminiscences, as quoted in Sekler 1982, p. 129.
8   As quoted in Hedwig Steiner, cf. note 2. For the picture that later was hanging in the Primavesi family's city domicile in Olmütz, now The Museum of Modern Art, New York, see Novotny-Dobai No. 155, there without mention of the Primavesi provenance, but with the information that until 1914, the picture was still unsold.
9   WStLA, post-mortem protocol.
10   Verbal communication from the granddaughter Claudia Klein-Primavesi, Vienna.
11   Werner J. Schweiger, Wiener Werkstätte. Kunst und Handwerk 1903–1932, Vienna 1982, p. 96f; see also Brandstätter 1992, p. 331, Nebehay, 1992, p. 144f, and Gmeiner/Pirhofer 1985, p. 240.

Eugenia Primavesi, photograph
by d'Ora, Vienna, c. 1920
Vienna, private collection

12 Schweiger, cf. note 11, p. 72.
13 WStLA, registration office,
communication of 22 October
1999. According to other sources,
the date of death was 9 February.
Buried in the family vault in
Olmütz.
14 Schweiger, cf. note 11, pp.
121f.
15 *Die Wiener
Werkstätte-1903-1928—Modernes
Kunstgewerbe und sein Weg*, commemorative volume, Vienna 1929,
p. 11. The picture's title is "Mäda
Primavesi".
16 Schweiger, cf note 11, p. 126.
See also Brandstätter, 1992, p. 331;
according to Gmeiner/Pirhofer,
p. 240, until 1928.
17 Communication Claudia Klein-
Primavesi, Vienna. For the city residence in Olmütz, see Zatloukal,
Pavel (ed.), *Vila Primavesi v Olo-
mouci*, exhib. cat., Art Museum
Olmütz, Olmütz, 1990.
18 See letter from the Österreichische Galerie to Frau Primavesi of
26 August 1943, archives of the
ÖG, entry 301/1943, when Frau
Primavesi handed over three Klimt
pictures to the museum in order to
rescue them.
19 See WStLA, registration office,
communication of 22 October
1999.
20 Novotny-Dobai No. 193. See
also the documentation in Hedwig
Steiner, cf. Note 2.
21 Novotny-Dobai No. 216. See
the Hoffmann letter of 5 December
1917 published in Steiner, 1968.
22 Novotny-Dobai Nos. 99 and
221.
23 See Nebehay, 1992, esp.
p. 230. For the preliminary studies
purchased by the Museum für
angewandte Kunst, Vienna, in
1961, see Strobl, Vol. 2, Nos.
1810–18.

company's fortunes from that date, having anyway been one of its best customers. In order to maintain contact with the customers, she held parties and teas in the Wiener Werkstätte.[12] However, Eugenia Primavesi also failed, as a result of the adversities caused by financial difficulties and the company's elite conception of itself. Otto Primavesi died on 8 February 1926. Events in Vienna followed one another in rapid succession.[13] Within a few weeks, the composition proceedings had to be instituted over the Wiener Werkstätte. In April 1926, the banking house of Primavesi in Olmütz also had to file its petition.

Werner J. Schweiger comments the Wiener Werkstätte's financial disaster: "The composition constituted the end of a long series of internal disputes, private and business quarrels between the couple Eugenia (Mäda) and Otto Primavesi, and the resulting weaknesses in management, exacerbated by the difficult economic situation."[14] But once again, a composition agreement was reached for the Wiener Werkstätte. A financial group led by the young textile industrialist Kuno Grohmann, who was related to Eugenia, provided new capital. When, in 1929, a commemorative volume appeared on the occasion of the Wiener Werkstätte's twenty-fifth anniversary, it included a reproduction of Klimt's Primavesi picture.[15] In 1930, Frau Primavesi withdrew from the Wiener Werkstätte. Two years later, the liquidation of the company had become inevitable.[16]

After losing the Olmütz estates, Vienna became the principal domicile of the widow who at first lived at 2 Gluckgasse, Wien I.[17] Eugenia Primavesi died on 13 June 1963 and was buried in the Wiener Zentralfriedhof. During the Second World War, she lived at 39 Schredtgasse, Wien III.,[18] at last at 39 Neulinggasse.[19] Josef Hoffmann, who often visited her, lived just round the corner, in Salesianergasse.

Eugenia Primavesi and her husband owned one of the most important Klimt collections. It included her own portrait and the portrait of the daughter Mäda; then the above-mentioned allegory *Hope II*. The Primavesis bought a first landscape, *Litzlbergerkeller on Lake Atter*, in 1916.[20] A second one followed in the late autumn of 1917. This was probably the *Garden landscape with mountain peak*, again planned as a Christmas surprise.[21]

According to Novotny-Dobai, the Primavesi family also owned the early *Farmhouse with rosebush* and *The baby*, which had been purchased at the estate auction at Nebehay's in 1919.[22] The Primavesis also purchased the preliminary sketches for the Stoclet-Frieze (ill. p. 233) from Nebehay in 1920.[23] And finally, their are the Klimt drawings, some of which are still owned by the descendants.

Portrait of Baroness Elisabeth Bachofen-Echt

GUSTAV KLIMT

1914–16
Oil on canvas, 180 x 128 cm
Marked on the lower right:
"Gustav–/Klimt"
New York, private collection
(Novotny-Dobai No. 188)

The exotic portrait of Elisabeth Bachofen-Echt intertwines feminine beauty, elegant naturalness, and fresh youth, whose magic the painter exalts into the realm of fantasy. The portrait was ordered by the parents Serena and August Lederer in 1914 and was completed in 1916.[1] Reportedly, Klimt received 35,000 crowns for the portrait.[2]

Klimt depicts the young woman in front of an outlandish background with figurines staying respectfully behind. The garment is of exquisite splendour, yet Alessandra Comini is mistaken in interpreting it as wedding dress, since that event did not take place until several years later.[3] Tapering toward the bottom, the so-called hobble skirt with its gathers has a highly fashionable trouser-like appearance. A stole of diaphanous chiffon with floral embroidery is draped over the shoulders, enclosing the subject within a closed contour.

The spatial orientation of the uncontoured triangle behind the woman, composed by Klimt of a variety of ornaments, remains indefinite. The detail from a Chinese dragon garment appears like a magic cloak protecting the frail figure.[4] In the upper part, we see the sky with clouds, and underneath the earth and the sea. Moreover, we recognise lucky symbols such as stylised bats and flowers. Angela Völker suggests that a garment like this formed part of an Asiatica collection in Klimt's studio.

In this picture, Klimt cultivated his undying fondness for ornament and his inexhaustible concern with decorations and patterns of all sorts. He is comparable only with the ingenious Josef Hoffmann in his playful sense of the infinite within clear frame structures. Despite all material and spatial differences, Hoffmann's interior design of the Eduard Ast villa, for instance, and the painted portrait of Elisabeth Bachofen-Echt, show strong parallels.[5] Both Klimt and Hoffmann revel in combining luxurious patterns. In Hoffmann's salon, it is the strongly patterned Wiener-Werkstätte carpet, the large-flowered upholstered furniture, the lozenge-parqueted floor, with everything in contrast and unity with the rising walls of cold white Laas marble.

In a recollection published here for the first time, Elisabeth Bachofen-Echt, who was allowed to call the painter uncle, remembers the sittings: "Months passed with making drawings in various positions. Uncle cursed and swore, it was a real pleasure to listen to him. Several times, he threw the pencil away and said that one should certainly never paint people who are too close. Then mama came in and a quarrel flared up about position, toilet, etc. Sometimes the differences assumed quite serious forms and he shouted in his deep, majestic bass: 'I shall paint my girl as I like her and that's the end of it'. In the course of three years he changed his

Egon Schiele
Portrait of Elisabeth Lederer,
1913, Gouache over pencil on
paper, Private collection

1   Throughout the literature, the date of origin has varied considerably. In Pirchan 1956, p. 55, the picture was dated "1910"; in Hatle 1955, p. 97, "ca. 1915"; in Novotny-Dobai No. 188, "ca. 1914". Thanks to Erich Lederer's reminiscences, see Strobl, Vol. 3, p. 91, the above mentioned date is now generally accepted.
2   The information about the 35,000 crowns is based on Erich Lederer's reminiscences, yet it has repeatedly been related to the portrait of her mother (i.e. Serena Lederer); see, for instance, Novotny-Dobai No. 103, and Nebehay 1992, p. 225, note 3. However, Nebehay 1969, p. 192, note 2, already mentions the correction.
3   Alessandra Comini, *Gustav Klimt—Eros and Ethos*, Salzburg 1975, p. 18. Similarly in Ilona Sarmany-Parsons, *Klimt*, Munich 1989, p. 87, talking about a "future bride".
4   Sarmany-Parsons, cf. note above, p. 87.
5   Sekler 1982, No. 134.

concept over and over again, and these were the most pleasant and most instructive hours of my life. He would have changed it once more were it not for my mother who one day seized the picture, loaded it onto the car, and kidnapped it. When he saw it at home he said: 'Now it is even less her!'"[6]

Elisabeth, correctly Elisabeth Franziska, Lederer was born to August and Serena Lederer in Vienna on 20 January 1894.[7] Her artistic talent found a fervent advocate in Klimt, to whom the child felt particularly attracted. At the age of twelve, she had lessons with the sculpture Heinrich Zita, and as a fifteen-year-old, she continued her training at the Wiener Kunstgewerbeschule with Michael Powolny and finally with the sculptress Theresa Fjodorowna Ries.[8] On 16 July 1921, she withdrew from the Israelitic Community and became member of the Protestant Helvetian Church in Vienna.[9] On the following day, she married Wolfgang Freiherr von Bachofen-Echt, a member of the brewer dynasty of the same name.[10] Their Nußdorfer Brauerei AG, founded in 1865, had become one of Austria's biggest breweries.[11] The company founder Adolf Bachofen (1830–1922) had been honoured with the rank of a Freiherr and the title von Echt as early as 1906.[12] It was not until 1934 that Elisabeth Bachofen-Echt brought a son into the world, christened August Anton, who, tragically, died on 5 July 1938.[13]

Elisabeth Bachofen-Echt in her palais in Jacquingasse, Vienna, photograph c. 1925/30, Vienna, private collection

The political and everyday life of Elisabeth Bachofen-Echt deteriorated rapidly. She was divorced from her husband by a decision of the Döbling municipal court on 17 August 1938.[14] Exhausting all possibilities to escape from the Nazi terror, on 18 March 1940, she obtained from the Reichsstelle for genealogy a "certificate of origin" with the official statement that she was descended from Gustav Klimt who was "of German blood", rather than from her legal "Jewish" father August Lederer. Based on a statutory declaration by her mother and testimonies by numerous other witnesses, "photographs of both possible fathers as well as the examinee's two brothers Erich and Fritz Lederer, whose descent from the legitimate father is uncontested, have been examined"—as it says in the rather absurd examination report. "By this, the examinee's descent from Gustav Klimt is not improbable. The opinion based on graphology and heredity

6   Elisabeth Bachofen-Echt's written reminiscences, unpublished manuscript from April 1939. Many thanks to Frau Kirstein-Jacobs who made available not only the manuscript, but other important documents as well.
7   Communication from the city hall of Vienna, MA 61, registrar's office.
8   See E. H., "Die Bildhauerin Elisabeth Bachofen-Echt", in Österreichische Kunst, year 5, Vienna, 1934, No. 4, pp. 8f, with three figures, including a portrait bust of her husband Freiherr Bachofen-Echt.
9   IKG Wien, registrar's office, communication of 28 September 1999 and 4 July 2000; see also parish register of the Protestant Helvetian Church, Vienna.
10   See register of marriages of the Protestant Helvetian Church, Vienna. The husband was born in Vienna on 17 November 1895. See same place and WStLA, registration office, communication of 30 June 2000.
11   Brandstätter 1992, p. 330.
12   Czeike, Vol. 1, 1992, p. 224.
13   Administration of the cemetery of Hietzing, communication of 21 June 2000.
14   See the corresponding entry in the register of marriages of the Protestant Helvetian church, Wien I., 16 Dorotheergasse.
15   All cited documents privately owned in Vienna. Many thanks for making them available.
16   Cemetery of Hietzing, grave 14/49. Originally 12/197. Her father August Lederer has also been buried here.

The Viennese municipal architect
Eduard Ast's villa, living hall,
Photograph c. 1912

(AG/40 of 16 December 1939), prepared using specimens of handwriting, is also to be taken into account."

Earlier still, the art historian and racial researcher Paul Schultze-Naumburg, presented with sculptural works by Elisabeth Bachofen-Echt, had confirmed with pseudo-scientific long-windedness that the examinee's talent had no "Jewish characteristics", for which only "non-Jewish descent" could be responsible. "But if the fully Jewish Lederer was the father it would be absolutely incomprehensible how it was possible that, in her artistic works, there is no expression of a purely Jewish nature."[15]

Elisabeth Bachofen-Echt,
photograph c. 1914, Vienna,
private collection

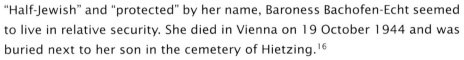

"Half-Jewish" and "protected" by her name, Baroness Bachofen-Echt seemed to live in relative security. She died in Vienna on 19 October 1944 and was buried next to her son in the cemetery of Hietzing.[16]

Portrait of Friederike Maria Beer

GUSTAV KLIMT

1916

Oil on canvas, 168 x 130 cm
Marked on the lower left: "Gus-
tav–/Klimt–/19 16"
Inscription on the upper right:
"Friedericke–/Maria Beer"
Tel Aviv Museum of Art, Mizne-
Blumenthal Collection
(Novotny-Dobai No. 196)

Friederike Beer-Monti in her
apartment equipped by the Wiener Werkstätte, photograph c.
1913. The cloth pattern of her
dress from the Wiener Werkstätte
was designed by Ugo Zovetti.

Friederike Maria Beer was born in Vienna on 27 January 1891. Her mother Isabella Beer, owner of the Kaiserbar at 3 Krugerstraße, died in Vienna on 23 August 1959. Her obituary in the name of the four children ("Federica Monti", Charlotte Böhler, Isabella Stevens, and Rudolf Brix) contained the proud boast: "Foundress and exclusive owner of the Kaiserbar and the Gelber Saal from 1904 to 1954".[1]

Since her childhood, Friederike, also Frederike or Federica, had been familiar with the Viennese art scene.[2] She was a rich and self-willed personality, dressed herself exclusively in fabrics from the Wiener Werkstätte at that time and regarded herself, in her own words, as a walking advertisement for them. Later, she liked to think back to that time of easy idleness: "Just living—going to the theatre, to art exhibitions, to the opera. In those days I was so wild about the Wiener Werkstätte that every single stitch of clothing I owned was designed by them. When I got an apartment of my own, all the furniture, even the rugs, was made by them."[3]

In 1914, she asked Egon Schiele to paint her portrait and shortly afterwards, in November 1915, she made a pilgrimage to Gustav Klimt to have herself "immortalised" also by him. She almost succeeded in persuading Oskar Kokoschka to paint her as well. He agreed, but was prevented by the war.[4] Fashion plays a major role in the two portraits that were painted. On 2 October 1914, Schiele wrote to his mother: "(...) I have now also received a portrait commission, a lady—I called upon her today and she showed me a collection of Wiener Werkstätte dresses. I chose four of them, which she will send me and in which I shall paint her tomorrow and in the next few weeks."[5]

The subject vividly remembered the sessions. Several slightly varying reports were given by Beer-Monti to different interview partners.[6] When Hans Böhler, her then boyfriend to whom she stayed attached all her life, wanted to give her a string of pearls she preferred a portrait by Gustav Klimt. In November 1915, she frequented Klimt's studio in Hietzing. Three times a week at two o'clock, she posed for him for two or three hours. In February 1916, she thought that the picture she hadn't dared to look at while it was being painted was ready and on her friends' advice it was snatched from Klimt. The wealthy Böhler settled the bill. The price difference was enormous. While Beer-Monti, paying for the Schiele portrait herself, had to spend 600 crowns, Böhler paid 20,000 crowns.[7]

Klimt had her try on numerous Chinese and Japanese dresses he owned in great number. Finally, she suggested that she should be painted in a dress she had recently acquired from the Wiener Werkstätte, which he accepted. She was proud of her new polecat jacket—after all, it was the middle of the war—but it was Klimt's suggestion that she should wear it inside out since the beautiful red tones of the Wiener Werkstätte's silk lining appealed to him.[8] Klimt deviated from the actual jacket only in the colour of the polecat, painting it grey rather than white because he thought it would look better. The dress, later altered, which Beer-Monti gave to the fashion department of the Metropolitan Museum in New York in 1946, had been tailored from the pongee "Marina" designed

1   Obituary in the *Adler*, Vienna, obituary collection.
2   Nebehay 1979a, p. 267.
3   As quoted in Alessandra Comini, *Egon Schiele's Portraits*, Berkeley/Los Angeles/London 1974, p. 127.
4   For Kokoschka, see Nebehay 1979, pp. 287f.
5   As quoted in Nebehay 1979, p. 312. For the portrait, see Jane Kallir, Egon Schiele, The Complete Works, New York, 1990, No. 276.
6   For Nebehay's reports, see *Klimt*, exhib. cat., Galerie Christian M. Nebehay, Vienna 1963, and Nebehay 1969, p. 444. In addition, Comini 1974, cf. above, p. 217; Comini 1975, pp. 18f; Strobl, Vol. 3, p. 99.

by Dagobert Peche. In a photograph showing Frau Beer in her apartment, she is wearing a housecoat made from the "Ant"-cloth designed by Wimmer-Wisgrill.[9]

The exotic Asian background with its bellicose soldiers in *horror-vacui* style originates from a Chinese vase.[10] Here again, the fashion for Japonisme, which had been all the rage in the Paris art world in the 1870/80s, reached an interesting variant that was not only "late" compared to the Pan-European development, but also original. Asiatic art's planar figure-ground relationship, at least, fitted Klimt's conception of pictorial space rather well. The fact that Beer-Monti is embedded in the fighting hordes is a vivid example.

Klimt gives her a closed calligraphic silhouette. Her clear contour keeps her from sinking completely into the background pattern. Moreover, she is standing with both feet near the front plane of the picture on a small greenish stripe that could be read as the border to the many-figured background.

From 1918 to 1920, Frau Beer worked in Gustav Nebehay's gallery where she had to arrange and stamp the drawings in the Klimt estate.[11] During a short marriage with the Italian Emanuele Monti in the 1920s, she lived on the island of Capri, where the couple ran a hotel and the legendary "Tom-cat Hiddigeigei", a meeting place for artists.[12] In 1931, Friederike Beer-Monti moved to New York where, in 1936, she founded the "Artist's Gallery" with Hugh Stix, which after 1938 became an important haven for many Austrian artists driven into exile by the Nazis, among them the Viennese Expressionist Max Oppenheimer.[13] However, the Artist's Gallery also made it its business to provide then unknown painters such as Willem de Kooning and Ad Reinhardt with first exhibition opportunities.

As well as her portrait, Frau Beer also owned a Lake Atter landscape by Klimt: *Schloss Kammer near Lake Atter II*.[14] In 1929, she lent both Klimt works together with the Schiele portrait to the Österreichische Galerie for the reopening of its modern department. In 1933, she sold the pictures to Hugh S. Stix.[15] With wise foresight, he claimed the pictures back on 30 November 1937 in order to take them to the United States. On 24 January 1938—just a few weeks before the *Anschluß*—the works were handed over to the shipping agency.[16] Later, the pictures seem to have returned into Frau Beer-Monti's hands. When she lent the two portraits to the Guggenheim Museum for the first exhibition by an American museum devoted to Egon Schiele and Gustav Klimt, she was mentioned in the exhibition catalogue as "Federica Beer-Monti, New York and Vienna". When already advanced in years, she sold the two pictures again in order to provide a comfortable retirement for herself.[17] More than ten years later, the ninety-year-old committed suicide in her home in Kaneohe, Hawai, on 12 July 1980.[18]

Gustav Klimt and Friederike Beer-Monti at Weißenbach near Lake Atter, photograph 1916, Vienna, private collection

7   See Strobl, Vol. 3, p. 99; Nebehay, 1979, p. 284, fn. 11; and also Comini 1975.
8   Nebehay 1979a, note 14, p. 268.
9   Nebehay, note 56, fig. 143. Also Comini 1974, cf. above, p. 127.
10   Nebehay 1969, p. 436, who talks about a Korean vase.
11   Nebehay 1992, p. 218.
12   Marie-Angnes von Puttkamer, Max Oppenheimer–MOPP (1885–1954), thesis, University of Bonn 1994, p. 105.
13   Numerous letters from Max Oppenheimer to Beer-Monti from 1936–38 are in the archives of the Universität für angewandte Kunst, Vienna.
14   Novotny-Dobai No. 166.
15   Communication about the changed ownership in a letter from Stix to the Österreichische Galerie of 30 March 1933, see archives of the ÖG, entry 128/1933.
16   See archives of the ÖG, entry 31/1938.
17   The picture came to the Tel Aviv Museum of Art as part of the Mizne-Blumenthal donation. See Guralnik, Nehama, *The Mizne-Blumenthal Collection*, Tel Aviv, 1995, pp. 50–53.
18   Communication from Frau Aaron Shapiro, as quoted in Strobl, Vol. 3, p. 99. See also Nebehay 1992, p. 220.

Portrait of Ria Munk III

GUSTAV KLIMT

1917/18 (unfinished)

Oil on canvas, 180 x 90 cm
Unmarked
Linz, Neue Galerie der Stadt Linz
(Novotny-Dobai No. 209)

Ria, correctly Maria, Munk was born in Vienna on 6 November 1887.[1] She took her own life on 28 December 1911. The *Wiener Fremdenblatt* reported: "The twenty-four-year-old Marie(!) M., daughter of commercial counsellor Alexander M., put a bullet from a five-millimetre calibre revolver through the left side of her chest yesterday at noon in her apartment in Währing. The emergency service was called, but the inspecting doctor could only pronounce her dead."[2]

Arthur Schnitzler noted the tragic event in his diary, blaming an unhappy love for the writer Hanns Heinz Ewers (1871–1944) for the suicide.[3] Her bereaved parents came up with the idea of ordering a portrait of the deceased from Klimt.

The parents were Aranca and Alexander Munk who ran large-scale activities in the timber and firewood trade.[4] The Munk family's prominent social position also shows in Ria's last resting place, directly adjoining Theodor Herzl's in the cemetery of Vienna-Döbling.[5] Ria's mother Aranca, née Pulitzer, was a sister of Serena Lederer's, probably Klimt's most important patroness. Most believe that the latter established the contact with Klimt.[6] Yet, it has been overlooked that the Munk couple had already been painted by Klimt in 1888 for the interior view of the old Burgtheater.[7]

Alice Strobl has made a thorough examination of the complicated history of the posthumous Munk portrait, of which there are three known versions.[8] At first, Klimt created a half-length portrait showing the deceased surrounded by flowers on her deathbed.[9] Here, an allegorical meaning has been ascribed to the floral element, since Ria seems to be floating in a sea of flowers like Shakespeare's Ophelia.[10] Shortly afterwards, Klimt painted another portrait of Fräulein Munk, this time full length and standing.[11] Since the picture allegedly failed to meet the patrons' expectations Klimt altered it into *The danseuse*.[12] Klimt himself confirms the pains he took with the Munk portraits. As he complains in a card to Emilie Flöge of 28 February 1913, "(…) it's not coming along! Can't make it look like her." On 4th March of the same year, he once again talks about the slow process.[13]

A third version of the Munk portrait is the one that is now in the Neue Galerie Linz. Almost completed in the upper region and the face, it remains sketchy and unfinished in the garment and the lower third. The succulently shining splendour of flowers (peonies, chrysanthemums, bellflowers, tulips, carnations, cinerarias, and bottle gourds) with the Asian heron motif on the lower right is only remotely reminiscent of a deceased's last greeting. In Ria Munk's death, Klimt may also have seen the utmost fulfilment of love.

1   See entry in the register of births of the IKG Wien, communication of 28 September 1999.
2   *Fremdenblatt*, Wien, 29 December 1911. See also the post-mortem protocol No. 879/1911, WstLA.
3   Arthur Schnitzler, *Tagebuch 1909–1912*, Vienna, entry of 1 January and 14 January 1912, pp. 294 and 296.
4   Lehmann 1910. The residential address is Wien XVIII., 52 Sternwartestraße.
5   Cemetery of Döbling, group 11, grave No. 32.
6   Strobl, Vol. 3, p. 111, and Brandstätter 1992, p. 330.
7   Nos. 124 and 125 in the explanatory mirror for the heliogravure after Klimt's oil painting. See Historisches Museum, Vienna, Inv. No. 72.703/a and b. Serena Lederer there as No. 128.
8   Strobl, Vol. 3, pp. 111ff.
9   Novotny-Dobai No. 170, there erroneously dated "ca. 1910".
10 See esp. Strobl, Vol. 4, p. 187.
11 Novotny-Dobai No. 208, there erroneously dated "ca. 1916/18".
12 As quoted in Strobl, Vol. 4, p. 187.

Gustav Klimt
The danseuse, c. 1914/16
Oil on canvas, Private collection

Gustav Klimt
Ria Munk on her deathbed,
1912, Oil on canvas
Private collection

141

Portrait of Johanna Staude

GUSTAV KLIMT

1917/18

Oil on canvas, 70 x 50 cm
Unmarked
Vienna, Österreichische Galerie
Belvedere, Inv. No. 5551
(Novotny-Dobai No. 211)

Blouse with the Wiener-
Werkstätte cloth "Leaves",
Vienna, Private collection

Johanna Staude was born in Vienna on 16 February 1883.[1] At the time when Klimt painted her portrait, according to Lehmann's Viennese address book, the thirty-four-year-old was registered as a "language teacher" in Wien IV., 20 Viktorgasse. There, she lived with her mother, of the same name, whose profession was given as "wife of a civil servant".[2] Many years later, Johanna Staude moved to Wien VI., 2 Chwallergasse. In the 1950s, the address remains unchanged, but Frau Staude now calls herself a "painter".[3] The same profession is mentioned in the death certificate. It seems, however, that none of her works are extant. Furthermore, the death certificate states that Frau Staude was Roman-Catholic and widowed. On the back of an old photograph of the picture in the Österreichische Galerie Belvedere, she is referred to as "Johanna Staude-Widlicka, Vienna".

Johanna Staude was painted by Klimt as well as by Schiele.[4] She also was closely attached to the Wiener Werkstätte, a passion shared by many Klimt models. The jacket she is wearing in the Klimt portrait comes from there. The cloth can be easily identified: having been designed by Martha Alber and given the name "Leaves", Klimt reproduces it in his painting brilliantly, yet without any changes of his own. It is conceivable that Johanna Staude bought only the cloth and tailored the blouse herself.[5] The turquoise and violet fields contrast with the scarlet background, providing an additional colour contrast.

Unfortunately, there was no opportunity to interview Frau Staude who, in the picture, faces the observer with a fashionably short haircut. When Nebehay met her she was already too confused to give details about the picture's history.[6] Nevertheless, he relates the following anecdote: When asked by Frau Staude why he never completed her picture, especially the mouth, Klimt replied: "Because you wouldn't come to my studio any more."[7]

Johanna Staude died in an old people's home at 28 Graf Starhemberggasse, Wien IV., on 2 July 1967.[8] She had already sold her Klimt portrait to the Österreichische Galerie Belvedere in 1963.[9]

Gustav Klimt,
Study for the portrait of Johanna
Staude, 1917/18
Pencil, 500 x 325 mm
Vienna, Albertina,
Inv. No. 34.667
(Strobl No. 2723)

1   Communication Magistratsabteilung 61, registrar's office, city hall, Vienna. See also the declaration of death, registrar's office, Wien-Penzing, of 2 July 1967.
2   Lehmann 1918.
3   See acquisition dossier ÖG, entry 77/1963
4   The portrayed's report to the author, Strobl, Vol. 3, p. 132, and Frodl 1992, p. 60.
5   Völker 1984, p. 262.
6   Nebehay 1969, p. 436.
7   Exhib. cat., Zurich 1992, p. 184.
8   Declaration of death, registrar's office, Wien-Penzing of 2 July 1967.
9   Cf. note 3.

Female Portrait en face (unfinished)

GUSTAV KLIMT

1917/18
Oil on canvas, 67 x 56 cm
Unmarked
Linz, Neue Galerie der Stadt Linz
(Novotny-Dobai No. 212)

Gustav Klimt's death prevented him from completing the picture. Only the white-painted face, to which Klimt added cool blue tones while the red tones are still only hinted at, has been worked through. In this condition, the picture produces the effect of a drawing. The atmosphere is that of a passionless eroticism far removed from the dark and mettlesome quality of Klimt's earlier "femme-fatale" portraits.

The semi-circular headgear, close-fitting like a cap, has as yet only been formulated with a single brushstroke. Here again, nothing reminds us of the voluminous feather hats preferred by Klimt in his pictures around 1910. Yellow priming above the ears prepares for the rendering of the thick, wavy hair. The painter chose the face as the starting point of his working process while, for the time being, sketching the body only with a few strokes. The ornamental background would have been the last step. A completely different procedure was followed by Paul Cézanne who used to work on all parts of the picture at the same time in order to be able to control the picture's structure and balance at any moment.

Gustav Klimt, Female portrait in white, c. 1917/18
Oil on canvas, Vienna,
Österreichische Galerie Belvedere

Initially, Klimt had planned a representation in full length, as Stroble was able to show by means of the paper studies that are still in existence.[1] The great number of unfinished pictures in Klimt's studio in 1918 illustrates the painter's penchant for working on several pictures simultaneously. The Österreichische Galerie Belvedere's unfinished female portrait has also been part of the inheritance. It shows the subject bending deeply forwards, dividing the picture with respect to composition and colour.

1   See Strobl, Vol. 3, pp. 131f, and Vol. 4, p. 188.

Portrait of Amalie Zuckerkandl

1917/18 (unfinished)
Oil on canvas, 128 x 128 cm
Unmarked
Vienna, Österreichische Galerie
Belvedere, Inv. No. 7700
(Novotny-Dobai No. 213)

Gustav Klimt,
Study for the portrait of
Amalie Zuckerkandl, 1917/18
Pencil, 568 x 371 mm
Vienna, Historisches Museum der
Stadt Wien, Inv. No. 114.949
(Strobl No. 2482)

Amalie, correctly Miriam Amalie, Zuckerkandl was born to the playwright Sigmund Schlesinger on 1 August 1869. On 2 July 1895, she converted to Judaism, and a week later she married the surgeon and urologist Dr. Otto Zuckerkandl who later became university professor and head of the surgical department of the hospital of the Jewish communitiy.[1]

Amalie and Otto Zuckerkandl's close relationship with Gustav Klimt had been arranged by Amalie's sister-in-law Berta Zuckerkandl (1864–1945), the anatomist Emil Zuckerkandl's wife. Known as the "revolutionary privy councillor",[2] Berta Zuckerkandl also fought within the wealthy Zuckerkandl clan for active support for modern trends and the avant-garde.

The portrait of Amalie Zuckerkandl remained unfinished. The face and the décolletage are worked through while the arms and the garment are only sketched and the background just indicated. The subject is sitting upright facing the viewer, the easy chair disappears behind the wide-sweeping flower-trimmed garment and her scarf. The scarf constitutes a moment of casualness in the strong en-face structure, seemingly slipping from her shoulders.

Concerning the picture's history, Alice Strobl observed that there are two stylistically quite different groups of preliminary sketches. In the first group are those dating from 1914 when Klimt started work on the picture, having perhaps already received the order in 1913. During the First World War, however, Amalie Zuckerkandl followed her husband to Lvov where she served as a nurse in his hospital in 1915/16. Klimt seems to have continued on the project only after the Austrian loss of Lvov and the couple's return to Vienna.[3] On 5 November and 12 December 1917, the painter received payments of 2,000 crowns each.[4]

The fact that the picture remained unfinished symbolises the decline of Klimtian aesthetics and the world they arose in, which in its belief in an elite art ceased to exist after 1918. But it may also stand for the radical failure of Jewish assimilation. In 1942, the Nazis deported Amalie Zuckerkandl together with her younger daughter to Theresienstadt and presumably murdered them in the Belzec extermination camp.

1   See IKG Wien, proselyte protocol Ottakring 7/1895, and register of marriages, entry 618/16/1895. For Otto Zuckerkandl, see WStLA, biographical collection. Born in Györ (Hungary) on 28 December 1861, died in Vienna on 1 July 1921. The marriage was divorced in 1919.
2   Nebehay 1992, p. 211.
3   Communication from Hermine Müller-Hoffmann, Amalie's daughter, as quoted in Strobl, Vol. 3, p. 85. See also Brandstätter 1992, p. 334.
4   See list of income 1917 in Klimt's sketchbook, as quoted in Strobl, Vol. 3, p. 242.

Portrait and Pose. On the representational Image of the "Feminine" at the Fin de siècle

MONIKA PESSLER AND THOMAS TRUMMER

"We regard portrait painting basically as an historically closed whole."[1] The Swiss art historian, Jakob Burckhardt, began his 1885 lecture on the beginnings of the portrait with the claim that the genre had found its final consummation. According to Burckhardt, photography and its faster, mechanical procedure had taken the place of portrait painting. For precisely the haste of modern living did not leave any time for potential subjects to find time for portrait sittings.

The series of paintings by Manet via Whistler and Munch to Kokoschka and Schiele shown in the context of the Klimt exhibition starts roughly in that period which Burckhardt proclaimed to be the provisional end. Thus, strictly speaking, every single one of these paintings contradicts his judgement, for, of course, the portrait did not die with Burckhardt's dictum. At the turn of the century, it even experienced one of its most illustrious periods. Collectors, the general public and patrons continued to demand portraits. And yet, Burckhardt was not completely wrong when he said that the genre was about to be pushed aside—but, as can be seen, initially it was not pushed downwards to the edge of marginality, but upwards, into the light of outstanding exclusivity.

Art of the end of the nineteenth century accommodated the feminine in various representational spaces. The image of woman is, as we know, in the very first place, the image that men have of woman. And none of the paintings discussed in the following comes from the hand of a female artist. All of them represent a male view. Realism gave outward significance priority over inward significance. However, the conflicts of class and the working world are not to be encountered in this selection. Life full of friction on the street, class struggle and proletarian misery were held at a distance from the noble interiors of the salons and reception halls. "Animal" femininity is encountered in the allegories, a group of sensuously satiated paintings. Woman in this type which Klimt took up, say, in the water snakes or Judith, appears as a mythical role bearer, interwoven in the interstices between willing and being, between anxiety and domination. The allegorical woman belongs to the imaginary world; she is a metaphorical figure, but also interwoven with actual reality. Her latent richness of allusion and the psychic imponderables, however, can only be united with the image of the refined, educated woman with some difficulty. Mother, enigmatic sphinx, coquette, exotic purity and many other role clichés could be mentioned here. All of them can flow more or less into the image of woman, but they can also keep a low profile as intermediate tones.

Finally, there is the type of the elegant representational image of the "feminine". What the quality and special character of this type consist in becomes clearer most easily by investigating Klimt's female portraits for oneself. The paintings of Fritza Riedler (ill. p. 113), Margarethe Stonborough-Wittgenstein (ill. p. 107) and some other specimens demonstrate that Klimt was an extraordinary master in this art. Most of the works drawn on in the following by way of comparison can be attributed to this genre. The main character is the lady. She is of bourgeois origins, well-to-do and has refined tastes. In his study on the art of Edouard Manet, T. J. Clark spoke of the "femme honnête"[2].

Often handled as a commissioned work, a special feature of this type lies in the agreement between the artist on the one hand and the commissioning customer on the other. On the precondition that the painting is preceded by an agreement, it does not necessarily follow that form and style also have to end up conventional. Many of the portraits are even pioneering in their progressive casting of forms. Characteristic for the representational image of woman is its Apollonian, purified sphere and the magic of a casual air. Cultivated, slinky, slender body forms, occasionally calculating coolness or seclusion from the world are its defining features. It can scarcely be overlooked that erotic allusions are interwoven in the majestic pose of gesticulation and manner. The aloof dignity derived iconographically from the courtly portrait of the eighteenth century and earlier epochs is, in its sublimated form, closer to the libido of medieval courtly love that the feudal portrait. It is the courtesy which makes these portraits comparable with courtly song.[3] The commercial agreement, an incidental expression of the capitalist economic cycle, reinforced the unequal relationship which makes the model into a figure of adoration and the painter into an adorer. It is interesting that the apologetic homage to woman is maintained even when sociological or personal reasons might contradict it. In this case, an 'as if' takes the place of the social contract. Khnopff idolises his sister like a lover; Manet elevates courtesans to the status of 'femme honête' in order to make them worthy of portraiture in the sense of a representative image of woman. If, however, the painter risked consolidating the relationship in the private sphere and demand just wages for his artistic adoration, he had to be punished. Kokoschka loses his loved one, Alma, precisely because of his unbridled desire. In a similar way Gerstl is helpless against his own emotions. Klinger's companion, Elsa Asenjeff, appears as a sensuously enticing courtesan who not just coincidentally resembles the threatening Salome.

In general, however, the pictures give the sense of being secure and self-contained. With the soundless figurines it is a similar situation as with the foil that surrounds them. They absorb our attention rather than violently demanding it.[4] Decisive for this type is therefore the room. The room provides protection; in it, the nervous bustling of everyday life and its changing impulses recede. In the interior, nothing happens; a calm constancy of state prevails; the woman depicted is merely present. Things are not subjected to action; the world is self-sufficient in its mere existence. These are artistic constellations which reality does not provide in this form; they can be given reasons rather through symbolic ascriptions. In fact, the room is a place of male and economic control. In the order founded on social and gender relations, women are obliged to maintain domestic idleness. What can be seen are luxury, stillness and introverted contemplation. Only seldom do we encounter the extroverted 'version', understood literally as the turning of the body towards the viewer, such as in Manet's portrait of Nina de Callias. The presentation of the body or the indication of an invisible happening (as in Kees van Dongen's *Gitane*) actively stimulate the voyeur. The activity is founded, however, on mimic appeal and not on any sort of physical activity.

The portraits are representational because the woman portrayed stands for something other than herself.[5] She poses for the gaze. Sitting, standing, posture and gestures, the dialogue with the viewer and the surroundings as well as the often extravagant outward appearance are never accidental, but visibly arranged. Roland Barthes has pointed out (significantly, in connection with his thoughts on photography) that the posing body is formed already before the depiction.[6] This transformation, the arranging

1   Jacob Burckhardt, "Die Anfänge der neueren Porträtmalerei", in *Die Kunst der Betrachtung*, Henning Ritter (ed.), Cologne 1997, pp. 318–334, esp. p. 318.
2   T. J. Clark, *The Painting of Modern Life. Paris in the Art of Manet and his Followers*, Princeton 1984, pp. 109f.
3   The song of the Provence troubadours is supposedly a transference, "a striving of emotion for the withdrawing of absolute meaning". Kristeva, Julia, *Geschichten von der Liebe*, translated from the French by Dieter Hornig and Wolfram Bayer, Frankfurt/Main 1989, p. 270.
4   Cf. the concept coined by Michael Fried, first elaborated in "Absorption. A Master Theme in Eighteenth-Century French Painting and Criticism", in *Eighteenth-Century Studies 9* (Winter 1975/76), p. 139–177, and ibid. "Absorption and Theatricality. Painting and the Beholder in the Age of Diderot", in *Studies on Voltaire and the Eighteenth Century*, no. 154 (1976), pp. 753–777.
5   On artistic representation in general: W. J. Thomas Mitchell, "Representation", in Frank Letricchia and Thomas McLaughlin (eds.), *Critical Terms for Literary Study*, Cambridge 1990, on the connection between representation, theatre and the fine arts: Thomas Trummer, "Das Drama des Als-Ob. Einige Beobachtungen zum Verhältnis von Theater und Bildender Kunst seit der Moderne", in Grazer Kunstverein (ed.), *Mise en Scène. Theater und Kunst*, Graz 1998, pp. 19–40.

of the person, may be the expression of self or the other, but independently of this, the setting-up of the body is the sole and essential action in these paintings. Ultimately, this results in a threefold sense of the concept "setting-up": firstly as the set-up of design and shaped living space visible in the painting; secondly as the laying down of position and posture, and thirdly as the painter's compositional decision to frame what is seen in a visible pictorial arrangement on the canvas.

Precisely because the room is not a space of action, in the paintings of Sargent, Whistler, Khnopff, Hodler and other painters it becomes a powerfully significant presence. Although profoundly private, physical and psychic stirrings are arranged in it in such a way that they find a form suitable for their public appearance.[7] The "mise en scène" becomes a "mise en commun" through presentation, however with the important addition that the image maintains its inimitable originality and exclusiveness.[8] Particularly in Klimt's work, elitism is a basic characteristic trait. The room and the figure are contrived as in the service of an outward effect worthy of social status which confirms the social hierarchy. These paintings thus have to be called 'representative' in a second, wider sense, namely as showing prestige. The generalising gesture of the representations, however, was also a consequence of the pressure emanating from mass images. The more photography took everyday visuality into its gaze, the more the female portrait was called on to avoid contingency and arbitrary appearance. Apart from the potential of being other, the photo also included the interchangeability of person and image.[9] It was only a small step from the arbitrariness of the snapshot to a devaluation of what was portrayed.

By maintaining not only the surplus value of the (artistic) image, but also the prominent position of the person portrayed, the representational portrait withdrew from these equations. The form proffered in each instance is shown to be the unique and the best one among all those possible. The room is only really emptied by the expressionists Gerstl and Munch. Radicalised in this form and distorted to unrecognisability, the room becomes speechless and withdraws from any conventional symbolic interpretation. The figures are no longer at home, neither in this reality nor in any transcendent beyond. The consequence is deprivation and oppressive isolation. It is important to mention that this rupture with the old concept of the representative image is articulated above all through an urge towards the emancipation of artistic technique. Thus, it is not mechanical reproducibility (as Burckhardt thought) but the new, artistic will of the avant-garde to conceive the painting as a self-enclosed totality which marks the end of the will to imitation and, along with that, puts an end to the portrait genre that can be observed today.

6   Roland Barthes, *Die helle Kammer. Bemerkung zur Photographie*, translated from the French by Dietrich Leube, Frankfurt/Main 1985, p. 19, cf. also Kaja Silverman, "Dem Blickregime begegnen", in Christian Kravagna (ed.), *Privileg Blick. Kritik der visuellen Kultur*, Berlin 1997, pp. 4–64.

7   Wolfgang Kemp refers to Hannah Arendt's thoughts (*Vita Activa*, Stuttgart, 1960, S. 50) in the foreword to his book: *Die Räume der Maler. Zur Bilderzählung seit Giotto*, Munich 1996, p. 10; cf. also the study by Griselda Pollock on the impressionist representation of space by women artists: "Modernity and the spaces of femininity", in *Vision and Difference*, London/New York 1988, pp. 50–90.

8   For this reason, the "mise en commun" never corresponds to a "common attitude".

9   On the equating of woman and image cf. Silvia Eiblmayr, *Die Frau als Bild. Der weibliche Körper in der Kunst des 20. Jahrhunderts*, Berlin 1993.

Portrait of the Infanta Maria Teresa

DIEGO RODRÍGEZ
DE SILVA Y VELÁZQUEZ
(1599–1660)

1652/53

Oil on canvas
127 x 98.5 cm
Vienna,
Kunsthistorisches Museum
Gemäldegalerie, Inv. No. 353

The Kunsthistorisches Museum owes its famous collection of Velázquez portraits to the dynastic intermingling of the Spanish and Austrian line of the Habsburgs. In their structure, the portrayals of the infantas correspond to the traditional type. The format, the posture of those portrayed and the depiction of the ambient are tied to prestigious representation. The portrait of the infanta, Maria Teresa, was sent by her father, Philipp IV, to her uncle, Emperor Ferdinand III of Austria, on 22 February 1653. Further versions were sent to Brussels and Paris. The portrayed figure was a marionette in the finely balanced policy of royal marriage. Seven years later, she was married to the French Sun King, Louis XIV, her cousin.

The many sparkles of the ivory-coloured dress create an astonishing realist effect, while the composition as a whole is designed to achieve balance and a sculptural structure. The impression of a closed corporeality is produced by the solidity of the tightly waist-fitting dress; the gracefully raised arms emphasise the majestic quality of the figure resting within itself. Velázquez devoted himself to his task with unerring painterly economy. Whereas the brushstrokes are mimetically dense in the hair and the sleeves, the details of the skirt are only sketched. "One must not take any further individual stroke literally," wrote Heinrich Wölfflin in 1915.[1]

Klimt's interest in this painting becomes immediately apparent in a drawing made already in the 1880s in the course of decorative work for the Pelesch Castle in Romania. There, Klimt is at pains to transfer the painterly bravura of the painting into the medium of drawing. He tries to capture Velázquez's differentiated treatment of the surface by altering line thicknesses in the outlines. The "painterly" dimension, a category which Wölfflin worked out in his "Basic Concepts", is transferred to its counterpart, the dimension of "drawing". The sheet is thus neither a copy nor a sketch but a linear extract.

For the portrait of Fritza Riedler (ill. p. 113), Klimt recalled after two decades the infanta's extraordinary hairdo. The semi-circular outlines of the hair volume in Velázquez's painting returns as the richly adorned wall ornament in Klimt's work. The elegant embellishment is even perceived as autonomous, especially because the colourful glass stones, in an astounding puzzle effect, can be seen not only as part of the wall panelling but also as jewellery of the portrayed woman. "Portrayal and ornament coalesce into each other, and their separation by the understanding is a practical postulate that does not capture their essence."[2]

Gustav Klimt, Drawing from the portrait of the Infanta Maria Teresa by Velázquez
Vienna, Dr. Rudolf Leopold Collection (Strobl No. 3270)

1   Heinrich Wölfflin, *Kunstgeschichtliche Grundbegriffe. Das Problem der Stilentwicklung in der neueren Kunst*, Munich 1915, p. 48.
2   Julius von Schlosser, *Präludien. Vorträge und Aufsätze*, Berlin 1927, p. 224, cited after Werner Hofmann, "Das Fleisch erkennen", in Alfred Pfabigan (ed.), *Ornament und Askese. Im Zeitgeist des Wien der Jahrhundertwende*, p. 120–129, here p. 121.

Symphony in Flesh-colour and Pink: Portrait of Mrs. Frederick R. Leyland

JAMES ABBOT
MCNEILL WHISTLER
(1834–1903)

1872/73
Oil on canvas
195.9 x 102.2 cm
New York, Frick Collection

The American artist, James Abbot McNeill Whistler, is regarded as the most important representative of refined Victorian aestheticism and was one of the first representatives of Japonism in England. Whistler began the portrait of Mrs. Frederick Leyland in November 1871. At that time he was briefly engaged to be married to her. Mrs. Leyland wanted to be portrayed sitting in a black velvet dress. Whistler, however, preferred a luxurious morning dress made of cream-coloured gauze, which with its ruffled sleeves and the long, thin sash was modelled on courtly art of the eighteenth century and the taste of Antoine Watteau. The painting shows the portrayed subject standing in front of a wall in an unusual three-quarter view from the back. Mrs. Leyland's clearly sketched head is turned with a gentle inclination to the side. The dark, softened sfumato contours and the proximity to Japanese cherry blossoms emphasise the facial outline. Dignity and elegiac inspiration elevate the subject from the compulsions of lived reality. Dreamily lost in thought, her gaze drifts into vacuity.

In a preliminary drawing that was executed in pastel, Maud Franklin, the artist's lover, is wearing Mrs. Leyland's dress. Whistler chose this solution when the commissioning customer was not available. The colour, tone, texture and refinement were more important to him than the subject represented. In the title *Symphony in Flesh-colour and Pink*, too, Whistler lets us know programmatically that he is concerned with the mediation of the finest chromatic nuances. According to information from a pupil, he "used very flowing colour and even the most solid part of a picture such as the whites in linen, were sufficiently transparent for the ground underneath to show." "The paint," another pupil reports, "should not be applied thick. It should look like breath on the surface of a pane of glass".[1]

Through the veil of light, the interior forms into an unreal sphere. All linguistic means emphasise the melting and gradual flowing over into a mood untouched by purpose and reason. Beauty, weighed down by melancholy, becomes the reflection of poetry. Whistler interpreted his paintings by analogy to the means of expression in music and poetry. He entitled them "Symphonies", "Notes" or "Nocturnes", and his idea of the mutual interpenetration of the arts influenced fin de siècle Vienna.

1   Mortimer Menpes, *Whistler as I Knew Him*, London 1904, p. 72, and Otto H. Bacher, *With Whistler in Venice*, 2nd ed., New York 1908, p. 31.

155

Portrait of a Lady
with Red Plumed Hat

HANS MAKART
(1840–1884)

c. 1873
Oil on canvas
151 x 99.5 cm
Vienna, C. Bednarczyk

The lady with the red plumed hat steps out of the darkness of her surroundings. The precise use of light and the mute gesture follow the painter's planned dramaturgy which is presented in the painting as a fleeting moment. The gold-laced brocade shines in the light of its own colour. The velvety Bordeaux of the skirt, too, which resembles Titian's choice of colour, is impressive in its palpable appearance. Under the title 'Makart red', this characteristic chromatic tone is a well-known label to the present day.

When the native of Salzburg, Makart, was called to the court in Vienna, his influence was to leave its mark not only on the art but also the lifestyle of the *Gründerzeit*, the period when many industrial firms were founded. His Viennese studio, a strikingly staged display room, became the mid-point of social rendezvous and parties. Makart liked to give his accoutrements the flair of earlier centuries. Typical styles of the sixteenth and seventeenth centuries and fashionable accessories of these epochs were taken up by way of citation. Renaissance was doubly filtered: Thus, the magnificent plumed hat, the trademark of many of his presentations, had already been borrowed by Rembrandt from the Italian art of the Cinquecento. Apart from the multiple historical coding, the phenomenon of an emptying of meaning also arose. The attributes added to the painting such as the book and the rosary became decorative clichés used solely for the purpose of enhancing the painterly effect. To achieve chromatic effect, Gustav Klimt, too, put a small book in the hand of Sonja Knips in her portrait (ill. p. 85). Knips holds the artist's small sketch book as an already secularised motif.

Makart put his suggestive portraits at the service of the typical tendency of the times to mask reality. But his way of living too embodied the unstilled yearning for genius and glamour, a longing which he consciously cultivated. "He was stronger than the predominant lie and deceived it. He deceived the deception," wrote Hevesi, not without recognition.[1] The social contradictions of the variously broken life-worlds collided in two events on 5 April 1874. On this memorable day, the operetta, *Die Fledermaus*, by Johann Strauss had its premiere, where it was enthusiastically celebrated by the Viennese bourgeoisie, while at the same time, in the small town of Neudörfl in Burgenland, the Social Democratic Workers' Party held its first meeting.

1   Ludwig Hevesi, "Hans Makart und die Sezession (14 June 1900)", Hevesi 1906; cf. also Allan Janik, and Stephen Toulmin, *Wittgensteins Wien*, Munich/Vienna 1984, p. 122.

Lady with Fans (Nina de Callias)

EDOUARD MANET
(1832–1883)

1873/74
Oil on canvas
113 x 166 cm
Paris, Musée d'Orsay
R. F 2850

When Edouard Manet painted *Lady with Fans* in 1873, it was also a portrait of Anne Gaillard who was known to her contemporaries as Nina de Callias. Her husband, from whom she was separated, Héctor de Callias, was an art critic, author and editor of *Le Figaro*. Madame is wearing the costume of the Spanish Maja. She has a scarf wrapped around her right upper arm. Like a brisk maelstrom, the whitish grey tulle flows down her body. At first glance it is a peaceful and calculable painting. The model rests parallel to the frame on a soft sofa and supports her left arm on a pile of cushions, a motif which Manet had already employed in the famous *Olympia* of 1863. The greenish wall behind the reclining woman is decorated with fans and other Japanese ornaments. The outline of arm and head of the portrayed woman is repeated in the angular position of the leaves and stalks. The crane, 'le grue', familiar to everybody in its meaning as a symbol for courtesan, crops up again in another portrait of a Parisian courtesan. Nina too was a lady of the demi-monde, but was no less famous as poetess and muse. Many Bohemians and artists of the time frequented her salon, including the poets Charles Cros and Bazire, her lovers, and Manet perhaps also was one. She was friends with Mallarmé and Verlaine.

Edouard Manet, Nana, 1877,
Oil on canvas, 154 x 115 cm
Hamburger Kunsthalle

Nina surrounded herself with animals, jewellery and oriental goods. She studied philosophy and mathematics, learned fencing and had a teacher for the Cabbala and spiritism. Manet is able to very credibly depict that galant atmosphere of Bohemian intellectualism, seduction and provocative flair. It was precisely the bizarre and artistic atmosphere of the boudoir that stimulated him to present his mastery in portraying palpable materiality. The brush hatching on the sofa in all directions provides evidence, however, of a new interpretation of reality. Liberated from pure mimesis, these quick strokes are the result of a visual act emanating from the painterly dimension.

Nina puts herself on display provocatively—with an eccentric dress, powdered skin and deep red lipstick on her lips—apparently unimpressed by the fact that her attractiveness is about to wilt. The straightforward depiction of the empirical truth of living, however, did not prevent the painter from taking up with the reclining figure a well-known classical topos which, particularly in the form of the resting Venus, the oriental odalisque and his own *Olympia*, was very common in nineteenth-century France as a phenomenon of fashion.

Charlotte Wolter as Messalina

HANS MAKART
(1840–1884)

1875
Oil on canvas
143 x 227 cm
Vienna, Historisches
Museum der Stadt Wien
Inv. No. 16.803

Hans Makart, original costume:
Adelheid, 1879 (designed for
Charlotte Wolter)
Vienna, Österreichisches Thea-
termuseum, Inv. No. 0–2677

The portrait of the Hofburg actress, Charlotte Wolter, as Messalina, refers back to the play *Messalina and Arria* that premiered in Vienna in December 1874. The author, Adolf von Wilbrandt, created with this drama, which was successful in his own time, a literary counterpart to Hans Makart's historicist painterly inventions. In the tendency of bourgeois derivative theatre to up-date the historical subject, the stage presentation oriented itself frequently towards the works of historical painting. Conversely, the foundations of theatrical presentation—the character of the performance, the staging and the literary text—left their mark on the style of the fine arts. The synergistic effects of the historical crossover were also subject to criticism, however. Franz Dingelstedt, Wilbrandt's predecessor as director of the Burg Theatre, did not like the exaggerated fashion of reconstruction. "The poetry ... is misused to hang the motley gubbins of an industrial exhibition of cultural history on it. This procedure characterises the orientation of present-day theatre ... which places the decorative painter, the machine operator, the costume manager and the props man above the poet and the actor."[1]

Antonio Canova,
Paolina Bonaparte, 1808
Marble, Rome, Galleria Borghese

Charlotte Wolter presents herself majestically and delicately in a pose inspired by antiquity. For the sitting position and gesture, Makart took Antonio Canova and his sculpture, which imitates Roman antiquity, as a model. The self-assured, but frozen gesture is framed by a powerful column and an architectural prospect illuminated by torches which dramatise the scene. The high cypresses in front of a night sky recall the dark manner of Böcklin's landscapes. The eclectically composed forms of costume, architecture and laurel wreath are supposed to assure the unsurpassed artistic achievements of the ancient styles even in the present day. For Makart, the portrait of Wolter was therefore a universally valid symbol that celebrates with a bright aura a homage to eternity and beauty. Charlotte herself saw the work rather profanely and did not haveany illusions about her effect on the public on the occasion of a guest appearance in Germany, "All Berlin is running to see it because it is so indecent and I am so magnificent as Messalina".[2]

1   F. Dingelstedt, *Shakespeare's Historien*, Berlin 1867, p. 17, cited after Vana Greisenegger-Georgila, "Die Bühne als lebende Historienmalerei", in exhib. cat. *Der Traum vom Glück. Die Kunst des Historismus in Europa*, Hermann Filitz, (ed.), Künstlerhaus Wien, Akademie der Bildenden Künste, 1996/97, pp. 275–290, p. 278.
2   E. Niederle, *Charlotte Wolter. Leben, Werk und Briefe der großen Tragödin*, Berlin/Vienna/Leipzig 1948, p. 148.

Lady in a Fur Coat

EDOUARD MANET
(1832–1883)

c. 1880
Pastel on canvas
55.8 x 45.8 cm
Vienna, Österreichische
Galerie Belvedere
Inv. No. 3867

As a realist, Manet denied himself all forms of imaginative power which approach reality euphemistically or add invented elements. In striving to achieve a truthful image via the medium of painting, reality as it is found is grasped in its actual state. Manet's artistic intention is not based on a store of experience. The present impression is all that guides his painting hand.

Luminousness and a transparent density which leaves the ground of the painting unencumbered are the characteristic traits of pastel. Even the shadows are painted in colour to produce a greater luminosity. Spontaneity and a sketchy mode of working can be clearly detected, especially in the background. The floral decoration is indeterminate and not solidified in a form. To the left of the oval of the rounded face, the confused lines coalesce to become the legible depiction of a lilac flower.

Hevesi was enthusiastic about the relaxation of the gesture. He welcomed it as a diversion from the routine of the salons in which "several Viennese had also done their training" and "licked everything smooth" with "inflexible attitudes" and "prescribed 'ideal' motifs".[1]

The painting is in fact striking by virtue of its directness. The woman gathers the fur together underneath her breast, presumably pretending that she has been surprised by the viewer's gaze. She plays coquettishly with showing and hiding and with the fleetingness of the moment.

A "sociological" gaze allows Manet to choose those situations which can be described as ambivalent, precarious or insoluble. Manet painted transversely to social ascriptions; he portrayed bourgeois private life along with Bohemia and the demi-monde. His actors are never artificial figures but real, live people, often friends and acquaintances in their habitual surroundings. In the *Lady in a Fur Coat*, this social ambivalence can be sensed. Whether the unknown model belonged to the upper class and is toying with the erotic gesture of the mistress, or whether, as often occurs with Manet, she is representing a courtesan pretending to be a bourgeois lady, remains an open question.

1   Ludwig Hevesi, "Auguste Rodin in Wien (8 June 1902)", in Hevesi 1906, p. 395.

Portrait of Mathilde Stern, née Porges

ANTON ROMAKO
(1832–1889)

c. 1886

Oil on canvas
100 x 73 cm
Inscribed in the lower right:
"A. Romako"
Vienna, Österreichische
Galerie Belvedere
Inv. No. 3317

Romako's art of counterposing form-dissolving painting with accentuated drawing is strikingly visible in this portrait. The portrayal of Mathilde Stern, the wife of the Viennese neurologist, Prof. Samuel Stern, was also called *Lady in a Spanish Costume*[1]. The fine drawing of her face shown in a three-quarter view corresponds to the white highlighted lace on the dress and continues in the web of lines in the floral motifs of the background. The fine, graphic details form a striking contrast to the amorphous brown of the armchair in the lower third of the painting. The skewed strip of black dress mediates between these two poles, between a strictness of form and formlessness, between white highlighting and glaze, partaking of both modes of painterly design.

The upward gaze of the reclining woman which focuses off in the distance is infused with a melancholy trait. The hyper-realist formulation of the chased tendrils before the greyish-green wall of colour transposes the painting into something surreal. It is a paradox of Romako's art that precisely the univocal legibility sets an imagination into motion which is not related to empirical experience. Thus, the motif of the floral hedge in front of which the portrait appears is not to be read only literally. One would have to speak here of a "hidden symbolism" since the rich world of objects serves as a pretence for other, deeper meanings. The portrait grows through these "attributes" into a metaphor for general atmosphere and psychic attunement.

In contrast to Hans Makart, who elevated harmony and Dionysian beauty to the crucial point of art, Romako's work announces the contradictory spirit at the end of the century which was marked by social ruptures and a pluralism of styles in art. Viennese society did refuse to recognise Romako right up to his death in 1889, but in its critical reception by critics and artists, the oeuvre was given a re-evaluation. "Formlessness" was to crystallise in the European avant-garde into a category, just as the "fine sensibility" is to be regarded as a predecessor of the psychologising narrative style of Austrian modernity, in particular with respect to the work of Oskar Kokoschka.[2]

1   The present portrait is cited in the Œuvre Katalog Anton Romakos by Fritz Novotny as No. 352 "Dame in spanischem Kostüm (Frau Stern)". In *Der Maler Anton Romako. 1832–1989*, Vienna/Munich 1954.
2   Cf.: Yves Alain Bois/Rosalind E. Kraus, *Formless. A User's Guide*, Catalogue of an exhibition in the Centre Georges Pompidou, Paris from 22 May to 26 August 1996, New York 1997, and Fritz Novotny, *Der Maler Anton Romako. 1832–1889*, Vienna/Munich 1954, also exhib. cat. *Der Außenseiter Anton Romako 1832–1889. Ein Maler der Wiener Ringstraßenzeit*, Österreichische Galerie Belvedere, Vienna 1992.

Portrait of Marguerite Khnopff

FERNAND KHNOPFF
(1858–1921)

1887

Oil on canvas
96 x 74.5 cm
Signed on the upper left:
"FERNAND KHNOPFF"
Brussels,
Fondation Roi Baudouin,
Musées royaux des Beaux-Arts
de Belgique

A slender door-frame, the upper lintel of which is cut off, frames the young woman standing in the room. Marguerite Khnopff, the artist's sister, was his preferred model. With a kind of immanent optics, elements suggesting space and surfaces are harmonised with each other. The gentleness of the abstract structure is repeated in the chromatic concept. The white of the linen, the brightest colour in the painting, is blended in carefully into the only slightly darker colours of the background. Colours, symmetries, horizontal and vertical beams, proportions and the spatial layers designed for minimum depth follow an aesthetic of conscious harmonisation.

Khnopff himself viewed the portrait as particularly successful. He placed it in his "Blue Room", that room that was "especially set aside for dreaming"[1] and he even took the painting with him when he went travelling.

Although the composition is conceived as a strict frontal view, the figure turns away from the viewer. Marguerite's gaze glides beyond the boundaries of the scene and loses itself in happenings not visible to the viewer.

Khnopff interpreted the sitter as someone who is about to leave her everyday individuality. Like a medium in a trance, a super-sensible dimension seems to have taken hold of her thoughts. Khnopff wanted "to forget the everyday, the mundane in painting and called up deep feelings in his soul, the memory of the eternal" is how it was described in the December, 1898 issue of Ver Sacrum.[2] The gown with its high collar and the gloves clothe the figure like an armour. In this aloof appearance, ascetic sternness and idealised virtue are united. Khnopff's enigmatic iconography, enriched with medieval religiosity, met with intense interest in fin-de-siècle Vienna. The "high mystic from Brussels" paints "full of graceful insolubilities" which the Viennese public "strenuously try to interpret", wrote Hevesi.[3] Indeed, the majestic figure depicted that ideal-typical image of romantic withdrawal from the world and transfiguration which struck the nerve of the apocalyptic feeling at the fin de siècle.

1   Wolfram Waldschmidt, "Das Heim eines Symbolisten", in *Die Kunst, Angewandte Kunst* 15, 1906, p. 165.
2   From: *Ver Sacrum*, December 1898, "Der Argwohn", p. 3.
3   Ludwig Hevesi, "Fernand Khnopff Ausstellung der Secession", in Hevesi 1906, p. 30.

Portrait of Alice Sethe

THEO VAN RYSSELBERGHE
(1862–1926)

1888

Oil on canvas
195 x 98 cm
Signed and dated in the middle
to the left: "V.R. 1888"
Saint-Germain-en-Laye,
Musée Départemental de Prieuré,
Inv. No. 978.12.1

He wanted to work not so much empirically but scientifically, said Théo van Rysselberghe.[1] His concept envisaged that the evanescence of the impressionist image be replaced by a stricter and more precise form. Van Rysselberghe adopted the technique of allowing a jumble of patches to mix in the eye from Seurat and Signac.[2] A grid-like closedness in these paintings prevents the softening of material contour familiar from Monet and Pissarro. The loose weave of the pigments is tamed by the uniform, dabbed application.

The nineteen-year-old Alice Sethe steps directly in front of the viewer. The narrow portrait format underlines the slender figure. The elegant, lilac-coloured ball gown and the girl's alert mood give the painting a festive character. The carpet of dabs covering the entire painting gives rise to a bright, palely shimmering surface of great optical focus. In contrast to the older impressionism, the contourless contiguity of the pigments produces a clear, sometimes hard plasticity. In this painting, the lavish neo-baroque furniture is striking which through its massiveness makes the figure of the mademoiselle seem a little doll-like.

In a large wall-mirror, the back view of the girl, the neatly combed hair and the pale skin of her neck become visible for the viewer. If the representation obeyed the laws of optics, this view would only be possible if the mirror were mounted at an angle to the viewing axis. This cannot be concluded from the spatial composition of the painting, however. This situation is different in the portrait of a lady by Jean-Auguste-Dominique Ingres from 1845. which reveals a striking similarity in accessories and dress as well as in the precise drawing. Edouard Manet demonstrated in an exemplary way the manipulation of the mirror effect in *A Bar in the Folies-Bergère* from 1881–82. The perspectival logic is broken by the lateral displacement of the mirroring in order to consciously raise the viewer's involvement in the picture even more.

Pointillistically shortened brushstrokes can also be found in Klimt's works. Klimt valued the form-dissolving effect of the technique. In contrast to van Rysselberghe, he tended, however, towards gently flowing transitions which consciously preserve the materiality of the colours.[3]

Edouard Manet
A Bar in the Folies-Bergère,
1881–82, Oil on canvas,
94.21 x 125.94 cm
London, Courtauld Institute

Jean-Auguste-Dominique Ingres
La Comtesse d'Haussonville, 1845
Oil on canvas, 131.8 x 92 cm
New York, Frick Collection

1 Marie Saint-Clair (Mme Théo Van Rysselberghe), Galerie Privée, Paris 1947, p. 118.
2 Georges Seurats *Un dimanche à L'Ile de la Grande Jatte* (1884/85) gave van Rysselberghe the impulse to turn toward this new style. The famous painting was to be seen in 1903 together with works by the Belgian in the Secession. Cf. G. Tobias Natter: "Weltenstaub und wirbelnde Atome—Zur Rezeption des Pointillismus in Wien", in exhib. cat. *Farben des Lichts. Paul Signac und der Beginn der Moderne von Matisse bis Mondrian*, Erich Franz (ed.), Westfälisches Landesmuseum für Kunst und Kulturgeschichte Münster, Musée de Grenoble, Kunstsammlungen zu Weimar, 1996–1997, pp. 357–363.
3 These painterly traits can be seen in particular in the portrait of Marie Henneberg (ill. p. 94).

Portrait of Gertrude, Lady Agnew of Lochnaw

JOHN SINGER SARGENT
(1856–1925)

1892/93
Oil on canvas
127 x 101 cm
Inscribed in the lower left:
"John S. Sargent"
Edinburgh,
National Gallery of Scotland
Inv. No. NG 1656

Lady Agnew of Lochnaw, née Gertrude Vernon, married Andrew Lord Noel Agnew, who was fifteen years her senior, in 1889 . Two years later, her husband was given the title of baron. This may have inspired the decision to commission the portrait. Once the portrait was on view in the Royal Academy in the spring of 1893, it helped Sargent to achieve his breakthrough as an artist.

The young lady is leaning back in a rococo armchair. Fine facial traits, glassy, shimmering skin and the somewhat shaded, dark eyes give the impression of refined beauty, but also exhaustion. In fact, in view of the lady's poor state of health, Sargent had to finish the painting in only a few sittings. The precious satin, the airiness of the sleeves and the ribbon wrapped around the hips underline an appearance of romantic luxuriousness which the fashion cultivated in the feminine salon portrait. Sargent's special skill consists in the various degrees of painterly elaboration and the ingenious, refined colouration: light pink, turquoise and white blend harmoniously. While the face is finely shaped in detail, the gossamer-like ornamentation in the upholstery of the armchair is characterised by a much higher resolution. The pattern of lines, which is dense in some places and less dense in others, sets a contrast to the generous streams of colour in the drapery of the dress. The pale lilac of the sash produces a particularly fine contrast and enriches the chromatic gradations within the cool spectrum with a subtle tone.

As a member of the aristocratic upper class, Lord Lochnaw represented those benefactors and that social class who, in turning away from a historicising repertoire of forms and motifs, wanted more credibility from their lived world for self-presentation. On the other hand, the glamour of their own, well-to-do lifestyle was by all means to be shown. In order to secure the favour the commissioning aristocratic stratum with its ambivalent taste, Sargent chose an artistic arrangement camouflaged as a casual, spontaneous scene. Sargent took pains to situate himself within the great tradition of English portrait painting which, especially since Gainsborough and Reynolds, could look back on a rich and flourishing period. The heritage also flattered the customers who in this way could partake in the tradition of great portrait art. Thus, Malcolm Warner wrote, "John Singer Sargent's portraits flattered people that they were like aristocrats from the time of Velázquez and Van Dyck."[1]

1   Malcom Warner, "Signs of the Times", in exhib. cat. *The Victorians. British Painting 1837–1901*, Washington 1997, p. 31.

Portrait of Ragnhild Bäckström

EDVARD MUNCH
(1863–1944)

1894
Pastel on canvas
87 x 70 cm
Oslo, Nasjonalgalleriet
Inv. No. NG.M.02814

Berlin, January 1894: Ragnhild Bäckström sends Munch a message and asks him to visit her the next day in connection with the portrait. She also mentions on this occasion that her husband is pressing very strongly for the commission to be fulfilled.[1] Feminine traits and fragility characterise this portrait. Light, curly brown hair frames the pale physiognomy with sparse lines. The sensitive appearance is additionally enhanced by the soft, graphically veined pastel technique. The dress in dark green and rust-red encloses the anaemic-looking body. The puffed sleeves dissimulate form as if under the diffuse silhouette a solid body were keeping itself hidden. Symmetry and bulges freeze to give an enigmatic likeness which, through the position of the hands and the floral adornment around the throat, seems simultaneously staid, lyrical and mysterious.

In accordance with the sensibilities of the times, the timid, sensitive female type was ascribed an erotic air. Helge Bäckström saw a second "Eve" in the portrait of his wife. The lips slightly open, Ragnhild looks at the viewer from below half-closed eye-lids. In the oil portrait by Dagny Juel Przybyzewska, which was painted one year earlier, the eyes have been narrowed to thin slits. The figure of this full portrait, however, is on the whole more vibrant; the smile is formulated more freely than in Ragnhild's portrait. Mystical femininity is still captured in these paintings. This situation is different in the work *Madonna*, which was painted in 1894/95. As a pure allegory liberated from the duty of mirroring personal qualities, Munch now discovers woman as a symbol of sexual seduction, linked with the thoughts of destruction, suffering and death at the moment of conception.[2] Perhaps knowing about the artist's symbolist inventions in the same period and probably worried about his daughter's reputation, Ragnhild's father asked the painter not to show the portrait at the exhibitions planned for Oslo and Paris. Munch granted this request and withdrew the work. His contemporaries showed great interest in this portrait, however. Even Henrik Ibsen made enquiries about the painting's whereabouts when paying a visit to the exhibition.

Edvard Munch
Portrait of Dagny Juel (Przybyszewska), 1893, Oil on canvas,
148.5 x 99.5 cm
Oslo, Munch-museet

1   Cf. Arne Eggum, "1890–1895. Impresjonisme og Dekadanse", in exhib. cat. *Edvard Munch Portretter*, Arne Eggum, preface by Alf Boe, Munch-museet, Oslo 1994, p. 59.
2   Cf. Alf Boe, "Edward Munchs Werk", in Alf Boe, *Edward Munch*, translated from the English by Petra Hustede, Recklinghausen 1989, p. 21.

Gertrude Elizabeth Blood,
Lady Colin Campbell

GIOVANNI BOLDINI
(1842–1931)

c. 1897
Oil on canvas
182.2 x 117.5 cm
London,
National Portrait Gallery
NPG 1630

Grey, white and sparkling anthracite define this painting chromatically. Gertrude Elizabeth Blood, Lady Campbell, leans against the high back of a chaise-longue. The slender curve of the shaped timber has been painted with verve, as if in one stroke. The lady's appearance also seems dynamic and radiates self-assured elegance.

Before Giovanni Boldini moved to Paris in 1871, he had loosely belonged in Italy to the group of Macchiaioli, an anti-academic movement. The Macchiaioli applied paint in the form of patches and restricted themselves to a dark palette of browns and greys. In France, Boldini came across new sources of inspiration. He came into contact with Corot and also with the German, Adolph Menzel, and was fascinated by the alla prima painting of Frans Hals. At this time, Boldini began painting large-format portraits of society ladies. The special characteristic of these paintings lies in the compositional contrast of carefully illuminated faces against loose, scarcely defined surroundings. Boldini's social intercourse brought him into contact with other portrait painters, especially those from the circle of English art. He became friends with James Abbott McNeill Whistler and John Singer Sargent, whose *Madame X* (*Mme Pierre Gautreau*, 1884) was to profoundly influence his later works.

However, the sternness and emblematic quality of the likeness as Sargent presents it to us cannot be found in Boldini's painting of Lady Campbell. More than a decade later, the Italian discovered for himself in Paris a more liberal way of painting and a fresher dramaturgy. In the place of Sargent's silhouette he places a blossoming figure, made more appealing by folds that split like minerals and a gesture of agitated movement. Of the admired model, the twilight ground, the plain colouration and the erotic effect remain. The high illusory power of the pale, low-cut neckline which both painters mastered brilliantly led to comparisons with the marble surface of classicist sculptures.[1] Indeed, the strong contrast of light and dark is the quintessence of expression. This means that the viewer's eye only notices the yellow and pink blossoms on the breast after some time and pauses briefly at this colourful animation before it resumes following the greater compositional lines.

John Singer Sargent, Madame X (Mme Pierre Gautreau), 1883–84
Oil on canvas, 208.6 x 109.9 cm
New York, The Metropolitan Museum of Art. Arthur Hoppock Hearn Fund, 1916

1   "A statue of Canova transmitted into flesh and blood and bone", *New York Herald*, 30 March 1880, cited after exhib. cat. *John Singer Sargent*, Elaine Kilmurray and Richard Ormond (ed.), Tate Gallery, London 1998, p. 101.

Elsa Asenjeff

MAX KLINGER
(1857–1920)

c. 1900

Parisian marble with pigment
residues (main parts), inlaid
opals (eyes), Pyrenees' marble
(hair), polychrome marble of
unknown origin (gown)
Munich, Bayerische
Staatsgemäldesammlungen
Neue Pinakothek

"One highly interesting work of the master is ... a magnificent polychrome female bust with demonic allurements", proclaimed Ludwig Hevesi in January 1901.[1] The bust of Elsa Asenjeff was to be seen in a side-gallery of the Secession; the homage in the main gallery was to Rodin's *The Citizens of Calais*. A year later, when the XIVth Exposition of the Secession took place in honour of Max Klinger, his Beethoven sculpture occupied the main gallery. Throning in "timeless nakedness",[2] the composer embodied genius which was able to save humanity by means of art.

Elsa Asenjeff, who was descended from the Austrian upper middle class, was married to a Bulgarian diplomat. Living later in Leipzig, she assumed a leading role in the women's movement. She met Klinger in 1898 and lived with him for almost fifteen years. Together they created the large folder work, *Epithalamia* (*Wedding Song*), for which Asenjeff wrote the text. A study of Klinger's *Beethoven* was also written by her hand.[3] It is reported that the muse and poetess liked the role of shrew. Ostensibly, she shocked Frank Wedekind, the author of *Lulu*, one evening at a social event by threatening him with a dagger.[4] Meant half jokingly and half seriously, the attack confronted the writer, so to speak, with his own invention, the idea of a barbarically unleashed femme fatale.

Characteristic for the closeness to actual reality of the Klinger bust is the use of various kinds of marble. Denounced by the supporters of a classically pure image of antiquity, colourful Greek sculpture had become more and more credible since the eighties and not only in archaeological terms. Excavations and speeches by Gottfried Semper had stimulating effects. Klinger was concerned with regaining that colourful dimension of sculpture and also that rapturous heightening of the demonic element. "All this flesh is coloured tenderly, half human, and half ghostly."[5] The scopophilia and the fears of male, bourgeois society are provoked in equal measure. In fact, the sculpture reveals a thematic connection with Klinger's earlier *New Salome* from 1893. The mythification of his partner is thus intentional. In an ex-libris design Asenjeff assumes the triumphant pose of a huntress who has pushed to the ground the man who is at her mercy and who bears Klinger's features. The battle of the sexes and the erotic power of seduction also leave their mark on Klimt's preoccupation with the female portrait. His *Judith*, which was done only one year later, causes confusion in a similar way through the danger of sensuous enticement. In this milieu, Hevesi was even able to surmise a movement to grab a dagger below the right arm of the Asenjeff bust.[6]

Max Klinger
Ex libris for Elsa Asenjeff, 1894
Etching and engraving,
Kunsthalle Bremen, Kupferstich-
kabinett

Max Klinger
The new Salome, 1893
Marble, Leipzig, Museum der
Bildenden Künste

1   Ludwig Hevesi, "Die Ausstellung der Sezession (13 January
1901)", in Hevesi 1906, p. 299.
2   Alfred Lichtwark, "Max Klingers Beethoven", *Jahrbuch der bildenden Kunst*, 1903, p. 41.
3   Elsa Asenjeff, *Max Klingers
Beethoven. Eine kunsttechnische
Studie*, Leipzig 1902.
4   This was circulated by Kurt
Martens, *Schonungslose Lebens-
chronik 1870–1900*, Vienna 1921,
p. 212; cf. also Brigitte Schweitzer,
"Im Glanze seines Ruhmes ... Elsa
Asenjeff (1867–1941) im Zwielicht",
in Frauke Severit (ed.), *Das alles
war ich. Politikerinnen, Künstlerinnen, Exzentrikerinnen der
Wiener Moderne*, Vienna/Cologne/
Weimar 1998, pp. 163–201, esp.
p. 169.
5   Ludwig Hevesi, "Aus der
Sezession. Klinger (27 November
1900)", in Hevesi 1906, p. 310.
6   Ibid.

Portrait of the Fey Sisters

RICHARD GERSTL
(1883–1908)

1905
Oil on canvas
175 x 150 cm
Inscribed on the back:
"Richard Gerstl, IX,
Nußdorferstr. 35"
Vienna, Österreichische
Galerie Belvedere
Inv. No. 4430

Slightly displaced from the centre, the two female figures are shown in rigid frontality. Their bright, strange, incorporeal presence is enclosed by an undefined darkness; the gloomy ground of the painting isolates the two figures. Their sitting posture is disclosed only by following the common course of the contours. The painting does without any colourful invigoration; only the contrast between the greyish white and the dirty brownish-black determines the strangely fear-inducing appearance. Gerstl renounces layering depths and restricts himself to a confrontation without any transition. The ghostly, dotted eyes become the unforgettable focal point of the painting. The visionary aura recalls the ineluctable vis-à-vis which we are familiar with from Edvard Munch's paintings. Even though on closer inspection, small differences can be observed; hair-styles and pairs of eyes differ from each other, the physiognomic features of the women are blotted out by the painter. The hands remain hidden below the shawls, the noses and mouths are only hinted at schematically. Gerstl also desists from specifying the social status and origins, as was usual for a female portrait. The sisters are rather the projective surface for the artist's personal view. Gerstl, who is concerned with painful truth, forms them into a distorted image of his own vulnerable ego. It can scarcely be deciphered from the painting that at the time it was made, Pauline and Karoline Fey were only twenty-three and twenty-four years old, respectively, and thus at an age which they share with the painter.

Gerstl goes far beyond the representational conventions of the time in the unrestrained painterly language as well as in the treatment of the subject. The means to this end are non-conformity, refusal and shock. The decision in favour of plain art combines not only a harsh critique of the conciliatory style of the secession, but also the idea that art could be content with reproducing visible perception. In a narcissistic mirroring, the mask-like demons embody Gerstl's own world-view, marked by anxiety, alienation and the experience of suffering.

Portrait of Ellen Warburg

EDVARD MUNCH
(1863–1944)

1905

Oil on canvas
180 x 100 cm
Inscribed in the lower right:
"E. Munch 05"
Kunsthaus Zürich
Donation by Alfred Rütschi

Edvard Munch,
Mother and Daughter, 1897
Oil on canvas, 135 x 163 cm
Oslo, Nasjonalgalleriet

Edvard Munch very much welcomed the commission for the portrait of Ellen Warburg, since in the preceding months many commissions had been withdrawn. His increased consumption of alcohol and attacks of nervousness had impaired his ability to work. According to diary entries, the portrait was finished on 18 January 1905. Munch's notes also provide us with an insight into his state of mind, "Painted the young Miss Warburg in the morning. Daughter of the banker Warburg ... Beautiful, large, dark eyes. Calm, still picture. Hallucinations in the night."[1]

Ellen Warburg stands before the viewer like a column. The room hinted at by the horizontal division of the surface makes the figure appear to be in front of the pale-coloured wall. Warburg seems almost lost in the divided emptiness of the room. Her motionlessness which is played down a little through the eye contact with the viewer is far removed from the ennui of the century that had come to an end. Munch's more deeply fathoming epistemological interest breaks through the superficial aestheticism and reaches to the core of an existential questioning. "The penetration of the inexplicable into what is lying clearly in view," wrote Hevesi. "The beyond that lies behind all sensible worldliness."[2]

The frontally presented female figure with the mute, mournful gaze is a theme of many of Munch's works. The posture of the woman goes back to the 1892 portrait of Inger Munch. The artist reproduced his younger sister in a similar way with hands folded in front of her body and wearing a high-necked dress. In the double portrait *Mother and Daughter* from 1897, the full-figure portrait in a white dress is supplemented by the mute dialogue with the mother and nature. Here, too, Munch employs a soft enclosing line thus emphasising the figures' exposed nature.

A photograph shows Munch next to the portrait with the artist's insignia—palette and brush. The painter's pride was not shared by the owner. The mother of the woman portrayed, who had commissioned the work on the occasion of her daughter's marriage, later told the art dealer, Gustav Schiefler, that the painting of the portrait had given her joy, but its possession much less so.[3] After an exhibition at Paul Cassirer, the portrait thus reverted to Munch's possession.

Edvard Munch in front of the
portrait of Ellen Warburg, 1905

1   Cf. Arne Eggum, "1890–1895. Impresjonisme og Dekadanse", in exhib. cat. *Edvard Munch Portretter*, Arne Eggum, preface by Alf Boe, Munch-museet, Oslo 1994, p. 123.
2   Ludwig Hevesi, review of 26 March 1904, in Hevesi 1906.
3   Edvard Munch/Gustav Schiefler, *Briefwechsel*, Vol. 1, 1902–1904, Hamburg 1987, p. 106.

Half-portrait of a Lady
(Mathilde Schönberg?)

RICHARD GERSTL
(1883–1908)

Summer 1907
Oil on canvas
100 x 140 cm
Vienna, private collection

Since the summer of 1907 at the latest, Mathilde Schönberg and Richard Gerstl were having an affair. The year before, the young Richard Gerstl with his passion for music was able to gain admission to the circle around Arnold Schönberg. After finding out about the liaison, Schönberg gave his wife an ultimatum. Mathilde returned to her husband. The Schönberg circle also took sides against Gerstl who, now isolated, took his own life.

Gerstl's art is characterised by a radical form of image which expresses itself above all in the dissolution of the relations between things. The colour, driven by physical energy, spontaneous and partially out of control, becomes independent of its task of depicting objects. In the *Portrait of the Schönberg Family*, the maiming by the act of painting attains its climax. Coarse, almost smeared into itself, the chromatic material occupies the surface of the painting so that the persons portrayed are distorted almost to the point of unrecognisability. The gestural slide of the visible into wildness is accompanied by a clarification of the artist's sensibilities, but it also has consequences for the painting's expression. Things are not questioned for their factual nature but for their expression-enhancing value.

Richard Gerstl, Portrait of the
Schönberg Family, c. 1908
Oil on canvas, 88.8 x 109.7 cm
Vienna, Museum Moderner
Kunst Stiftung Ludwig Wien

In the present portrait (the comparison with other works suggests that the subject is Mathilde Schönberg), the pointillist dabs condense to form solid masses of colour. The dress and headgear are composed of a dense conglomerate of swarming, bluish-black dabs of colour, some of which are loosened from their structured position and penetrate into the free space. The same violent use of colour models the facial features. The wide-open eyes as a striking and legible detail in the painting penetrate the unsettled flickering. Like a magnetic force-field, the darkly vibrating figure seems to have absorbed into itself and with it the change, agitation and endangerment of human existence.

The Gypsy or the Curious One

KEES VAN DONGEN
(1877–1968)

c. 1910/11

Oil on canvas
55 x 46 cm
St. Tropez, L'Annonciade
Legs Grammont 1955
Inv. No. D 1955.1.6

In Kees van Dongen's life-affirming world-view, French fauvism provided an experience of colour marked by sensuality and harmony. Like Matisse, he also felt an inclination towards the Mediterranean feeling for life. The impressions which he absorbed in Spain differ, however, from those which Matisse portrayed. Van Dongen had less of a preference for green groves, seashores flooded in light, and foreign boudoirs. His principal theme was the representation of people, especially the faces and bodies of women.

Here we have a small, intimate painting. Cautiously, a girl looks out from behind a turquoise-coloured cupboard whose thick stripe of colour indicates a raw surface and thus spatial difference. The girl, called *La Gitane* (*The Gypsy*), is wearing a luminous-orange Spanish shawl around her shoulders. The coarse fringe and the lineament of the decoration indicate a date around 1910 when van Dongen began to refine the pure effect of vibrantly coloured surfaces with graphic accents. The two dark vertical lines work equally to structure the painting spatially and as a flat pattern.

The hesitant posture of the slightly tilted head causes the viewer to surmise that the girl wants to remain unseen, that, as the one observed by the viewer, she is observing something herself. The object or happenings in which she is interested remain out of sight of the viewer's eye. Thus we do not find out anything about the reason for her hesitation.

In the mythological scenes of Susanna and Bathseba, the observer is able to enjoy the view of the women. The girl in the present painting slips, so to speak, into the role of the "two old men" who are lying in wait for the bathing Susanna. In the painting, however, she is herself the object of desirous attention and thus also comparable with the role of Susanna. The one privileged most of all in this enticing play of showing and hiding and conflicting identities is the viewer. Undisturbed, the (male) gaze can satiate its own curiosity in the role of the eavesdropper. The viewer supplements what can be seen of her and projects his own voyeuristic yearnings. In this sense, the girl becomes not only an identification figure for the desiring gaze but also an object of desire.

In contrast to Klimt, who broke through taboos with his auto-erotic and homo-erotic drawings, van Dongen remains within the framework of admissible healthy mores. Aesthetically tamed, he restricts himself to the erotic effect of a suggestive illusion.

Madame Matisse in Manila Shawl
(The Spaniard)

HENRI MATISSE
(1869–1954)

1911

Oil on canvas
118 x 75.5 cm
Signed and dated
in the lower left:
"Henri Matisse 1911"
Rudolf Staechelin Family
Foundation, Basle
Fort Worth Kimbell Art Museum

Matisse spent the winter months of 1910/11 in Spain, mainly in Seville. After his return, he tried to review the impressions of the journey in Issy-les Moulineaux. His wife, Amélie, served him as model in various poses and costumes. The portrait resulting from these "stagings" does not follow the type of female portraits that represented social status. Here, Mme Matisse is presented rather as an extra in a folkloric performance. Twisted in a dance-like pose, she supports her hands on her hips. Matisse captures the moment of pause in the movement very credibly. The captivating flamenco rhythm pulsating up and down is evoked by the hint of a jolt-like gesture and the head is tilted with some tension. Already in 1909, Matisse had visualised something similar in the painting *The Dance* in which naked figures join to form a pulsating circle. The monochrome contiguity of primary and secondary colours from the group picture is replaced in the portrait of his wife by an animated interplay between jagged and rounded lines, plane chromatic surfaces and a colourful interior composition. "Composition is the art of arranging the various elements available to the artist for the expression of his feelings in a decorative way," remarked Matisse.[1]

Amélie has wrapped the fashionable souvenir from Manila, the shawl which gives the painting its name, around her body. The figure itself, with the exception of the face and neck, is left unformed. Its flat outline interposes itself before the blue wall and the red floor which meet each other in a perspectival diagonal. The abstract principle of the composition is counterposed, as in many other works, to the realistic principle of three-dimensionality.

Henri Matisse,
The Dance, 1909/10
Oil on canvas, 260 x 391 cm
St. Petersburg, Hermitage

The head and bust have a blue-and-white striped curtain as background. The effect of the image within an image preoccupied Matisse, who never wanted to leave the interaction of the rhythm of the surface and the limits of the image to chance. "Think of the hard lines of the chassis or the frame; they have an influence on your motif's lines."[2]

The balance of decoration and spatial reality is expressed in the work of Matisse, who had several stays in North Africa, also as a rival encounter between oriental and occidental aesthetics. Many special individual features of his painting were accordingly received with some astonishment: the purportedly defective working-out of anatomy, the refusal of nuanced colouration and the stark patches and surfaces. Precisely these properties, however, also found their admirers. Thus, a critic wrote in 1911 that the painting, despite all objections, was "un superbe morceau".[3]

1   Matisse, Henri, "Notizen eines Malers, 25 December 1908", in *La Grande Revue*, cited after Jack Flam (ed.), *Henri Matisse: 1869–1954*, New York/Cologne, 1994, p. 77.
2   Related by Pierre Dubreuil, cited after Yves Alain Bois, "Matisse and 'Arch-drawing'", in ibid., *Painting as Model*, Cambridge, Mass./London 1990, p. 24.
3   Georges Lecomte, "Salon des Indépendants", in *Le Matin*, 20 April 1911, cited after exhib. cat. *Henri Matisse 1904–1917*, Centre Georges Pompidou, Paris 1993, p. 474.

Portrait of Trude Engel

EGON SCHIELE
(1890–1918)

1911
Oil on canvas
100 x 100 cm
Linz, Neue Galerie der Stadt Linz

Before 1911, only family members and friends served as models for Schiele. Probably to relieve the financial strain, he accepted the commission to paint Trude Engel.

A uniform ochre-coloured background forms the base for the painting. Its lower edge is the basis of a triangle running upward to an acute angle which provides the figure with a background like a cape. The structure of the transparent, red material can be read as a reminiscence of the ornamental ordering of Klimt's portraiture. Even the square format is in harmony with the secessionist artistic intentions. In contrast to Klimt, from whose slavish dependency he freed himself in 1910, Schiele separates his models from their worldly surroundings. His art disempowers the beautiful illusion of Viennese linear aesthetics with a new understanding which interprets the body as a sign and the psyche as the driving force for the somatic element.

Two levels of reality interpenetrate each other. One of them is articulated bodily in the representation of head, body and limbs; the other level consists of a network of defined formal axes which formalise the outer appearance. Symmetry and tension define the close, spaceless composition. By bracketing with the surrounding space, Trude Engel is formed into a brittle, artificial figure. Her right hand on her hip, she looks at the viewer with big eyes. Individual strands of her untamed abundance of hair break through the strict compositional schema in an arabesque line. The fingers raised before her belly emphasise her corporeality. At the same time, red and yellow coloured lights dematerialise the body to a thin membrane. The glow symbolises aura and is perhaps also a playful hint which associates the name of the woman portrayed with her angelic appearance. In one of his rare statements, Schiele hinted that the luminous framing witnessed the "revelation" of a human. For Schiele, transfiguring coloured light was a means to allow the invisible radiation, the "astral light", to become visible. In a letter to Dr. Engel, Schiele wrote in congruity with this vitalist life philosophy: "The painting must give light from within itself; the bodies have their own light which they consume in living."[1]

1   Egon Schiele, letter to Dr. Engel, September 1912, cited after Alessandra Comini, *Egon Schiele's Portraits*, Berkeley/Los Angeles/London 1974, note 40, p. 232.

Portrait of Mrs Luther

LOVIS CORINTH
(1858–1925)

1911

Oil on canvas
115 x 86 cm
Inscribed in the upper left:
"Lovis Corinth–/1911 pinxit"
Hanover, Niedersächsisches
Landesmuseum

In contrast to the calligraphic Jugendstil, Lovis Corinth employed a spontaneous way of painting which brings the movement of the brush-holding hand into play. Sureness in the presentation, intensive expression and a fresh, sometimes powerful brushstroke are the hallmarks of his painting. The large-format portrait of Mrs Luther was commissioned by her husband, Hermann, who owned a trading company in Antwerp. The sugar exporter's letter to the artist makes it clear that Corinth was highly valued for the idiosyncratic features of his style and not for a will to imitate naturalistically. "I have the intention of having you do a portrait of my wife. I am guided solely by the wish to acquire from you an interesting art work which will then give me aesthetic satisfaction. Proceeding from this point of view, I allow your absolute freedom in the interpretation and execution. Do what you want and paint how you think best, but not in a banal way, but in your case there is no danger of that."[1] In fact, Corinth avoided aestheticising the reproduction by means of well-meaning dogma. Despite the closeness to reality, he remained tied to tradition in the motifs.[2] The balancing act which swings back and forth between academic conformity and provocation is typical for Corinth's oeuvre. Naturalism, as in the depiction of the hands, for instance, was to be harmonised with an unfettered way of painting.

The portrayed woman, who seems wooden in her need to show off her social status, is represented with a wide-brimmed plumed hat. Corinth uses the somewhat grotesque-looking accessory to bring his painterly self-assuredness into play. The violet swirls in the drawing seem spontaneous and fresh. In a letter of reply, Corinth himself described the extravagant dress of Mrs Luther as "capricious" which stimulated him to accept the commission.[3] Stately and with assured self-control, the lady presents herself as a member of the moneyed bourgeois nobility. It becomes unmistakable that her self-confidence does not come from a feminine ideal of beauty but is an outgrowth of etiquette and social status.

1   Thomas Corinth (ed.), *Lovis Corinth. Eine Dokumentation*, Tübingen 1979, p. 140.
2   Georg Bussmann, *Lovis Corinth: Carmencita. Malerei an der Kante*, Frankfurt/M. 1985, p. 35.
3   Cited after exhib. cat. *Lovis Corinth*, Peter-Klaus Schuster/Christoph Vitali/Barbara Butts (ed.), Haus der Kunst, Munich, and Nationalgalerie, Staatliche Museen zu Berlin, Munich/New York 1996, p. 184.

Portrait Gertrud Müller

FERDINAND HODLER
(1853–1918)

1911
Oil on canvas
175 x 132 cm
Solothurn, Kunstmuseum
Dübi-Müller Foundation

The collector, Gertrud Müller, and Ferdinand Hodler met for the first time in 1902. Another meeting seven years later in Geneva marked the beginning of a long friendship. The fact that Gertrud Müller finally possessed thirteen paintings by the artist is a visible expression of this friendship. The works include the portrait she commissioned from him which was done in 1911.

Gertrud is sitting, leaning back a little, on a red couch. It is a precarious posture situated between movement and motionlessness. The room is completely empty; the sand-coloured wall is lacking in any decoration. Only the floor is structured ornamentally by a pattern of red squares and short, blue stripes. The pink dress is an element that defines the painting. Hodler employs a bright, chalky palette and the colours create a crystalline effect. Like a broad, soft, swinging diagonal, the lustreless pink joins the lower left-hand corner with the upper right-hand corner of the painting. In stages, the waves of the body, which is emphasised by contours, lead the eye into the depths. A lilac shawl wrapped around the lower arm repeats analogously the curvature of the whole painting. Its violet verve responds chromatically to the pink where, interestingly, its hue changes at the point where it wraps around the greenish yellow skin of the lower arm. This balance of planimetry and perspective is made possible by the body's twisted position. An inner dialogue unfolds in which colour and form, surface and body start to communicate with each other.

Hodler was guided by the idea that the same spirit penetrates everything. A parallel order which is able to express itself artistically in symmetry and rhythm permeates humankind, nature and society unified in solidarity. Even in the feelings of the individual, idealised by beauty and exaltation, the sole, determining thought of pantheistic unity mediates. In following this thought, the even features refrain from any habitual contingency. Clear definition and peaceful, aesthetically pleasing lines preserve an iconic character removed from time. Ludwig Hevesi had already associated mosaics like those in Ravenna as possible models for Hodler's figural types.[1] The Byzantine art, which tends towards wall painting, experienced a renaissance in secessionist aesthetics, as in the Beethoven frieze.

The detail of the fingers on the right hand is worth mentioning. The somewhat parted index and middle fingers recall the bony phenotype as also used by Klimt, and later exaggerated by Schiele into a highly expressive element. The fact that the artists held each other in mutual high esteem is proven by one of Hodler's remarks. He said of Klimt, "I especially love his frescos; in them everything is still and flowing."[2]

1   Ludwig Hevesi, *Fremdenblatt*, 22 November 1901, cited after Jura Brüschweiler, "Ferdinand Hodler im Spiegel der Wiener Kunstkritik. Ein entscheidendes Kapitel in Hodlers Rezeptionsgeschichte", in exhib. cat. *Ferdinand Hodler und Wien, Katalog der 165. Wechselausstellung der Österreichischen Galerie Belvedere*, Vienna 1993, p. 39.
2   Ferdinand Hodler in an interview with Else Spiegel, 26 November 1904, published in *Wiener Feuilletons- und Notizen-Correspondenz.* Cited after *Ferdinand Hodler 1853–1918,* exhib. cat. Secession, Wien 1962/63, Vienna 1962, p. 23.

Portrait of Alma Mahler

OSKAR KOKOSCHKA
(1886–1980)

1912
Oil on canvas
62 x 56 cm
Tokyo, The National Museum
of Modern Art

Early in 1912, Kokoschka began a passionate relationship with Alma Mahler, who was seven years older than him. The liaison found expression in a series of paintings. The most important work of the series is the *Wind Bride*. In this double portrait, Alma cuddles up to the breast of her lover. The longing for sensuous union tempted the artist to elevate himself and his lover into a mythically religious dimension. In the midst of a turbulent nature, the couple find peace.

The portrait from Tokyo, which was begun in the same year on a journey together to Switzerland, shows us Alma Mahler as a bust portrait. Blue-eyed with reddish brown wavy hair, the girlish lover is idealised as a Madonna. The adoration which Oskar Kokoschka shows for Alma Mahler can be sensed in the lack of direct eye contact. The possessive artist who desires the model so greatly moderates his urge and remains at a distance like an admiring viewer.

Leonardo da Vinci,
Mona Lisa (Portrait of Lisa
del Giocondo), 1503–06
Oil on wood, 77 x 53 cm
Paris, Musée du Louvre

Oskar Kokoschka
The Wind Bride, 1913/14
Oil on canvas, 181 x 220 cm
Basle, Öffentliche Kunstsamm-
lungen Kunstmuseum

The bust and the relationship between the figure and its surroundings awaken the recollection of well-known portraits from the Italian renaissance. In particular, Leonardo da Vinci's *Mona Lisa* probably had a stimulating effect. The painting, which at that time was already the most famous painting in the world, had been stolen from the Louvre a year earlier and was thought lost until it cropped up again in 1914. The portrait of Alma must have been done under the impact of this event. Similarly to Leonardo's painting, we look across a river into an Alpine landscape and at a mountain range dissolving into the misty distance.

In *A Childhood Recollection of Leonardo da Vinci*, which was published in 1910, Sigmund Freud had interpreted the enigmatic smile of the *Mona Lisa* as a sign of repressed wishes and unconscious drives.[1] Freud had reached the conviction that for the painting Leonardo had reawakened the hidden memory of his mother's image. In a similar way, Kokoschka understood the image·of a person as the fixation of a state that never becomes completely clear in which magical thoughts, inklings and smouldering memories have their effects. "The state of the soul," he said in a lecture, is formed "bodily in the face ... as if it made use of the mother's eyes".[2]

In contrast to the artist who painted *La Gioconda*, employing dark tones and sfumato, Kokoschka regarded colour as a material. He allowed the pigments to have concrete and hardened effects, sometimes also pasty and cracked. The opaque build-up of painted layers results in a chalky, crystalline effect with iridescent brilliance reminiscent of frescos. The darkening and greying of the palette was only to return when the relationship found its unhappy end and the loss of tension transformed into hurt agitation.

1   Sigmund Freud, "Eine Kind-
heitserinnerung des Leonardo da
Vinci", in *Schriften zur Kunst und
Literatur*, Frankfurt/M. 1987,
p. 132ff.
2   Oskar Kokoschka, "Von der
Natur der Gesichte, Vortrag Wien,
Ingenieur- und Architekten-Verein,
26. 1. 1912", in *Das schriftliche
Werk*, 4 Vols, Heinz Spielmann
(ed.), Vol. 3: *Aufsätze, Vorträge,
Essays zur Kunst*, Hamburg 1975,
p. 9f.

MONIKA PESSLER, THOMAS TRUMMER

Portrait of Berta Zuckerkandl

ANTON KOLIG
(1886–1950)

1915
Oil on canvas
150 x 81 cm
Vienna, Historisches Museum
der Stadt Wien
Inv. No. 77.879

Berta Zuckerkandl, today the quintessence of the "salon lady" in Vienna at the turn of the century, was regarded by her contemporaries as the "Viennese Cassandra".[1] In her memoirs which were published posthumously in 1970, she describes the milieu of the intellectual circles with the words: "For many years I have been meeting here with friends ... trying to give solace, must, however, as a journalist with an all too strong temperament, also offend people now and again."[2] Zuckerkandl's multifaceted activities included pronounced political commitments. In the first years of the war she wrote pacifist articles; towards the end of the First World War she was even active as a secret diplomat. In 1938 she fled to Paris and from there on to Algeria. She was never to see Vienna again and died in exile at the age of 81 shortly after the end of the war.

Anton Kolig describes her at the age of fifty-one as a worldly wise and experienced woman. Her hands lying loosely in her lap and her head inclined a little to the side, she turns towards the viewer. The reflective gaze seems lost in thought, engaged introvertedly with memories. The portrayed woman's radiating presence is represented by a moving aureole of dense traces of colour, particularly around the head and shoulders. The armchair which is only hinted at with broad brushstrokes in green, encloses the permeable outline of the body like a frame. The background is formed by a dissolved chromatic space in a range from green through blue to bright ochre. "He put his model in the posture, the background, the clothes which he felt psychically and spiritually to be the colours and chromatic tensions corresponding to the model,"[3] reports one of Kolig's pupils. Dissonant surroundings and bright colours are a favourite means for him to attain the desired result.

When Kolig painted Zuckerkandl's portrait in 1915, the linearity of secessionism had been overcome by a younger generation of artists. Interestingly, Gustav Klimt never painted a portrait of Berta Zuckerkandl even though she had given her support to him and other protagonists of the Viennese modern school.

1   Olaf Herling, "Berta Zuckerkandl (1864–1945) oder die Kunst weiblicher Diplomatie", in Frauke Severit (ed.), *Das alles war ich. Politikerinnen, Künstlerinnen, Exzentrikerinnen der Wiener Moderne*, Vienna/Cologne/Weimar 1998, p. 53f.
2   Berta Zuckerkandl, *Österreich intim*, Vienna 1970, p. 186.
3   Rose Sommer-Leypold, "Gedanken über Anton Kolig", in exhib. cat. *Anton Kolig. 1886–1950. Das malerische Werk*, Neue Galerie am Landesmuseum Joanneum, Graz 1981, no page no.

Klimts Studies for the Portrait Paintings

MARIAN BISANZ-PRAKKEN

Those interested in examining the studies that Gustav Klimt executed in preparation for his large portrait paintings will find Alice Strobl's four-volume catalogue raisonné, which forms the main factual basis for this essay, an invaluable source of information.[1]

    The *Portrait of Sonja Knips* (ill. pp. 85 and 206/207) which was first shown at the Secession in the autumn of 1898, is widely regarded—because of its innovative approach, monumental size and square format—as the first truly modern portrait painting by this artist. In terms of draughtsmanship, too, it is of key importance, for it documents the first time that Klimt sought to capture his sitter as distinctively as possible in multiple preparatory studies. Although he had painted and drawn portraits of male and female sitters before this, hardly any studies for portrait paintings survive. One rare example is the previously unpublished drawing that is very probably a preliminary study for his 1894 *Portrait of Frau Heymann* (ill. p. 81).[2] Drawn in painstaking detail, this unbiased and objective portrayal with its white highlights bears the same facial traits as the painted version. The sophisticated handling of light, the contrasting effects and slightly upward-looking angle make the sitter appear more aloof and at the same time more sensual. Even so, this drawing cannot really be regarded as a forerunner of the studies of poses for the *Portrait of Sonja Knips*.

    Time and again, in these drawings, Klimt explores the outlines and the basic inner structure anew.[3] His line is fluid and brimming with vitality, and his main medium is thin black chalk, though he sometime uses blue crayon. This marks the beginning of the "inspired" line in Klimt's drawings, as manifested in the nude studies for his monumental *Philosophy* painting in parallel with the drawings for the Knips portrait. In the course of the work, Klimt maintains a balance between the overall form of the figure and chair in relation to the picture plane. Initially wavering between a horizontal landscape format and a vertical portrait format, he finally plumps for the square. Generally, the edge of the paper forms the frame for the planar structure, and Klimt only occasionally draws a frame with chalk. A distinctive aspect of most of the studies is the way the skirt and chair are cropped on the right. The result is strangely ambivalent. On the one hand, this presses the figure close to the edge of the picture, while on the other hand it acts as a barrier, creating a distance between the spectator and the sitter. This dialectical handling of proximity and distance is even more noticeable in the painting. In spite of the emphatic presence of the figure, the spatial disposition remains unclear. The face is focused with an almost photographic sharpness that contrasts starkly with the blurred outlines of the clothing.

    The method of having the figures overlapped by the picture frame can be traced to the Belgian symbolist Fernand Khnopff, who enjoyed enormous success at the first Secession exhibitions. The controlled and solemn gestures of Khnopff's irreal, hieratic figures and the interaction between various levels of reality had a considerable influence on Klimt. Together with the preparatory drawings, the *Portrait of Sonja Knips* conveys a sense of a "world beyond" that is perfectly in keeping with the early Secessionist ideology of the "world of the artist".[4]

Gustav Klimt, Study for the Portrait of Frau Heymann (?), c. 1894

1   Alice Strobl, Gustav Klimt, *Die Zeichnungen 1878–1903*, Vol. 1, Salzburg 1980; Vol. 2, 1904–1912, 1982; Vol. 3, 1912–1918, 1984; Vol. 4, 1978–1918 (Nachtrag), 1989; Albertina publications no. 15. Quoted in Strobl 1, 2, 3, 4. Given my collaboration on the dating of the drawings, the author entrusted me with further processing the Klimt drawings that have been found since the publication of Vol. 4. An addendum is planned. Recent publications on Gustav Klimt's portrait paintings include Christian Brandstätter, "Schöne jüdische Jour-Damen" in exhib. cat. *Sehnsucht nach Glück—Klimt, Kokoschka, Schiele*, Frankfurt/M., Schirn Kunsthalle 1995, pp. 325–328.
2   Black chalk highlighted in white, 43 x 28 cm. Reproduced by courtesy of St. Etienne gallery, New York.
3   Strobl, Vol. 1, Nos. 409–426
4   On the influence of Fernand Khnopff on Gustav Klimt, see

From this first "modern" portrait of the early Secession years, Klimt's path to become the celebrated portraitist of women belonging to the circle of wealthy friends and patrons of the Viennese avant-garde took its course. His practice of drawing studies for his commissioned portraits differed enormously from his extremely casual approach to work with his models. His ability to achieve such exhilarating results in his drawings in spite of the distance from the sitter was due primarily to his portrayal of clothing—a field in which he was able to free himself from the constraints of external discipline. The dialectics of body language and gestures on the one hand, and the vitality of the clothing on the other hand thus became the hallmark of his portraiture. Klimt's women posed in a variety of robes and costumes, almost invariably at the very height of fashion.

Following his *Portrait of Sonja Knips*, Klimt took a decisive step in his drawings for the 1899 *Portrait of Serena Lederer* (ill. p. 89).[5] For the first time, a standing figure takes up the entire length of an empty picture plane, borne by the vertical, undulating lines of the pleated dress. The sweeping curve of fine pleating on the lower right that forms such an important aspect of the pervasive rhythm of the line would appear to have been achieved by draping the fabric of the skirt over some squat object.[6] The overall effect of the finished drawing is a far cry indeed from this distinctly "earth-bound" solution. The feet remain out of sight and the top of the head is slightly cropped by the edge of the paper, lending the impression of a figure floating past. This metaphysical sense of infinite motion corresponds to the simultaneous work for the faculty picture *Philosophy* (1900), Klimt's first monumental allegory in the spirit of modernism. In it he arrived at his solution of presenting the great chain of being as a vertical progression through the cosmos, symbolising the eternal cycle of becoming, being and passing away. The impression of progress is not conveyed by human activity, but by the overall contours of the vertically aligned figures which are rhythmically swept by a meandering flow of dark, veil-like lines. These parallel linear structures, inspired by the motifs of the Dutch symbolist Jan Toorop, also play a dominant role in the *Portrait of Serena Lederer*.[7] In the painting, the fine folds of the loosely draped white dress billow forwards like a wave, making the figure, already partly dissolved in the surrounding white, seem even more ethereal.

In some aspects of his drawings (ill. p. 208) for the 1901 *Portrait of Marie Henneberg* (1901; ill. p. 94) notably in the sweeping lines and areas of hatching, Klimt does not strays far from his Knips study.[8] In the summer of the same year, initial preparations began for the 'Beethoven exhibition', a project in which twenty-one Secession artists collaborated to create an aesthetic environment with Max Klinger's recently completed statue of Beethoven as its focal point. In accordance with the maxim of taking the architecture and the alignment of rooms into account, Klimt created a work that addressed, on three walls, the symbolism of man's redemption through art, with specific reference to Beethoven's Ninth Symphony. His *Beethoven frieze*, as it is known, was completed in 1902, with clear figure outlines, decorative contrasts and distinctly delineated, geometrically ornamented areas. These same characteristics can be found in the 1902 portrait of his partner Emilie Flöge (ill. p. 101), for which there is no known preparatory drawing. This portrait is a far remove from the earlier portraits of Sonja Knips and Serena Lederer. It clearly reveals the transformation from the "atmospheric" to the "monumental" that had emerged in every field of art in Viennese circles and, indeed, throughout

Fernand Khnopff, Solitude, 1890–91. Pastel and lacquer on canvas, 150 x 43 cm. Private collection

Gustav Klimt, Study for the Portrait of Serena Lederer, 1899

the German-speaking world from 1900 onwards. The Dutch artist Jan Toorop, the Belgian George Minne, the Swiss Ferdinand Hodler and the circle associated with the Glaswegian Charles Rennie Mackintosh were celebrated.[9] To what extent did these fundamental changes affect Klimt's drawing and, most especially, the studies for his portraits?

On the face of it, little changed. His primary medium was, as ever, thin black chalk. He still drew on sheets of packing paper. Nevertheless, the 1903 studies (ill. p. 208) for his *Portrait of Hermine Gallia* (ill. p. 104) and *Portrait of Adele Bloch-Bauer I* are to be regarded as important stages in his development as a draughtsman. What had emerged so tentatively in his studies of Sonja Knips and Serena Lederer had by now became a clear maxim: the edges of the paper had become a determining factor in the dynamism of the planar structure. In the drawings for the Gallia portrait, Klimt sought to achieve an ideal synthesis between the individual character of the sitter and her position in the overall geometry of the work. In some works, the main lines of the standing figure, portrayed in profile, describe a triangle, with a strictly vertical front line and a stylised slant formed by the sweeping outline of the coat at the back. This triangular structure creates an exciting negative-positive dialogue between the mutually interactive areas of the composition.

Gustav Klimt, Study for the
Portrait of Adele Bloch-Bauer,
1903/04

Marian Bisanz-Prakken, "Khnopff, Toorop, Minne und die Wiener Moderne" in exhib. cat. *Sehnsucht nach Glück—Klimt, Kokoschka, Schiele*, Frankfurt/M., Schirn Kunsthalle 1995, pp. 172–178. See also Edwin Becker, "The soul of things, Alma-Tadema and Symbolism", in exhib. cat. *Sir Lawrence Alma-Tadema*, Amsterdam, Rijksmuseum 1996/1997; Liverpool 1997, pp. 79–88. On the subject of the "world of the artist" see exhib. cat. *Heiliger Frühling, Gustav Klimt und die Anfänge der Wiener Secession*, Vienna, Albertina 1989/99, edited by Marian Bisanz-Prakken, pp. 16, 17.
5   Strobl, Vol. 1, No. 442–454; Strobl, Vol. 4, Nos. 3325, 3325a
6   Particularly evident in Strobl, Vol.1, No. 442 and Nos. 452–454.
7   On the influence of Jan Toorop on the *Philosophy* painting see Marian Bisanz-Prakken, "Gustav Klimt und die Stilkunst Jan Toorops", in *Mitteilungen der Österreichischen Galerie* 22/23, 1978/79, 66/67, Klimt-Studien, pp. 155–162.

Klimt skilfully applied these new principles in his Bloch-Bauer studies, which rank among the finest of all his drawings, revealing as they do the very quintessence of his artistic intentions.[11] With unprecedented levity, the artist accepts the constraints dictated by the limitations of the paper. The starting point of the compositional structure in almost all the Bloch-Bauer drawings is the point at which the forehead is cropped by the upper edge of the paper. In the actual face, certain parts are deliberately omitted or rendered only sketchily. The stylised, triangular mouth is strongly emphasised and is in itself an easily recognised trait and focal point of all the Bloch-Bauer studies.

A typical feature of almost all the drawings in which the model is seated is the way the loosely-draped, pleated robes spread out in waves from the shoulders across the picture plane, so that they are sometimes even cropped by the edge of the paper. The example shown here demonstrates the principle of parallel, overlapping, distinctly delineated layers of space, with the soft, flowing lines cleverly offset against angular geometric elements. In this complex of mutual dependence and dynamic tension, the negative space also plays an active role. This, in turn, is defined within by the outlines of the main form and externally by the edges of the paper.

It might be said that Klimt's figural studies, especially those created since the Bloch-Bauer drawings, took on an "environmental" aesthetic in parallel with his painting. The avant-garde art critics of the period used the term *Raumkunst* to describe this approach in which architecturally-oriented wall painting triumphs over the autonomous illusionist framed painting—most notably in the case of the 1902 *Beethoven frieze* and the 1903 faculty painting of *Jurisprudence*. The *Raumkunst* aspect of the Bloch-Bauer drawings goes hand in hand with a new quality of line. The chalk quite literally draws a fine line between individual characterisation and subjective impression on the one hand, and the higher laws of the overall context on the other hand. Klimt's faith in the notion of the gesamtkunstwerk and, in a broader sense, his belief in the relationship between art and life, protected him from the pitfall of indulging in the anecdotal and the trite. At the same time, his distinct awareness of sensual values meant he stopped short of lifeless universality and sweeping generalisations. This combination of sensibility and sublimating energy informs the lines of the Bloch-Bauer drawings. It is the line itself, beyond all figurative portrayal, that conveys sensuality and transcendence at one and the same time. The fine line mentioned above seems to have been an almost effortless process guided by sound intuition, yet requiring an enormous degree of concentration. Klimt appears to have fully absorbed the polarity of linear freedom and formal discipline that was to shape his drawings in future. The painting was not completed until 1907. The lyrical serenity of the drawings, in which it may be assumed that the personal charisma of the sitter played an important role, has given way to the dominance of gold and silver ornament. The sense of "other-worldliness" imbued in these drawings through the intoxicating power of the lines is heightened in the monumental painting to the point of the ineffably sacred.

Jan Toorop, Dolce, 1896, lithograph, 56,9 x 43 cm (Blatt), Rijksprenten-Kabinett, Amsterdam

The studies for the *Portrait of Adele Bloch-Bauer*, a point of crystallisation in the development of Gustav Klimt's draughtsmanship, are early works situated at the beginning of his golden period in painting. The melodic rhythm of undulating lines pays homage one last time to the sweeping curves of the early Secession period, while the geometric ornamentation of the furnishings (the Wiener Werkstätte was founded in 1903) is an indication of future developments. A synthesis of three major influences accompanied his experimentation.

As in Klimt's earliest symbolist phase, Fernand Khnopff was an important influence in his frontal portrayal of the seated figure as well as in the symbolically charged fragmentation of the forehead. The transcendence of the parallel linear structures, like the slender stylisation of body forms and angular poses, are borrowed from Jan Toorop, who was particularly important to Klimt in the period around 1903.[12] The angular, bony shoulders and the fragile geometry of the arms and hands recall the work of the sculptor George Minne, whose figures of youths had been so admired since 1900 in the Secession and the Wiener Werkstätte.[13] The influence of Minne is particularly evident in Klimt's allegorical figural compositions (e. g., the *Beethoven frieze*, *Jurisprudence*, *The Three Ages*, *Hope I* and *Hope II*, *The Kiss* and others).

In the monumental portraits from the early phase of his golden period—*Margaret Stonborough-Wittgenstein* (1905, ill. p. 109) and *Fritza Riedler* (1906, ill. p. 113)—the women in question are portrayed against a flat backdrop of large and small geometric forms. The compositions appear like a fragment from a larger tectonic context, in the spirit of *Raumkunst*. The technique employed—black chalk on packing paper—suggests that the studies for the *Portrait of Fritza Riedler* (ill. pp. 210/211) were created no later than 1904.[14] In these studies, the tendency towards monumentality is manifest in the calmly structuring alignment of the separate island-like particles of the clothing and the face and hands. The majestic aloofness of the seated figure—in the ornamentation around the head the painting echoes Velázquez' painting of the *Infanta Maria Teresa* (ill. p. 153)—is particularly effective because of the straight pose.[15]

Deliberately leaving some areas blank heightens the effect. This is particulary the case in one drawing in which the arm of the chair on the right is treated as a nega-

8   Strobl, Vol. 1, Nos. 732–740; Strobl, Vol. 4, Nos. 3442, 3443.
9   The changes around 1900 in connection with a new orientation towards international art were first addressed in the exhib. cat. *Heiliger Frühling*.
10   The studies for Hermine Gallia: Strobl, Vol. 1, Nos. 1017–1053; Strobl, Vol. 4, Nos. 3516–3519a. The studies for Adele Bloch-Bauer I: Strobl, Vol. 1, Nos. 1054–1151; Strobl, Vol. 4, Nos. 3520–3536.
11   Strobl, Vol. 1, No. 1138. Black chalk, 45,8 x 31 cm. Until 1999 in the Albertina, since then returned to the possession of the Bloch-Bauer family.
12   See Bisanz-Prakken 1978/79, pp. 198–205.
13   On the importance of George Minne for Viennese art around 1900 see Bisanz-Prakken 1995. At the show in the Wiener Werkstätte (1907) the *Portrait of Adele Bloch-Bauer I* was flanked by two kneeling youths by George Minne in Mannheim (illustrated in *Deutsche Kunst und Dekoration XX*, 1907, p. 331). Exhib. cat. *Sehnsucht nach Glück—Klimt, Kokoschka, Schiele*, Frankfurt/M., Schirn Kunsthalle 1995, pp. 172–178.

tive space and the eye contact between the sitter and the spectator is reduced to one eye, while the other half of the face is left empty.[16] This single detail reveals the full force of the dichotomy between the vitality of the moment and the claim to universality. Although Klimt was interested primarily in working out the pose and clothing of his sitters in the drawings, he often gave a glimpse of certain physiognomic traits or facial expressions in a few laconic strokes.

The studies for the *Portrait of Margaret Stonborough-Wittgenstein* (ill. p. 209) were created slightly later, in 1904–1905.[17] By this time, Klimt was already using Japanese woodcut paper on which he drew alternately in pencil, thin black chalk and red or green crayon. The shimmering overall effect of these drawings corresponds to the sheen of the gold and silver in the paintings he was producing at the same time. In slender, delicate lines, Klimt explores the essence of the transparent, variously patterned fabrics of the dresses in which the young woman posed. The delicate outlines of the standing figure and the immaterial character of the clothing seem to correspond perfectly with the spirituality of this woman from a famous and cultivated family. Unusually for Klimt, this particular portrait reveals painstaking attention to detail in the rendering of the distinctive and dark facial features, further accentuated by the contrasting thin fabric. In these drawings, the cut created by the edge of the paper along the forehead is all the more noticeable. Whereas, in the drawings, the sitter's gaze is directed at the spectator, it looks beyond the observer in the final painting. This in itself is an unusual approach for Klimt to take. Not only the detached gaze and the expression of majesty are reminiscent of Fernand Khnopff's painting of *Marguérite* (ill. p. 166). They also have in common the stringent fixing of the white-clad figures in the geometric structure of their surroundings, cropped by the lower edge of the picture. This is a formula that Klimt had already previously adopted from Khnopff. In this context, it is interesting to note that, in the earliest studies, the sitter is actually wearing a high-collared dress in the manner of the Khnopff figure.[18]

Where the major portrait commissions are concerned—with the exception of the 1907 Bloch-Bauer portrait begun in 1903—the turbulent years between 1906 and 1910–11 mark an important caesura. It was during this period that Klimt created the main works of his golden period, which he abandoned after visiting Paris in 1910. The portraits of women from the last years of his life reflect a French-inspired palette and brushwork. The all-over background patterns and the clothing of the sitters are often intensively interrelated. It is in these two areas that the life of the painting lies, while the faces and poses of the women remain remarkably passive. Here, too, as in the earlier portraits, we find different levels of reality, albeit with varying stylistic approaches.

Apart from some small compositional sketches, the question of the background plays no role in the studies for the late portraits. As before, Klimt continues to explore different aspects of the individual figure and its relationship to the plane. Right up to the end, the interfaces created by the edges of the paper at top and bottom convey the symbolism of the transitory. What has changed above all in comparison to the earlier drawings is the vibrant and often interrupted movement of the line that creates new vehicles of expression as well as new dimensions of space and light.

In the 1910–11 studies (ill. p. 212/213) for the *Portrait of Adele Bloch-Bauer II*, completed in 1912, Klimt took recourse to the group of standing figures which had been created in 1903–04 for the *Bloch Bauer I* portrait, and inspired by the figure of the

George Minne, Kneeling Youth, 1898/1900, marble, height 83 cm, Österreichische Galerie, Vienna

14 Strobl, Vol. 2, Nos. 1226–1246; Strobl, Vol. 4, Nos. 3542– 3543b.
15 On the influence of Velázquez see Strobl, Vol. 2, pp. 27, 28.
16 Strobl, Vol. 2, No. 1237.
17 Strobl, Vol. 2, Nos. 1247–1274; Strobl, Vol. 4, Nos. 3545, 3546, Thomas Zaunschirm, *Gustav Klimt. Margarete Stonborough-Wittgenstein. Ein österreichisches Schicksal*, Frankfurt/M. 1987.
18 Strobl, Vol. 2, Nos. 1247–1251 (standing); Strobl, Vol. 4, No. 3545.
19 Strobl, Vol. 2, Nos. 1101–1115; Strobl, Vol. 4, Nos. 3528–3530. Illustration: Strobl 115; black chalk, 44,7 x 31,2 cm. Until 1999 in the Albertina, now returned to the possession of the Bloch-Bauer family.

Empress Theodora in the mosaics of S. Vitale in Ravenna.[19] Here we clearly see the difference between the taut sweep of the lines and the confident expression in the earlier studies and the nervous, hesitant sketchiness of the later Bloch-Bauer studies, in which the passively dangling arms suggest a mood of resignation. The sensual aura of the drawings for *Adele Bloch Bauer I* with the strong focus on the mouth has given way to a tentatively suggested physiognomy in which the figure of *Adele Bloch-Bauer II* is concealed beneath several layers. Klimt dedicates all his energy as a draughtsman to these layers, using a number of different techniques to characterise the diversity of the distinctly delineated fabrics which he illuminates in various ways.

The drawings created in 1911 (ill. p. 214) for the 1912 *Portrait of Paula Zuckerkandl* (whereabouts unknown) also possess a positive and confident aura.[20] The nervous sketchiness of the Bloch-Bauer studies gives way here to a more fluid and calmly structuring draughtsmanship that seems better suited to the impression of calm conveyed by the sitter.

The drawings for the portraits of mother and daughter *Eugenia* (ill. pp. 129 and 215) and *Mäda* (ill. pp. 127 and 216/217) *Primavesi* completed in 1913–14 and 1913 respectively were begun in 1912.[21] The studies for the girl's portrait—Klimt's only major commission for a portrait of a child—appear more natural and immediate, even in their gaze, than his studies of grown women. It is extremely interesting to note the small compositional sketches for the painting in which he explores the various possibilities for the final version (frontal, legs apart, standing before a meadow) within the confines of a picture frame he has defined himself.[22] In each sketch, a certain aspect of the overall composition is elucidated, while others are deliberately omitted. Thus, the artist addresses the aspect of tension in the light and dark areas, the triangular contour of the girl in relation to the grassy background, and the rhythm of ornaments scattered throughout the composition. Such details indicate that, for Klimt, it was the confines of the picture plane that created the prerequisite for the development of dynamic lines.

Gustav Klimt, Study for the Portrait of Adele Bloch-Bauer, 1903/04

The synthesis of individuality and universality that Klimt pursued as his ideal was often difficult to achieve, as the studies of the buxom and matronly figure of Eugenia Primavesi indicate.[23] The three-quarter profile proved less than flattering, although the technical quality of this drawing cannot be faulted. The generally satisfactory solution in the painting uses a frontal pose—the heavy and frequently broken pencil lines of the contour merge with the outlines of a chair above the mid-point of the body, lending the overall form the solid and symmetrical aspect of a mountain. Klimt developed a comparable approach in the 1913–14 study (ill. p. 146) for the unfinished *Portrait of Amalie Zuckerkandl* (1917–18, ill. p. 147).[24] In the studies of the seated figure the layered spread of clothing merges almost imperceptibly with the form of a bench to either side, resulting in a varied and dynamic directional flow from the head downwards.

For Klimt, the 1916 *Portrait of Friederike Maria Beer-Monti* (ill. p. 137) was a personal challenge that prompted him to make several special studies of the distinctive, evenly rounded face (ill. p. 219).[25] The facial traits recall the masks used in Japanese Noh theatre, and indeed, Klimt actually owned such a mask. Decades later, in describing her sittings for Klimt at his studio, Friederike Maria Beer-Monti claimed that he had

20   Strobl, Vol. 2, Nos. 2053–2073; Strobl, Vol. 4, nos. 3636.
21   Strobl, Vol. 2, Nos. 2113–2140; Strobl, Vol. 4, 3639–3646.
22   Strobl, Vol. 2, Nos. 2132–2140. Technique, dimensions, owner unknown.
23   Strobl, Vol. 2, Nos. 2141–2157; Strobl, Vol. 4, Nos. 3647–3649
24   Strobl, Vol. 2, Nos. 2468–2493; Strobl, Vol. 4, Nos. 3684–3687
25   All studies for the *Portrait of Beer-Monti:* Strobl, Vol. 3, Nos. 2524–2561; Strobl, Vol. 4, Nos.

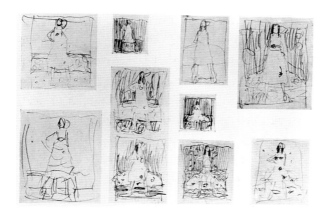

Gustav Klimt, Study for the
Portrait of Mäda Primavesi,
c. 1912

remarked "Now nobody can say that I only paint hysterical women".[27] What is remarkable is the fact that the Beer-Monti painting, like the 1916 *Portrait of Elisabeth Bachofen-
Echt* (ill. p. 132) includes the feet, so that the floating effect found in other portraits is
not present here.[28] The study drawings show this lively woman in full length—Klimt
even made separate special studies of the feet.[29] The hands, too, which he apparently
studied for a long time, are rendered with painstaking care. In the portraits of Beer-Monti
and Bachofen-Echt the background composition reflects Klimt's great love of Asian art.
Friederike Beer-Monti reports that Klimt had a long chest full of Chinese and other oriental costumes, many of which she tried on.

The 1917–18 *Half-figure Portrait of Johanna Staude* (ill. p. 143), a personal
friend of the artist, also has an "archaic" frontality that recalls the Khnopff-inspired faces
of the early years. It is clearly much less of a swagger portrait than the others.[30] In one
of the studies (ill. p. 142) two spatial layers overlap. The fundamental traits of the frontally rendered face are lightly sketched and reworked with heavier lines so that the
forms shift slightly. The result is a vibrant oscillation between light- and dark-grey pencil lines, which is particularly effective in the mouth and eye area.

The portrait of a woman wearing a kimono, which remained unfinished on the
death of the artist, has been identified by A. Strobl as the third posthumous portrait of
Ria Munk (ill. p. 141).[31] The studies created in this context show several models, each
wearing a kimono. In one of the loveliest drawings (ill. p. 219) in this group the consum-
mate draughtsmanship of the artist is particularly evident. Almost without interruption,
the soft and constantly turning pencil lines move over the paper to create a multitude of
patterns. The veiled body forms are revealed only by certain systems of movement and
changing concentrations of line thickness. Fragile transparency and stringent tectonics
hold a balance here, with the column-like figure cropped at top and bottom flanked by
two empty areas. Klimt offsets the central axis with the strongly accentuated eyebrows
that are a focal point of the composition. This late work is a finely wrought synthesis of
many previous insights. The horizontal and vertical edges of the paper determine the
relationship between figure and plane, and the principle of inclusion forms the energetic
line. Until the end of his life Klimt believed in the higher order of the gesamtkunstwerk
and the servile function of art—an attitude that was a fundamental principle of his early
career.

This notion of serving also underpins the courtly and transfiguring stance he
took as an artist in relation to the society ladies he painted (from 1898 onwards Klimt
painted only women). In the field of international portraiture of the early twentieth cen-

3688–3691. Studies of the face:
Nos. 2552–2561.
26 Strobl, Vol. 3, p. 100.
27 Cited in Strobl, Vol. 3, p. 100.
28 The drawings for the *Portrait
of Elisabeth Bachofen-Echt*: Strobl,
Vol. 3, Nos. 2494–2523; Strobl,
Vol. 4, Nos. 3694–3694a.
29 Strobl, Vol. 3, Nos. 2549, 2550.
30 Strobl, Vol. 3, Nos. 2723–2726.
31 Strobl, Vol. 3, p. 111, Nos.
2606–2619; Strobl, Vol. 4, p. 187,
No. 3695.
32 Julius Meier-Graefe, "Das Neue
Wien", in *Entwicklungsgeschichte
der Modernen Kunst, II*, Stuttgart
1904, p. 690.

tury his characteristic blend of modernity and hieratic detachment—with something of a sphinx-like aura of mystery—remains a unique phenomenon. "The cult of the female is part and parcel of Austrian culture just as it is in the Romance countries," wrote the famous German art dealer and cultural historian Julius Meier-Graefe in his 1904 treatise on "Das Neue Wien".[32] In the studies for the portraits, as mentioned above, the other-worldly air of the sitters is achieved by the device of fragmentation through which the figures are set in an indeterminate spatial situation. The thoroughness with which Klimt approached his subject in preparatory studies might seem superficially academic and almost anachronistic. In actual fact, in each drawing, he took up the challenge anew to integrate the figure standing before him into the overall "world of the artist". Within his unchanging, self-imposed limitations he sought a balance between emotional expression and a higher order. In other words, above and beyond the function of a preparatory study, each drawing took on the creed-like aspect of the urgent and the definitive.

Studies for the Portrait of
Sonja Knips
1898

Black chalk, 450 x 317 mm
Vienna, Historisches Museum der
Stadt Wien, Inv. No. 96.482/4
(Strobl No. 419)

Black chalk, 450 x 312 mm
Vienna, Historisches Museum der
Stadt Wien, Inv. No. 96.482/5
(Strobl No. 425)

Charcoal auf cardboard,
450 x 320 mm
Graz, Neue Galerie am
Landesmuseum Joanneum,
Inv. No. II/8313
(Strobl No. 415)

Black chalk, 443 x 311 mm
Vienna, Historisches Museum der
Stadt Wien, Inv. No. 74.930/158
(Strobl No. 414)

Studies for the Portrait of
Sonja Knips
1898

Black chalk, 306 x 463 mm
Vienna, Historisches Museum der
Stadt Wien, Inv. No. 74.930/45
(Strobl No. 421)

Black chalk, 320 x 452 mm
Vienna, Albertina, Inv. No. 34.933
(Strobl No. 420)

Pencil on tracing paper, grid
496 x 372 mm
Vienna, Historisches Museum der
Stadt Wien, Inv. No. 96.482/13
(Strobl No. 424)

Study for the Portrait of
Marie Henneberg, 1901/02

Black chalk,
300 x 450 mm
Vienna, Albertina,
Inv. No. 22.492
(Strobl No. 737)

Studies for the portrait of
Hermine Gallia, 1903/04

Black chalk, 319 x 452 mm
Vienna, Historisches Museum der
Stadt Wien, Inv. No. 96.482/15
(Strobl No. 1025)

Black chalk, 452 x 315 mm
Graz, Neue Galerie am Landes-
museum Joanneum, Inv. No. 8315
(Strobl No. 1049)

Studies for the Portrait of
Margarethe Stonborough-
Wittgenstein, 1905

Black chalk, 550 x 350 mm
Vienna, Albertina,
Inv. No. 29.842
(Strobl No. 1265)

Black chalk, 550 x 346 mm
Vienna, Albertina,
Inv. No. 29.735
(Strobl Nr. 1266)

Studies for the Portrait of
Fritza Riedler, 1906

Black chalk,
450 x 315 mm
Berne, Kunstmuseum Bern,
Inv. No. A7659
(Strobl No. 1226)

Black chalk on brown paper,
456 x 313 mm
Vienna, Historisches Museum der
Stadt Wien, Inv. No. 96.482/2
(Strobl No. 1231)

Black chalk,
448 x 317 mm
Wien, Albertina, Inv. No. 34.553
(Strobl No. 1237)

Studies for the Portrait of
Fritza Riedler, 1906

Black chalk,
450 x 313 mm
Berne, Kunstmuseum Bern,
Inv. No. A7658
(Strobl No. 1238)

Black chalk,
453 x 315 mm
Graz, Neue Galerie am
Landesmuseum Joanneum,
Inv. No. 8314
(Strobl No. 1229)

Black chalk on paper,
450 x 314 mm
Linz, Neue Galerie der Stadt
Linz, Inv. No. 65
(Strobl No. 1246)

Studies for the Portrait of
Adele Bloch-Bauer II, 1906

Pencil, 565 x 372 mm
Vienna, Historisches Museum der
Stadt Wien, Inv. No. 74.930/179
(Strobl No. 2078)

Pencil, 561 x 367 mm
Vienna, Historisches Museum der
Stadt Wien, Inv. No. 101.059/1
(Strobl No. 2075)

Pencil, 559 x 368 mm
Vienna, Historisches Museum der
Stadt Wien, Inv. No. 74.930/180
(Strobl No. 2104)

Pencil, 654 x 371 mm
Vienna, Historisches Museum der
Stadt Wien, Inv. No. 74.930/186
(Strobl No. 2093)

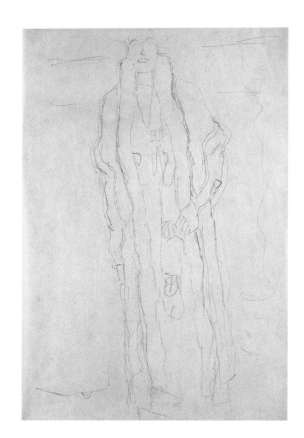

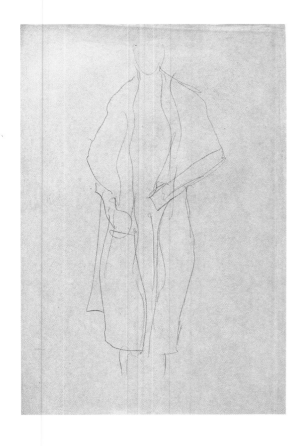

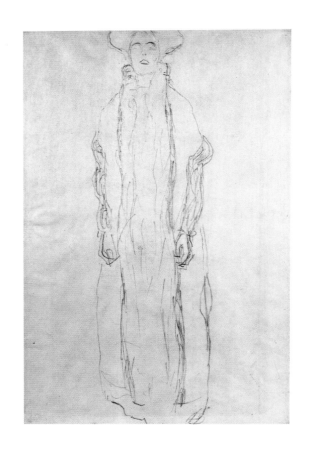

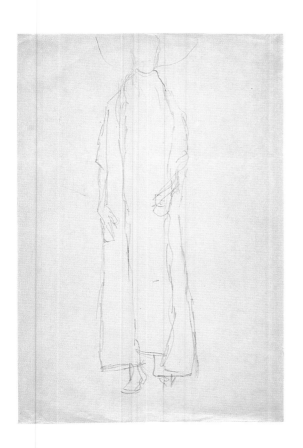

Studies for the Portrait of Adele Bloch-Bauer II, 1906

Pencil, 566 x 370 mm
Vienna, Historisches Museum der
Stadt Wien, Inv. No. 74.930/198
(Strobl No. 2074)

Pencil, 567 x 365 mm
Vienna, Albertina,
Inv. No. 23.542
(Strobl No. 2102)

Pencil on paper,
561 x 367 mm
Copenhagen, Statens Museum
for Kunst, Inv. No. 1972/51
(Strobl No. 2086)

Pencil on paper,
561 x 367 mm
Copenhagen, Statens Museum
for Kunst, Inv. No. 1972/52
(Strobl No. 2089)

Studies for the Portrait of
Paula Zuckerkandl

Pencil, 550 x 372 mm
Vienna, Albertina,
Inv. No. 29.731
(Strobl No. 2062)

Pencil, 569 x 373 mm
Vienna, Historisches Museum der
Stadt Wien, Inv. No. 74.930/184
(Strobl No. 2063)

Pencil, 558 x 374 mm
Vienna, Albertina,
Inv. No. 29.733
(Strobl No. 2076)

Pencil, 569 x 375 mm
Vienna, Albertina,
Inv. No. 30.246
(Strobl No. 2069)

Pencil, 558 x 374 mm
Vienna, Albertina,
Inv. No. 29.732
(Strobl No. 2072)

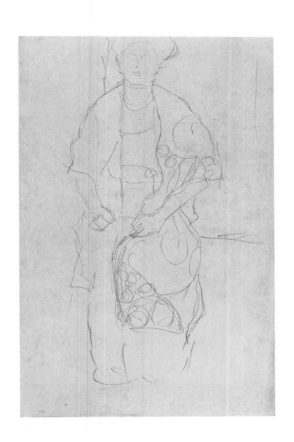

Studies for the Portrait of
Eugenia Primavesi
1913/14

Pencil, 566 x 370 mm
Vienna, Albertina,
Inv. No. 30.646
(Strobl No. 2150)

Pencil, 560 x 367 mm
Vienna, Historisches Museum der
Stadt Wien, Inv. No. 74.930/178
(Strobl No. 2153)

Pencil, 570 x 375 mm
Vienna, Private collection
(Nicht bei Strobl)

Pencil, 566 x 370 mm
Vienna, Albertina,
Inv. No. 30.645
(Strobl No. 2155)

Studies for the Portrait of
Mäda Primavesi, 1913/14

Pencil, 560 x 367 mm
Vienna, Albertina,
Inv. No. 30.446 (Strobl No. 2118)

Pencil, 559 x 367 mm
Vienna, Albertina,
Inv. No. 33.355 (Strobl No. 2114)

Pencil, 566 x 368 mm
Vienna, Albertina,
Inv. No. 30.445 (Strobl No. 2121)

Pencil, 558 x 366 mm
Vienna, Historisches Museum der
Stadt Wien, Inv. No. 75.403
(Strobl No. 2119)

Pencil on paper,
559 x 367 mm
Vienna, Albertina,
Inv No. 30.443 (Strobl No. 2122)

Pencil on paper,
568 x 371 mm
Vienna, Albertina,
Inv. No. 30.444 (Strobl No. 2125)

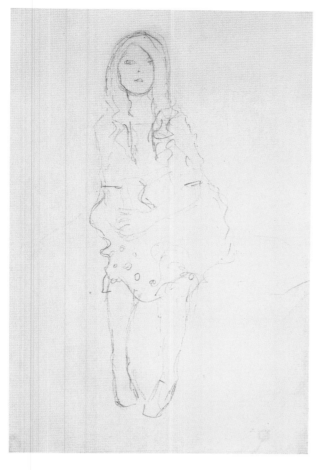

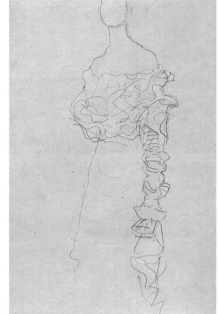
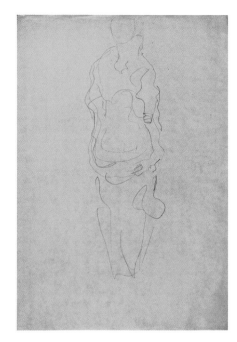

Studies for the Portrait of
Baroness Bachofen-Echt

Pencil on paper,
485 x 275 mm
Inscribed lower right:
"Gustav Klimt"
(not in his own hand)
Linz, Neue Galerie der Stadt
Linz, Inv. No. 1804
(Strobl No. 2494)

Pencil, 482 x 334 mm
Vienna, Historisches Museum der
Stadt Wien, Inv. No. 74930/185
(Strobl No. 2495)

Pencil, 570 x 374 mm
Vienna, Historisches Museum der
Stadt Wien, Inv. No. 74930/177
(Strobl No. 2496)

Studies for the Portrait of
Frl. Lieser

Pencil, 500 x 325 mm
Vienna, Historisches Museum der
Stadt Wien, Inv. No. 74.930/182
(Strobl No. 2588)

Pencil, 500 x 323 mm
Vienna, Historisches Museum der
Stadt Wien, Inv. No. 101.059/7
(Strobl No. 2593)

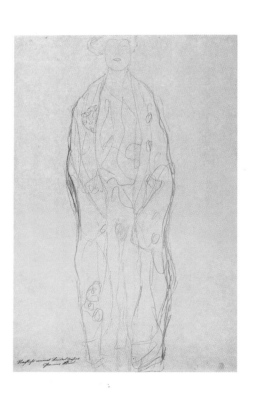

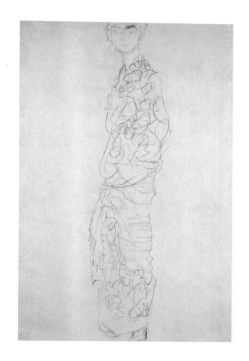

Study for the Portrait of
Ria Munk III
1917/18

Pencil, 498 x 322 mm
Vienna, Albertina,
Inv. No. 22.396
(Strobl No. 2617)

Studies for the Portrait of
Friederike Maria Beer

Pencil on paper,
605 x 290 mm
Inscribed lower right:
"Gustav Klimt"
(not in his own hand)
Linz, Neue Galerie der Stadt
Linz, Inv. No. 1805
(Strobl No. 2544)

Pencil, 570 x 370 mm
Vienna, Albertina,
Inv. No. 34.555
(Strobl No. 2532)

Judith

DANIELA HAMMER-TUGENDHAT

According to Felix Salten, one could fully illustrate the modern element in Klimt's art by reference to his *Judith*: "How he takes a figure from the present, a living person, the warmth of whose blood is capable of intoxicating him, and how he then shifts that figure into the magical shade of distant centuries, so that it seems heightened and transfigured in all its reality. ... A slim supple woman with an exhilarating fire in her dark eyes, a cruel mouth and nostrils that tremble with passion. ... This illustration of the eternally human, this emphasis on a continuity that is otherwise beyond our comprehension is modern style."[1] Salten's interpretation communicates some impression of how Klimt's *Judith* was perceived by his (well-meaning) contemporaries.[2] The text quoted (incompletely) here describes *Judith* as the incarnation of the femme fatale.[3]

In the following I would like to pursue the question of whether Klimt's Judith figure in fact represents "the eternally human", whether she is really located in a "continuity". In order to estimate the cultural significance and function of this figure of the femme fatal at the turn of the century, it is highly edifying to recall the story of Judith.

Klimt's Judith—The incarnation of the "eternally human"? A look back.[4]

Our current image of Judith is coloured by the notion that she slept with Holofernes before killing him, an interpretation that only emerged in the second half of the nineteenth century. This association of the sexual act and murder, a paradigm of the femme fatale, also crops up in scholarly literature. By contrast, in the text of the Old Testament, the pious widow from Bethulia who, in order to save her people from the threat of annihilation by the Assyrian leader, steals her way into the enemy camp with her servant and bewitches Holofernes with her cunningly clever words and her beauty, remains untouched by him. During the festive meal which he has served in her honour, he drinks so much wine that he falls asleep before ever even touching her. Judith chops off his head with his own sword, escapes with her servant and so helps the Israelites to victory over the Assyrians, who were without a leader as a result of her act. In the "original story"[5] Judith is described as modest, God-fearing and heroic, a heroine and saviour of her people. In Catholic reception, Judith becomes an allegory of the victory of purity over vice, or modesty over pride, and thus a prefiguration of Mary. Medieval depictions, in keeping with the illustrations of virtue and vice in the *Psychomachia* of Prudentius, show Judith standing on Holofernes or else they present the whole Judith cycle in narrative form. In the early modern era, she assumes an eminent significance. At the start of the Reformation and Counter-Reformation, Judith appears as a symbol of freedom, justice and the right faith. Above and beyond the symbolic denominational meaning, the Judith figure also articulated current political conflicts, as for example when Hans Sachs identifies the Assyrians with the Turks. The triumphant Judith becomes a femme forte, the incarnation of the strong woman, and as such, an identification figure for female rulers.[6]

1   Felix Salten, "Eine schöne jüdische Jourdame / Was will er denn eigentlich?", Salten, *Gustav Klimt. Gelegentliche Anmerkungen*, Vienna and Leipzig 1903, quoted from Otto Breicha (ed.), *Gustav Klimt. Die Goldene Pforte. Bilder und Schriften zu Leben und Werk*, Salzburg 1978, p. 31.
2   For a critical evaluation of the reception of Klimt's works cf. by Gottfried Fliedl "Das Weib macht keine Kunst, aber den Künstler. Zur Klimt-Rezeption" in *Der Garten der Lüste. Zur Deutung des Erotischen und Sexuellen bei Künstlern und ihren Interpreten*, ed. by Renate Berger und Daniela Hammer-Tugendhat, Cologne 1985, pp. 89–149; *Gustav Klimt. 1862–1918. Die Welt in weiblicher Gestalt*, Cologne 1989; "Geste und Blick" in *Gustav Klimt*, Kunsthaus Zürich, 11. 9.–13. 12. 1992, ed. by Toni Stooss and Christoph Doswald, Zürich 1992, pp. 13–25.
3   It is not possible within the scope of this essay to go into the significance of the femme fatale, but reference is made, among others, to Bram Dijkstra, *Evil Sisters. The Threat of Female Sexuality and the Cult of Manhood*, New York 1996; Mary A. Doane, *Femmes Fatales. Feminism, Film Theory, Psychoanalysis*, New York 1991; Mireille Dottin-Orsini, *Cette femme qu'ils disent fatale. Textes et images de la misogynie fin-de-siècle*, Paris 1993.

The idea of a female heroine, a woman of political and historical significance, was inconceivable in the hegemonial discourse at the turn of the century.

In 1840 Friedrich Hebbel produced a whole new version of the Judith material in a theatre play, the radical reinterpretation of which was subsequently adopted in all realms of art. According to Hebbel, Judith, though a widow, was still a virgin, because her dead husband Manasse was impotent. A thus frustrated Judith is sexually attracted to the cruel superman Holofernes. After a rape which she herself stages, she murders him out of personal revenge: "Nothing drove me but the thought of myself." This annihilating insight grounds Judith's act in the realm of the psychological-subjective and instinctive. Any political or religious motivation is "unmasked" as an illusory attempt at legitimation. Sigmund Freud's interpretation of Judith in his *Tabu der Virginität* of 1917 is highly significant. Freud was of the opinion that Hebbel's play had uncovered the real truth of the text, the original text, as it were, the real meaning of the story: that a virgin beheads the man who robs her of her virginity, whereby beheading is a symbol of castration.[7]

The literary and artistic treatments of the theme since the second half of the nineteenth century correspond to this sexual explanatory mode. Thus Klimt's *Judith* does not reflect the "eternally human", she is in no way in a timeless continuity; instead Klimt and his contemporaries turned the Judith image into its opposite. Yet through an aesthetic mise-en-scène the whole aura of which is mythical in character, Klimt presents the characterization of the female as a femme fatale as an eternal truth.

Gustav Klimt
Judith I
1901
Oil and gold on canvas,
84 x 42 cm
Inscribed lower left:
"Gustav—/Klimt"
Vienna, Österreichische Galerie
Belvedere, Inv. No. 4737
(Novotny-Dobai No. 113)

Judith: a paradoxical figure

The notion of Judith as a femme fatale is not, however, a pure invention of the nineteenth century. The figure of Judith is a scandal; her story signals nothing less than the reversal of the gender roles. Contrary to the patriarchal rabbinical concept, Judith is an active woman, she acts independently, intervenes in political events, conquers one of the mightiest military commanders, kills a man. Judith not only embodies salvation, she is also a threat to male dominance. In the history of the reception of the Judith story, various strategies have been developed in order to rob this figure of its explosiveness and ward off the threat that emanated from it. Already in the Old Testament story, great store was laid by presenting Judith as an exception and returning her to the private realm after the murderous act. Unlike David, an analogous figure, Judith no longer plays a role in the public domain, but spends the rest of her lonely life as a modest widow. Above all, she carries out the murderous act in the name of the father: "The Lord, our God, killed him by the hand of a woman". God is so great that he can conquer his people's enemies even by the hand of a weak woman. The story of Judith was excluded from the Hebrew canon. The Catholic Bible too, merely integrated it as a deuterocanonical work. Luther eliminated her; her story is not included in most Protestant bibles, in some it figures as apocryphal.

At the same time, an interpretative pattern emerged in the early modern era that was diametrically opposed to the theological interpretations and allegorical representations. It focuses on those elements of the story which speak of how Judith cunningly played with her female charms and her deadly art of seduction. The story of Judith is taken up into the cycle of female wiles and she is thus equated with evil women who through cunning and deceit destroyed innocent men, like Delilah (Samson) and Phyllis (Aristotle). Artists such as Jan Massys and Baldung Grien depicted Judith as an aggressively seductive figure in lascivious poses. The image of woman in the early modern era, as in the Middle Ages, presented a dichotomy. The concept of the pure modest woman— be it in the traditional Catholic version of the Virgin Mary or the demure housewife of the Reformation—determined its counterpart, the sexualised woman, Eve, the seductress, the witch. Judith is one of the very few woman who could be identified with both, mutually exclusive meanings and thus oppose those one-sided categorisations. This ambivalence constitutes the explosiveness, the subversive potential of this figure.

In the early modern era this contradictory aspect is expressed in many works of fine art in which different, even contrary understandings of the Judith figure become superimposed. This polysemy can be seen, for example, in an engraving by Barthel Beham of 1525. Created in the historical year of the Peasants' War by a politically radical artist, this engraving can be read as an allegory of the victory of the weak over the violent oppressor. The composition is reminiscent of the iconography of the allegories of the virtues victorious over the figures of vice, familiar to us, for example, from Donatello's and Giorgione's versions of Judith—after the *Psychomachia*. The allusion to this pictorial tradition and the forceful expression on Judith's face underscore the political reading of Judith as heroine. At the same time, the link between the motif of sitting (or riding) and the naked, altogether sensually arranged body with the billowing hair awakens associations with the seduction-desire-murder complex.

Titian, Salome (?), c. 1511–15,
Rome, Galleria Doria Pamphili

4   For a detailed evaluation of the figure of Judith in the art of the early modern era cf. Daniela Hammer-Tugendhat, "Judith und ihre Schwestern. Konstanz und Veränderung von Weiblichkeitsbildern" in *Lustgarten und Dämonenpein. Konzepte von Weiblichkeit in Mittelalter und früher Neuzeit*, ed. by Annette Kuhn and Bea Lundt, Dortmund 1997, pp. 343–385.
5   It is different to arrive at the original concept of the Judith figure. The original Hebrew text has been lost. Researchers assume that the Greek version is based on the original Hebrew text. The text on which Hieronymus' *Vulgata* was based was written in Aramaic. The Hebrew versions are of a later date. The original is dated as second century B.C. On the history of the text cf. *Theologische Realenzyklopädie* Vol. XVII, Berlin/York 1988, pp. 404–408 (Erich Zeuger); Robert Hanhart, *Text und Textgeschichte des Buches Judith*, Göttingen 1979; *The Anchor Bible*, New York 1985. For feminist interpretations of the figure cf. Athalya Brenner, *A Feminist Companion to Esther, Judith and Susanna*, Sheffield 1995.
6   *Die Galerie der starken Frauen. La Galerie des Femmes Fortes. Die Heldinnen in der französischen und italienischen Kunst des 17. Jahrhunderts*, Kunstmuseum Düsseldorf, 10. 9.—12. 11. 1995, and Hessisches Landesmuseum Darmstadt, 14. 12.1995—26. 2. 1996, by Bettina Baumgärtel and Silvia Neysters, Dusseldorf 1995, pp. 238–279.

Judith or Salome?

Despite the inscription "Judith und Holofernes" on the frame, which Gustav Klimt designed personally, the *Judith* painting, dated 1901, was referred to as *Salome* at the Second German Künstlerbund Exhibition of 1905 in Berlin. The second version of *Judith*, dated 1909, also appears under both names.[8] The fusion of these vastly different female figures is not entirely Klimt's invention, as is so often assumed in the relevant literature,[9] but has its roots in the art of the early modern era. In the case of a number of sixteenth and seventeenth century paintings, for example, Titian's early works at the Galeria Doria Pamphili in Rome, researchers disagree as to whether Judith or Salome is intended. What is instructive is not so much the decision in favour of the one or other figure, but the fact that this question could arise at all. What does it mean when two so divergent figures as Judith and Salome can be confused? What happens to Judith, when she becomes so similar to the depraved Salome, who is guilty of the murder of Saint John? What happens to the villain Holofernes, symbol of the hated suppressor and the essence of vice and pride, when he reminds people of a saint, the victim?

Barthel Beham, Judith, 1525, copper-engraving

For artists at the turn of the century Salome, not Judith, constituted the essence of the femme fatale. One only has to think of the *Salome* paintings by Gustave Moreau, which inspired Oscar Wilde's dramatic ballad of 1893, the illustrations of which by Beardsley in turn inspired Gustav Klimt. Salome was also the figure chosen by Richard Strauss for an opera, by Franz von Stuck for his paintings and by Max Klinger for his famous sculpture. Salome was selected because the male protagonist, John the Baptist, was a pure, innocent victim, whereas Holofernes was associated with male desire and male violence. It was only possible to project (deadly) sexual desire onto the female figure alone, and suppress the male role in this drama of the sexes, by opting for the figure of Salome.

In Klimt, the images of these unequal sisters become completely superimposed. In his second version of *Judith*, the disappearance of the severed head, into an ornamentation recalling the bag of the traditional story, is a pointer to Judith; the restrained motifs of the dance, the gathering of the skirt and the figure's sideways movement, are pointers to Salome.[10] The fragmented heads with the closed eyes and the dark frame of hair in both of Klimt's paintings actually bear no traces of the villain Holofernes. Instead they associate with the *vera icon*, the true image of Christ. Memories of male aggression (both political and sexual) and of female heroism have been totally eliminated. So why Judith and not Salome? Perhaps because she evokes the personal act of killing and thus the merging of female desire and murder.[11] Judith/Salome points to a third figure, Delilah, as the embodiment of female deviousness and castration. The emphasis on the dark hair of the severed heads, into which Judith digs her fingers, recalls Samson, whose superhuman powers were in his hair. When he betrayed this secret to his wife, she cut his hair and could thus deliver him up to the mercy of her people and his enemies, the Philistines.[12]

The subversive ambivalence of the Judith figure, as she is portrayed in the paintings of the early modern era, has given way in Klimt to a simplification in the direction of sexualisation. But even Judith's sexual power is broken by the aesthetic presentation. In *Judith I* her body is fragmented and dismembered, as it were, by the ornamentation; the golden neckband separates body from head as if in a stranglehold—an aesthetic analogy to the beheading of Holofernes. (Notice the repetition of the ornamentation of

7 In Sigmund Freud, *Studienausgabe Bd. V, Sexualleben*, Frankfurt/M. 1972, pp. 213–228.
8 Johannes Dobai/Fritz Novotny, *Gustav Klimt*, 2 edition, Salzburg 1975, p. 320, No. 113 and p. 345. No. 160.
9 For example in Alessandra Comini, *Gustav Klimt*, New York 1975, pp. 22f.
10 Alice Strobl (*Gustav Klimt. Die Zeichnungen 1904–12*, Vol. 2, Salzburg 1982, pp. 151–153) draws attention to the link between the painting with the sketches of the dancer for the Stoclet frieze, in progress at the same time, and a watercoloured chalk drawing of a dancer.
11 The confusion of Klimt's Judith figures with Salome in the reception is interpreted by Comini 1975 as a repression of the fact that Judith killed her male victim with her own hands.
12 In a copper-engraving of c. 1627 Claude Mellan transformed a Judith with the head of Holofernes painted by Simon Vouet into a Delilah with the head of Samson. *Die Galerie der starken Frauen* (see note 6) p. 274, fig. 125.1 and 123.

her neckband on the band beside Holofernes' head.) That ornamentation coerces the body into the picture plane and prevents it from moving. The threat that emanates from the figure is averted by this forced paralysis and passivity. This freezing of movement, thereby restricting all scope for action, is even more crass in *Judith II*, given that here Klimt originally began with a dance motif.[13] Movement and vitality are transferred entirely to the abstract ornamentation.[14] The tension in the Viennese painting between the shimmering surface of the skin, the delicate robe and the golden ornamentation, between a certain naturalism in the portrait, under-scored by the lascivious gaze at the observer, and the abstraction, has given way in *Judith II* to a more all-encompassing ornamentalisation. The link to the observer is also missing; Judith's gaze is empty. What are strik-ing are her cramped hands digging into her own ornamented lap. The figure's aggression emanates primarily from these hands, on the bony fin-gers of which the severed head of Holofernes hangs.[15] Orgasmic ecstasy, pain, death and cruelty merge in a sado-masochist fantasy. For the protag-onist Severin in the classic text of 1870 *Venus im Pelz* by Sacher-Masoch, Judith functions as an ideal figure and as a biblical legitimation of his per-verse sexuality. [16]

The gold in both Judith paintings turns these treacherous and seductive murderers of men into almost sacred icons of womanhood.[17]

13   Cf. note 12.
14   This ornamentalisation of the female body is already present in Moreau's Salome. Cf. Karen Fromm/Barbara Höffer, "Die Femme fatale wird bezwungen? Salome als 'Verdrängungsfigur' und die Strate-gie ihrer ästhetischen Bannung bei Gustave Moreau" in *FrauenKunst-Wissenschaft 19 (Femme fatale. Entwürfe)*, Marburg a. L., May 1995, pp. 25–31.
15   Closely related in the aggres-sive gesture is Oskar Kokoschka's expressionist poster for the sum-mer theater that same year ("Mör-der, Hoffnung der Frauen"). Cf. Kathrin Hoffmann-Curtius, "Frauen-bilder Oskar Kokoschkas" in *Frauen, Bilder, Männer, Mythen* ed. by Ilsebill Barta i.a., Berlin 1987, pp. 148–178. The gesture of the hands looks like an aggressive vari-ation on the many masturbating women which Klimt depicted in his more private drawings. On the sig-nificance of female masturbation in Klimt cf. Laura Arici, "Schwanenge-sang in Gold. 'Der Kuss'– eine Deu-tung" in *Gustav Klimt*, Kunsthaus Zürich, 11. 9.—13. 12. 1992, ed. by Toni Stooss and Christoph Dos-wald, Zurich 1992, pp. 43–51.
16   Margarita Stocker, *Judith: Sex-ual Warrior. Women and Power in Western Culture*, Yale University Press, New Haven/London 1998, p. 177.
17   On the significance of gold in Klimt cf. Arici 1992.

Gustav Klimt
Judith II
1909
Oil on canvas, 178 x 46 cm
Inscribed lower left:
"Gustav–/Klimt–/ 1909"
Venice, Galleria Internazionale
d'Arte Moderna–Ca' Pesaro
(Novotny-Dobai No. 160)

The compositional Concept of The Kiss— Gustav Klimt and Edvard Munch

HANS BISANZ

Gustav Klimt's 1907–08 painting *Der Kuss (The Kiss)* (ill. p. 231) was purchased by the Staatsgalerie (now the Österreichische Galerie) at the 1908 Kunstschau exhibition organised by the Klimt group.[1] The success of this painting has remained unbroken ever since, with countless reproductions granting it virtually unparalleled popularity with a broad public.

In *The Kiss* the depiction of lovers embracing on a flower-strewn hillock—a tiny fragment of earth—against a starry sky becomes an allegorical portrayal of Love. In terms of Klimt's overall oeuvre, *The Kiss* can undoubtedly be placed within the context of such monumental works as his earlier *Beethoven frieze* and the mosaic he created around the same time for the Palais Stoclet, both of which conclude with similar portrayals of lovers. Yet this does not mean that, as an individual painting, *The Kiss* may be regarded as a mere offspin of these larger works, for its sheer size and wealth of expression make it a thoroughly independent painting in its own right. This painting is one of the key works of Klimt's golden period. Though the use of gold as a compositional vehicle can be traced back to his 1899 painting of *Pallas Athene*, it took on a whole new dimension in the years 1907–08. In the words of Fritz Novotny, "Gold, a colour from another world, a non-colour, already used quite often by Klimt in the past, now fills the picture in the richest possible degree, in sophisticated contrasts of matt and brilliant gold, interspersed with the sheen of small silver fragments." Novotny also points out the contrast between the "detailed and highly sensitive precision with which the bodies are portrayed, the heads and hands, and the incorporeal, rigid planarity of the ornament...," adding that "the monumentality of the work lies essentially in this supremacy of pure form and ornament, and in the fragile tenderness of the figures themselves, creating an emotive undertone."[2] This contrast, together with the calm portrayal of the figures, the halo around the heads of the lovers, and the starry background, all combine to create an iconic effect that lends the image a sacred aura.

Shortly before 1900, Klimt had chosen a similar background for his faculty painting *Philosophy*, of which the contemporary critic Ludwig Hevesi pointed out that it shows "a fragment of the universe charged with mystic fermentation... a welter of blue, violet, green and grey merging and brewing, in tides and waves brimming with a glistening yellow that heightens to real gold. They conjure up cosmic dust, whirling atoms, and elementary powers..."[3] Here, then, we already find the starry background that will later be used in *The Kiss* —a feature that is also evident in the golden painting of *Hope II* (1907–08; ill. p. 245) and in the background wall structure of the *Portrait of Adele Bloch-Bauer I* (1907; ill. p. 117) which was also exhibited at the 1908 Kunstschau.

In contrast to the standing lovers in the *Beethoven frieze* and the *Stoclet frieze*, Klimt has portrayed a kneeling woman in *The Kiss*, with the man bending over her. Alice Strobl has persuasively demonstrated that the couple portrayed in *The Kiss* is in fact a stylised and veiled double portrait of the artist and his partner, the fashion designer Emilie Flöge.[4] This claim is further supported by a letter that recently came to light,

1 Oil on canvas, 180 x 180 cm, signed lower right GUSTAV KLIMT, Novotny-Dobai no. 154, see Fritz Novotny/Johannes Dobai, *Gustav Klimt*, Salzburg 1967.
2 Novotny-Dobai, p. 39
3 Ludwig Hevesi, *Acht Jahre Secession*, Vienna 1906, p. 233 f.
4 Alice Strobl, *Gustav Klimt. Die Zeichnungen II*, Salzburg 1982, p. 162 and note 7.
5 Love letter from Klimt, sent from Munich on 4. 6. 1897 (date-stamp), to one Helene Kraus, poste restante, unequivocally identifiable as Emilie Flöge. In Wiener Kunst Auktionen—Palais Kinsky, 28th art auction, 16. 5. 2000, cat. no. 87.
6 In the leaflet accompanying the series published in two boxed editions.
7 Johannes Dobai, "Zu Gustav Klimts Gemälde Der Kuss", in *Mitteilungen der Österreichischen Galerie 1968*, p. 100.

clearly indicating that Klimt's liaison with Flöge was not public knowledge.[5]

Klimt had already addressed the subject of *Love* in 1895 in an oil painting that he used as a study for a print of the series *Allegorien, Neue Folge* published by Gerlach & Schenk in Vienna. The publisher, Martin Gerlach, had initially issued the primarily educational series *Allegorien und Embleme* as a late historicist pattern collection for craftsmen, illustrators and advertisers, albeit including innovative philosophical and literary themes such as Time, Eternity, The Ages of Man and Life and Death. He had then decided to issue the *Neue Folge* (1895–1900) treating more general and private subjects. In the foreword to this New Series he writes, "I initially chose a subject that breathes pleasure and life: Wine, Love, Song, Music and Dance, to which the figuratively inexhaustible

field of the arts and sciences, the merry march of the seasons and the joyful pursuit of sports were to be added later."[6] The change in Martin Gerlach's programme signified a departure from the so-called Ringstrasse art with its allegories and references to classical mythology aimed primarily at glorifying the aristocracy and the rising bourgeoisie. In his small oil painting of 1895, Klimt goes one step further by rendering visible emotional states. His painting of *Love* (ill. p. 227) can hardly be said to pursue a subject "that breathes pleasure and life", as called for by Gerlach, for, as Johannes Dobai writes, it "maintains a fairly melancholy tone, on the whole comparable to the mood that prevails in the stories by Arthur Schnitzler."[7] In the background of this portrayal of a young couple, terrifying masked heads cast their shadows (anticipating the menacing undertone present in some of Klimt's later works, such as the university paintings and the *Beethoven frieze*). Hofmannsthal's commentary on *Anatol* further consolidates the comparison of Klimt's *Love* with the works of Schnitzler when he describes that what really appeals to him "in the light of love … is not so much the direct radiation of light

Gustav Klimt, Lovers, 1901/02,
pencil on paper, whereabouts
unknown (Strobl No. 3467a)
Photography: Archives Dr. Strobl

as the colour bursts where it fragments on the fringes ... and the uncanny gloom behind it."[8]

Whereas the melancholy portrayal of the couple in the 1895 oil painting *Love* lends the scene a valedictory aspect, the couple at the end of the *Beethoven frieze* would appear to have something final and constant as a consequence of the notion of salvation presented in the frieze.

Edvard Munch (born in Løten, Norway, on 12 December 1863, making him a close contemporary of Klimt) had, on numerous occasions, treated the theme of lovers embracing, and had taken an approach broadly similar to Klimt's until, before 1900, he created a woodcut whose monumentality foreshadows Klimt's *The Kiss*. Yet Munch approached the subject from a totally different starting point. After all, historicism played a relatively minor role in nineteenth-century Norwegian art. Given Norway's Protestant tradition and its more democratic form of monarchy, art had remained very much the preserve of the bourgeoisie and with that, revolved largely around *Biedermeier*-style themes of domesticity, in stark contrast to the art of Vienna in the same period. Munch's later work, unlike that of Klimt, which is rooted in the allegory and mythology nurtured by the Ringstrasse era, has no trace of such mythological motifs as *Pallas Athene* or *The Sphinx*. Nevertheless, in Munch's *Frieze of Life*, which so clearly reflects the spirit of the times, one can find plenty of programmatic common ground. Munch's frieze was never intended to have a decorative function—the "Raumkunst" ideas of the Viennese Secessionists remained anathema to him—but merely as a sequence of images conceived as a frieze.

In 1889, in his St Cloud diary, he designed the programme for his murals and, in doing so, broke with bourgeois Scandinavian genre painting. "No more interiors with men reading and women knitting. These had to be people who could breathe, feel and love. I shall paint a series of these pictures; the sacred aspect of them must be grasped, and people should take their hats off before them as in a church." He also wrote that this planned frieze "is intended as a series of related pictures, which together should create a picture of life. Throughout the entire frieze runs a sweeping shoreline beyond which the waves of the eternally moving sea break; beneath the tops of trees, life breathes in all its diversity, in all its worries and joys. The frieze is perceived as a poem of life, of love and of death."

Here we can find parallels to the programme of the two series by Gerlach & Schenk with their titles such as Time, Eternity, The Ages of Man, or Life and Death as well as the emphasis on the significance of Love. In both cases, these are contributions to the symbolist decade of the 1890s, influenced by the ideas of the English pre-Raphaelites, the Belgian painter Fernand Khnopff and the Dutch painter Jan Toorop. On his second visit to Paris in 1889, Munch also discovered the works of Toulouse Lautrec, van Gogh and Gauguin. (On his first visit to Paris in 1885, he had seen works by Manet.)

The portrayal of the human individual was now to be liberated from the domestic constraints of the genre scene, just as Munch had claimed, and transposed into the timeless expanses of landscape, as certain aspects of the *Frieze of Life* so clearly convey.

The significance of landscape as a setting for his *Frieze of Life* resulted in the early '90s in the creations of pure landscape paintings such as *Strandmystik* (circa 1892)[9] or *Starry Night on Asgarstrand* (circa 1893).[10] The monumentality of the latter

8   Hugo von Hofmannsthal, "Von einem kleinen Wiener Buch (1892)", in *Reden und Aufsätze I*, Frankfurt/M. 1979, p.161.
9   Exhib. cat. Edvard Munch, Frankfurt/M., Steinernes Haus 1962, Fig. 10.
10   Exhib. cat. Frankfurt/M., no. 14.

Gustav Klimt
The Kiss
1907–08
Oil, silver and gold layers on
canvas, 180 x 180 cm
Inscribed lower right:
"Gustav–/ Klimt"
Vienna, Österreichische Galerie
Belvedere, Inv. No. 912
(Novotny-Dobai No. 154)

already echoes the cosmic expanses and starry skies in Klimt's *The Kiss*. Yet even the "eternally moving" sea, the setting for some of his *Frieze of Life* scenes, is intended as a means of portraying an openness far removed from urban constraints.

A number of the best known scenes from this series by Munch consist of figures in a landscape setting, such as *The Scream* (1893),[11] *The Storm* (1893),[12] *The Three Ages of Woman* (1894)[13]—thematically related to Klimt's composition of the same name—and *Dance of Life* (1899/1900).[14] His well-known painting *Evening on Karl Johan Street* (circa 1892)[15] is a street scene with a throng of people which he later transposed in 1894 under the title *Fear*[16] into a landscape setting that corresponds to the scene of *The Scream*—whereas other works, most of them earlier, including precursors of the *Frieze of Life*, tend to be innovative approaches to the traditional Scandinavian genre scene.

The Kiss, in which Munch, like Klimt, used a melancholy undertone, belongs to the latter category. Klimt's 1895 painting *Love* conveys a sense of valediction, and in 1890 Munch created a drawing which he himself entitled *Adjö* (Farewell).[17] A number of drawings and an oil sketch[18] finally led in 1892 to Munch's oil painting *The Kiss*.[19] It is still, in some respects, a genre scene, executed in soft and relaxed brushwork. It shows a couple, fully clothed, at the far right of the picture, in front of a curtain, next to which a large window reveals a view of an evening street. Three years later, in 1895, Munch produced an etching of this composition[20] (ill. p. 234)—but this time with an important shift in emphasis. This time, he placed the naked couple at the centre of the picture and structured the entire composition strictly symmetrically with the window mullions and windowsill as axes. This decision to use a symmetrical approach was clearly influenced by a new turn-of-the-century stylism. The curtain on the right—now given a counterpart on the left—no longer serves to shelter the lovers protectively, and they are exposed more than ever to the gaze of the spectator, with a vulnerability further underlined by their nudity. Yet at the same time, for these human figures, such exposure represents an emancipation from concealment and revelation, while their central position in the composition heightens their significance. Even in such a work, there are elements that foreshadow Munch's progress from stylism to expressionism, in which the human individual becomes the central theme of creative work.

Klimt adopts the theme of lovers embracing shortly before 1900 in his faculty painting *Philosophy* and the studies for it. In the vertical grouping of hovering figures, symbolising the sequence of human ages to the left of the Sphinx as the main figure, we can see a pair of lovers.[21] The critic Ludwig Hevesi described this composition as "...untroubled children, blossoming young bodies entwined, pleasure and torment, labour and strife, the struggle, creation and suffering of existence, and finally the withering, icy greyness of old age..."[22]

In a catalogue raisonné of Klimt's drawings, Alice Strobl ascertains in "one of the first studies of the kiss for the *Beethoven frieze* a reference

11 Exhib. cat. Frankfurt/M.,
no. 17.
12 J. P. Hodin, *Edvard Munch—
Genius des Nordens*, Mainz 1963,
T. 5.
13 Ibid., T. 13.
14 Ibid., p. 48.
15 Ibid., T. 4.
16 Exhib. cat. *Edvard Munch*,
Rotterdam, Museum Boymans-van
Beuningen 1958, no. 5.
17 Exhib. cat. *Edvard Munch—
Das zeichnerische Werk*, Kunsthalle
Bremen 1970, Fig. 1.
18 On this development, see
ibid., Fig. 1–6.
19 Exhib. cat. *Sehnsucht nach
Glück*, Frankfurt/M., Schirn Kunsthalle 1995, Fig. p.228.
20 Schiefler no. 22, Gustav Schiefler, *Verzeichnis des graphischen
Werks Edvard Munchs bis 1906*,
Berlin 1907.
21 Alice Strobl, *Gustav Klimt. Die
Zeichnungen IV*, Salzburg 1989,
p. 106.
22 Hevesi 1906.

to the couple at the top left hand corner of *Philosophy*". The author also points out Klimt's interest in the same motif of lovers in the work of Edmund Munch, when she compares another, albeit unused, drawing for the *Beethoven frieze* (ill. p. 228) with Munch's 1895 etching.[23]

From here on, the *Beethoven frieze*, the *Stoclet frieze* and *The Kiss* become a single, thematically related complex, for which a number of drawings—including drawings of reclining couples—are created as interim stages. In some drawings[24] the transition from *Beethoven frieze* to *Stoclet frieze* is particularly clear in the transformation of physical poses and body language. The fact that the *Stoclet frieze* and the painting *The Kiss* were created around the same time makes it difficult to identify preliminary studies for the latter work. "What does come close to it," writes Strobl, is a sketch in which "the motif of the kneeling woman is already present and her robe has been abstracted to a strict triangle". Compositional sketches and detail studies for the head of the man and for one foot of the kneeling woman are also further developments of the compositional idea of *The Kiss*.[25] Dobai associates the self-contained composition of *Fulfilment* in the *Stoclet frieze* with a woodcut of the same theme by Munch[26] (ill. p. 234), though Klimt's oil painting *The Kiss*[27] has far more in common with this woodcut, including the alignment of the figures and, to some extent, the position of the hands. Moreover, the way the figures jut into an open space like silhouettes, thereby taking on a certain monumentality, links these two works. The difference in size between a woodcut and an oil painting of 180 x 180 cm plays no role in this respect. Dobai writes, "In Munch's work, the print loses its illustrative aspect. He himself tended to choose a large format for his prints. Yet one could well say that the poignancy and precision of his woodcuts and lithographs permit any degree of inner magnification."[28]

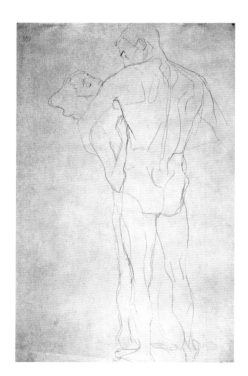

Gustav Klimt, Lovers, 1905–07,
pencil on paper, Vienna,
Historisches Museum
(Strobl. No. 1741)

Novotny[29] presents this woodcut as "counterpart and counterpoint" to Klimt's *Kiss* and sees in Munch's work a "rawness of ascetic expressionism taken to its extreme". In such a comparison, one is certainly struck by Munch's economic use of decorative forms, which are restricted to the "ornament" of a wood grain that has been left visible throughout the background and occasionally in the figures themselves. Yet in the course of Munch's artistic development, especially in the period around 1900 when his woodcuts were created, a decorative phase that stands in stark contrast to the rest of his oeuvre can indeed be found. Urbanek writes of this, with some regret, "... Vallotton and the Japanese constituted a temptation to indulge in decorative art that not even Munch could always resist, as the later woodcut version of *The Kiss* proves."[30]

Yet this is not an exception in his oeuvre, but merely an example of a stage of development in which Munch was clearly dabbling in a brief dialogue with turn-of-the-century stylism. For example, around 1900, he

23 Strobl 3467, 3467a.
24 Strobl 1739, 1741.
25 Strobl 1790, 1804–1806.
26 Dobai 1968, p. 99.—on the woodcut mentioned see Schiefler 102c.
27 Cf. Hans Bisanz, *Edvard Munch und seine Bedeutung für den mitteleuropäischen Expressionismus.* Unpublished doctoral thesis, University of Vienna 1959.
28 Ewald Rathke, in exhib. cat. Frankfurt/M. 1995
29 Novotny-Dobai, p. 39.
30 Walter Urbanek, *Edvard Munch—Lebensfries*, Munich 1955, p. 13.

Gustav Klimt
Fulfilment
1910
Working drawing for the
Stoclet frieze
Tempera, watercolour, gold
paint, silver bronze, chalk,
pencil, lithiphone, gold leaf and
silver leaf on paper,
195 x 120 cm
Vienna, MAK–Museum für
angewandte Kunst,
Inv. No. 37.197
(Strobl No. 1811)

Edvard Munch, The Kiss, 1900,
coloured woodcut, Vienna,
Albertina

Edvard Munch, The Kiss, 1895,
etching, Vienna, Albertina

painted a group of pure landscapes, which, unlike his other works, do not treat such issues as the human condition, the lot of the individual and the problems of life, but stand entirely on their own. They are, for the most part, groups of fir trees whose contours are outlined in sweeping strokes, as in *Winter Night* or *Locomotive*.[31] As in the final version of the woodcut *The Kiss*, this group of landscapes includes square formats and symmetrical compositions such as *Birch Tree in the Snow* and *White Night*.[32]

In other words, in this woodcut, which is both monumental and decorative at the same time, Munch actually approximates Klimt's intentions. In Klimt's painting *The Kiss*, the influence of the Belgian sculptor George Minne is added—in the motif of kneeling, which is reminiscent of the *Fountain of Youth* presented at the Secession in 1900, or in the gracefully angular arm position of the women.[33] In an earlier version of the painting,[34] the kneeling position seems less emphasised and the arm position more rounded.

In the basic concept of his painting *The Kiss*, in the portrayal of the human couple standing alone in the midst of nature, merged in a single planar unit, Klimt nevertheless follows Edvard Munch's thought process. Even though nature, in Munch's work, is visible only in the wood grain that recalls the tree, Klimt's flower-strewn mound serves as a pedestal for his monument to love. The flowers are the same flowers that we find in his landscape paintings of the Salzkammergut, where he spent the summer with Emile Flöge.

31 Exhib. cat. Frankfurt/M. 1995, no. 23, 24.
32 Exhib. cat. Frankfurt/M. 1995, no. 25; Hodin 1963, at p. 64.
33 On the importance of George Minne to the work of Klimt, see Marian Bisanz-Prakken, "Khnopff, Toorop, Minne und die Viennaer Moderne" in exhib. cat. *Sehnsucht nach Glück*, pp.172–178.
34 Illustrated in Novotny-Dobai, p. 343.

The Two-fold Woman (Water-snakes)

NEDA BEI

During Klimt's lifetime, the painting *Wasserschlangen I* (Water-snakes I) (ill. p. 236) was called *Pergament* (Parchment) or *Schwestern* (Sisters).[1] In the original frame, the upright format ended at the top in a flat curve. For this painting Klimt worked with lead pencil and watercolours, goal leaf and shell gold on parchment. The painting was first exhibited in 1907 at Galerie Miethke, and what we see today is the product of restoration work done by Otto Wächter in 1973 on the now somewhat distorted carrier.[2] The translucent parchment combines metallic gold and silver sheen, sheer and impasto pigment, lead pencil and brushwork. As a contrast to the areas filled with opaque ornamentation, in the inner, pigment-free areas Klimt has inscribed two delicately modelled women, one of whom has her face turned towards the viewer. The parchment is flesh-coloured. Dated between 1904 and 1907, *Parchment* can be characterised as a work of Klimt's golden period in view of the tension between the planar ornamentation and the expressively modelled face and hands; it is comparable to the *Portrait of Adele Bloch Bauer I* (1907; ill. p. 117) and has details such as stylised creeper motifs similar to those in *The Kiss*. The closed eyes and slightly parted lips are ciphers of the lust and sexual aura of the painting. Although this woman is not asleep, but pleasurably awake, still her closed eyes confront us with the same dilemmas as he who observed Albertine. The polarity between female genus and individual women, so constitutive of western gender metaphysics, returns here as a tension between nude and face.

Gravity is eliminated under water

Women floating in or weaving through water are a recurrent motif in Klimt's work after 1897.[3] For the rigorous square format of *Ver sacrum* he drew *Fischblut* (Fish Blood) using pen and ink in 1898.[4] That same year he painted *Bewegtes Wasser* (Moving Water) in oils. Apart from the difference between abstract graphic art and painting, their composition is similar, with female nudes grouped along a diagonal of streams of hair and water. Furthermore, both works have a "heterogeneous goggle-eyed spectator". In *Fish Blood* a huge—compared to the women—fish progresses inwards from the edge of the picture, its lower jaw to the fore, while out of its profile a circular eye gazes past us into the void; in *Moving Water* the "goggle-eyed spectator", a dark merman or triton reminiscent of Böcklin, a nixie with a certain similarity to a human, gazes from the depths at the floating women. The one-eyed fish in profile penetrating the scene from the edge of the painting recurs in *Parchment*. It may well be that its circular staring silver-blue eye is now cloudy or blind, and sharp teeth are visible in its jaw; tentacles conjure up associations with sucking and grasping, and with Hokusai's *Dream of the Fisherman's Wife*[5] in which the woman is portrayed in rapturous surrender to a huge octopus. In other variations of this motif the "goggle-eyed spectator" has disappeared. Iconographically, the upright oil painting *Nixen* (Mermaids) (ill. p. 237), done around 1899, is autonomous. The only human things here are the faces of two women merging into a black phallic form. The silver streaks in the dark-green gold-speckled water may have inspired the

Teach me to heare Mermaides singing.
John Donne, Song

I have heard the mermaids singing, each to each.
T.S. Eliot, The Love Song of J. Alfred Prufrock

Gustav Klimt
Water-snakes I
c. 1904–07
Mixed media, gold layers on
parchment, 50 x 20 cm
Inscribed lower right:
"Gustav–/ Klimt"
Vienna, Österreichische Galerie
Belvedere, Inv. No. 5077
(Novotny-Dobai Nr. 139)

title of the work, which Susanna Partsch sees as a paraphrase of the *Portrait of Rose von Rosthorn-Friedmann* (1900/01; ill. p. 93). The *Goldfish* (1901/02) are three largely exposed callipygian nudes floating upwards in an upright format. The figures in *Water-snakes II*, dated like *Parchment* between 1904 and 1907, weave their way through a taut landscape format in a stylised and richly coloured flower ornament (a nude from the rear, a nude in profile, and two heads).

All these paintings lend expression to the fantasy of being in the water. What we see, however, are bodies supported by a kind of ether or dense air; they hover or float in characteristic pictorial spaces, or rather non-spaces, in which plasticity and depth are largely dissolved in planes. Sketches show that Klimt used relaxed reclining nudes to study this state of immersion in water.[6]

The eye of the draughtsman

The mermaids are only represented as a pair in *Parchment*. Their relationship to one another excludes a third party; to observe their mutual abandon one must imagine oneself as the mute fish with the blind eye. In this, the *Parchment* motifs point beyond the series of mermaids to the depictions of a couple turned towards one another, and above all, to the exclusive seclusion of the relationship represented in *The Kiss*. And even if the yearning which overcomes the women in *Parchment* does not resemble the cramped embrace in which the man and woman in *Erfüllung* (Fulfilment) or *The Kiss* hold one another, the similarly inclined head is still more reminiscent of an Eros that breaks rather than relaxes the extremities. The arm characteristically angled in an expressive-hieratic gesture and adapted from a preliminary study[7] to *Parchment*, recurs in the unfinished *Braut* (The Bride) of 1917/1918 (ill. p. 248)

Klimt was a manically productive draughtsman. The nude drawings document an almost uninhibited visual drive, a clinical curiosity about human, above all, female sexuality. The relationship between eye, hand, pen and initially empty sheet of paper is open to many and varied interpretations as to its unconscious meaning. Drawing can be understood orally, as a sublimated bite or grab at the mother's breast. In the context of the fantasy of the common skin shared by mother and infant, the line carved into the picture carrier or put down on the paper would be a scar, a trace, a symbol of separa-

Gustav Klimt
Mermaids
(Silverfish)
c. 1899
Oil on canvas, 82 x 52 cm
Vienna, Bank Austria
Kunstforum
(Novotny-Dobai No. 95)

tion. A child who plays at leaving traces behind on a sheet of paper is not alone. The page that suffers that child's attacks would be a transitional object that helps the child to experience himself as separate from the mother. In the completed work, the attacks on the mother, imagined as angry and dismembering, would be made up for; separation, anger and sadness would be worked through (Serge Tisseron)[8]. In front of *Parchment*, the gaze, having glided along the creepers and ornaments, can then suckle at an uncovered female breast and find rest. On the other hand, concealment and exposure are fetishist themes: holding fast that final moment before the cover falls to reveal the sight of the genitals of a grown woman—and to terrorise, above all, the male child. In this way, the borderlines between naked and covered body become important, fragmenting it and ensuring that the moment of horrific discovery is always postponed. Here in *Parchment* as in many of his other works Klimt was operating within this dynamism. In the wave pattern of the "skirt", the carefully painted naked *Bride* (ill. p. 248) grows a penis in front of her gaping genitals, which we can only see and associate so clearly because the painting was left unfinished.

The song of the sirens

The mythical figure of the mermaid is an ancient one. Sirens and Undine-figures may recall shamans, who participate in the nature of both man and animal. In the sea, in lakes, rivers, springs and wells, they deceive men about their bird-like claws by means of their seductive voice. These phallic, that is false, women with their dragon's tails signify powerful seduction, marital infidelity, bad luck, and death (Michel Bulteau). In the Middle Ages, the mermaid was the emblem of sensual passion (Exeter cathedral)[9]; in the fifteenth century sirens were fashionable in literature. René Magritte beaches the mermaid, fish up top, woman down below, as a *Collective Invention*[10]—at the end of a story in which yearning divides the odour of the sea into a fishy and a human half. Their narcissism shaken by the women's movement, the decadent artists of the *fin de siècle* revived the perilous seductresses in the image or stereotype of the *femme fatale*. Salome, like Judith a cipher of castration anxiety, costs a man his head, gender and identity.[11] Mario Praz found that the imagery of decadence was more multifaceted in literature than in the fine arts—including references to the lesbian and sadistic features of the femme fatale. In *Parchment* Klimt's imagination too, is not without sadism: the nude depicted from the rear seems like a torso, the waxy skin a pointer to necrophilia (cf. John Everett Millais' *Ophelia*)[12]. Yet like embryos or newborn infants, the women in *Parchment* seem to be able to breathe under water. Two individuals, one gender, they weave, hair like tendrils, between the snake skin and the slimy animal life of the deep, beneath and up through aquatic plants, beyond the straight picture edge, waxy, glassy, perhaps more tamed nature in an aquarium than oceanic emotion. The artist-master-voyeur has painted himself as a mute and blind fish, as a creature of another kind, floating with them in the river of longing for lost happiness and for an unattainable mother. Whether they are speaking is an open question, for painting, like the primary process, does without words. "Neither the spoken nor the written word come easy to me, especially when I am supposed to communicate something about myself or my work," writes Klimt, who can hardly have been unaware of the contemporary linguistic scepticism of Viennese modernism. In 1906 Robert Musil preceded his first work with these words by Maurice Maeterlinck: "As soon as we articulate something, strangely enough, we

1   *Freundinnen*, Österreichische Galerie Wien, Inv. No. 5077.
2   Cf. Registry of the Österreichische Galerie Belvedere, on Inv. No. 5077: Report by Otto Wächter, Institut für Restaurierung der Österreichischen Nationalbibliothek, dated 04/05/1973, and an expert on the state of preservation, dated 07. 04. 1981.
3   Gerbert Frodl, *Gustav Klimt in der Österreichischen Galerie in Wien*, Salzburg 1992, p. 32; Catherine Dean, *Klimt*, London 1996, p. 82, with reference to Egon Schiele, *Wassergeister I* (1907), gouache, 24 x 28, privately owned (fig. 28). In general cf. Michel Bulteau, *Die Töchter der Wasser. Mythologische Gestaltungen des Unbewußten*, Bad Münstereifel 1987; William G. Niederland, "Flußsymbolik" in Wenda Focke (ed.), William G. Niederland, *Trauma und Kreativität*, Frankfurt/M. 1989.
4   Illustration in *Ver Sacrum* 1898, issue 3; Nebehay 1987, fig. 30; Gottfried Fliedl, *Gustav Klimt. 1862–1918. Die Welt in weiblicher Gestalt*, Cologne 1998, p. 63, with the reference "pen and ink drawing, dimensions and owner unknown".
5   Edward Lucie-Smith, *Eroticism in Western Art*, London 1972, fig. 257.
6   Christian M. Nebehay, *Gustav Klimt. Das Skizzenbuch aus dem Besitz von Sonja Knips*, Vienna 1987, fig. 32; Fliedl 1998, p. 62, fig. *Liegender weiblicher Akt—Armstudie*.
7   Susanna Partsch, *Gustav Klimt. Maler der Frauen*, Munich 1994, fig. 25.
8   Serge Tisson, *Psychoanalyse de la bande dessinée*, Paris 1987.
9   Lucie-Smith 1972, fig. 255.
10   Lucie-Smith 1972, fig. 254.
11   Mario Praz, *The Romantic Agony* (translated by Angus Davidson), New York 1956, reference to Gustav Klimt's *Judith und Holofernes*, p. 476, addendum to note 99.
12   Rudolf Zeitler, *Die Kunst des 19. Jahrhunderts*, Propyläen Kunstgeschichte 11, Frankfurt/M./Berlin 1966, fig. 174.

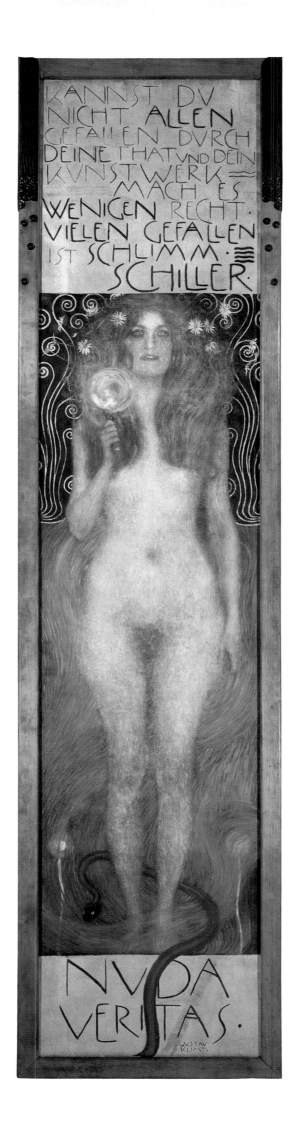

KANNST DU
NICHT ALLEN
GEFALLEN DURCH
DEINE THAT UND DEIN
KUNSTWERK —
MACH ES
WENIGEN RECHT.
VIELEN GEFALLEN
IST SCHLIMM. ≋
SCHILLER.

NUDA
VERITAS.

Gustav Klimt
Nuda Veritas
1899
Oil on canvas, 252 x 56.2 cm
Inscribed lower right:
"Gustav—/ Klimt"
Vienna, Theatermuseum
(Novotny-Dobai No. 102)

Gusatv Klimt
Danae
c. 1907–08
Oil on canvas, 77 x 83 cm
Inscribed lower right:
"Gustav–/Klimt"
Vienna, Sammlung Dichand
(Novotny-Dobai No. 151)

devalue it. We believe we have descended into the depths of the abyss, yet when we return to the surface, the drop of water on our pale fingertips no longer resembles the sea from which it emerged. We think we have discovered a wonderful treasure-trove, yet when we return to the light of day, all we have brought with us are false gems and pieces of broken glass; and nevertheless, the treasure shimmers unchanged in the darkness."

The Three Stages of Life

ALESSANDRA COMINI

"Enough of censorship ... I want to come clear," explained an exasperated Klimt in a 12 April 1905 interview with the sympathetic critic Berta Zuckerkandl concerning his withdrawal of three ceiling panels for the University of Vienna—an increasingly controversial project commissioned by the Ministry of Education which he had been working on for the past six years. The hostility and studied misunderstanding with which his somber, undulating, multi-figured, Eros-premised allegories of Philosophy, Medicine, and Jurisprudence had been received, combined with repeated government interference, brought to an end Klimt's career as a public artist; henceforth he would respond only to private commissions and personal choices, devoting himself primarily to exquisitely elegant portraits of women and genetically-studded landscapes.

And yet Klimt was not finished with allegory—it was in his blood. A month after the Zuckerkandl interview he travelled to Berlin for the opening of an exhibition featuring his works in which a large (180 x 180 cm) new oil painting was on prominent display. Visitors scanning the Deutsche Künstlerbund catalogue before seeing the painting might have assumed from the title, *Die Drei Lebensalter* (The Three Stages of Life), that Klimt's new allegory would take up the traditional three ages of man theme by showing a male or males in youth, maturity, and old age (as Edvard Munch would soon do in his Bathers triptych of 1907–08, ill. p. 244). Not so. The dramatis personae inhabiting *The Three Stages of Life* are all female. Set within the center of a white silvered ground of evanescent grey-brown tree trunks past which stream tiny flecks of pollen, and confined to a vertical column of colourful decorative fill, are the three ages of woman, not man. Nor are the three ages represented the usual ones: instead of youth or adolescence, there is a naked curly-haired baby who dreamily but insistently reaches for her mother's breast; instead of maturity, there is, facing us—her head inclined upon that of her child's—a nude, slim-hipped, blonde, very young mother, perhaps not yet out of her teens. Only old age seems to be represented in the customary fashion: to the left of the mother-and-child unit and facing them, is a naked figure in silhouette with rounded, concave back, sagging breasts, swollen belly, and blue-veined neck, arms and feet. And yet this pathetic figure (pictorial homage to Rodin's *The Old Courtesan*) with silver-streaked but still brown hair, who buries her face in one hand in despair (a gesture borrowed from *Philosophy* and *Medicine*), could range in actual age anywhere from fifty to seventy. In Klimt's world view, fixated as it was on biological regeneration, the cause for female despair is not so much age as it is loss of sexual attractiveness and the ability to reproduce. This for woman, as not only Klimt but most turn-of-the-century males thought, is the beginning of death. Describing Rodin's 1889 sculpture entitled *Dried-Up Springs,* Edmond Goncourt had written dismissively: "Two old women with dried-up breasts who have lost all sex." Contemplating Klimt's old woman in *The Three Stages of Life*, an impressed Peter Altenberg mused: "The old woman deplores her physical destruction. Once having lost her nimbus, what could a deep soul and a deep recognition serve her?"

1   From English edition of the author's *My Life and History,* New York 1939, pp. 180–181, end of Chapter two.

Gustav Klimt

**The Three Stages
of Life**
1905
Oil on canvas, 173 x 171 cm
Rome, Galleria Nazionale
d'Arte Moderna
(Novotny-Dobai No. 141)

But between life and death there is the dream-a seductive concept that had exercised tremendous appeal in the city that fostered Grillparzer's popular play, *Der Traum ein Leben* (Dream, a Life), Hofmannsthal's epigrammatic poem, *Leben, Traum und Tod* (Life, Dream and Death), and, most recently, Freud's *Die Traumdeutung* (Interpretation of Dreams). As he had done in the University panels, Klimt suggests in his new allegory the unconscious dream state through which human destiny passes: both mother and child have their eyes closed, as if in sleep, while the old woman's eyes cannot be seen behind the protective cascade of hair and supporting hand, as she blots out perception.

A similar helpless averting gesture can be observed in the old woman with closed eyes who faces the separated young mother and child on the lower left pilaster of Rodin's *Gate of Hell,* and it is indeed conceivable that the Austrian artist ("painter of the unconscious," a hostile critic had dubbed him) was consciously paraphrasing the work of the renowned French sculptor he had admired and met in person at the Secession exhibition of his allegorical Beethoven frieze three years earlier. Berta Zuckerkandl has left a graphic description of their afternoon together at a Prater garden cafe where from a nearby piano Schubert melodies floated in the air: "Klimt and Rodin had seated themselves beside two remarkably beautiful young women—Rodin gazing enchantedly at them. Klimt had created an ideal of this type—the "modern" woman, with a boyish slimness and a puzzling charm. ... And, that afternoon, slim and lovely vamps came buzzing round Klimt and Rodin, those two fiery lovers. ... Rodin leaned over to Klimt and said: "I have never before experienced such an atmosphere— your tragic and magnificent Beethoven fresco; your unforgettable, temple-like exhibition, and now this garden, these women, this music ... and round it all this gay, childlike happiness ... What is the reason for it all? And Klimt slowly nodded his beautiful head and answered only one word: 'Austria.'"[1]

If Klimt's explanation of Vienna's unique ambience was understandably chauvinistic, his subscription to the sexual determinism announced in *The Three Stages of Life* was a highly personal interpretation of Nietzsche's idea of eternal recurrence coupled with an appreciation of Ernst Mach's "flux of sensations" theory of experience. With a fatalistic sense of the connection between humans and nature, the artist posited his cyclic recurrence of female destiny against a rain of fecundation (the tree "pollen") and within a mosaic-saturated cocoon of multifarious drifting ova. Embracing the notion that life and death are equally present in the great continuum of biological renewal, he had already expressed this theme, as well as a first interest in the three ages of woman, in the "realist" allegory, Love, completed some ten years earlier in 1895. Above the heads of an embracing couple is a serial unfolding of the ages—and the aging—of woman from eager child to emaciated hag. (How different from Munch's insistence on an inevitable character transformation from innocence to lust in his *Three Stages of Woman* of 1893–05 or *The Dance of Life,* 1899–1900.)

August Rodin, pilaster study for The Gates of Hell (1883–1917), plaster, c. 1885.

Edvard Munch, Bathers triptych, oil on canvas, 1907-08: Youth, Bergen, Rassmus Meyers Samlinger; Maturity (Bathing Men), Helsinki, Ateneum; Old Age, Oslo, Munch-Museet.

Why, we might ask, did Klimt choose to show a baby rather than a youth (a precedent can be found in Arnold Böcklin's much-admired variation on the "ages of man," *Vita somnium breve*, of 1888, in which both sexes are represented by two infants playing by a stream)? And why did he elect to depict a pubescent mother rather than a mature woman? Did Klimt have any real-life "ages of women" examples from which to draw as he set about composing his compelling cycle-of-life allegory? The answer is yes. An infant girl had impinged upon his bachelor life in the form of an adored niece, Helene, for whom he was appointed guardian after the untimely death of his younger brother Ernst in 1892. His own dearly beloved, deeply opinionated mother Anna, who would live until 1915, was sixty-nine when he completed *The Three Stages of Life*. (He had made a moving portrait sketch of her seated in an armchair the year before.) One of her daughters—his sister Johanna—had produced four offspring (a girl, Eleonora, was born in 1902), and we can in fact contemplate three Klimt generations in a photograph of around 1900 (ill. p. 250) showing Anna, with silver-streaked but still brown hair, and two of her young (male) grandchildren with their mother and aunt.

Arnold Böcklin, Vita somnium breve, oil on canvas, 1888, Basel, Kunstmuseum

Beyond such proximate family paradigms there was the alluring—for Klimt—three-generational exemplar of the ages of woman afforded by his friendship with the painter Carl Moll and his new family: Moll had married the widow of Austria's greatest landscape painter, Emil Jacob Schindler, and his stepdaughter was none other than the vivacious Alma, object of a vigorous if frustrated courtship by Klimt, who pursued the seductive seventeen-year-old on a family trip to Italy in the summer of 1897. After Alma married Gustav Mahler in 1902, Klimt was an occasional dinner guest in their home, and by 1904, a year before painting *The Three Stages of Life*, he observed what a witness at the same dinner party has described as a radiant, unselfconsciously pregnant hostess, who would soon give birth to her second daughter, Anna. That Klimt remained tenderly aware of Alma and her life is confirmed by a touching condolence letter he wrote her upon the death of her older daughter, Maria, in 1907.

One other life-cycle paradigm—seared into the collective consciousness of all subjects of Kaiser Franz Josef and hanging nostalgically over the protracted demise of his huge empire—was the image of the ill-fated royal family and its three generations captured in a much-recycled and circulated photograph of 1861 (ill. p. 250) showing the emperor's domineering mother, Archduchess Sophie, his ravishingly beautiful but ano-

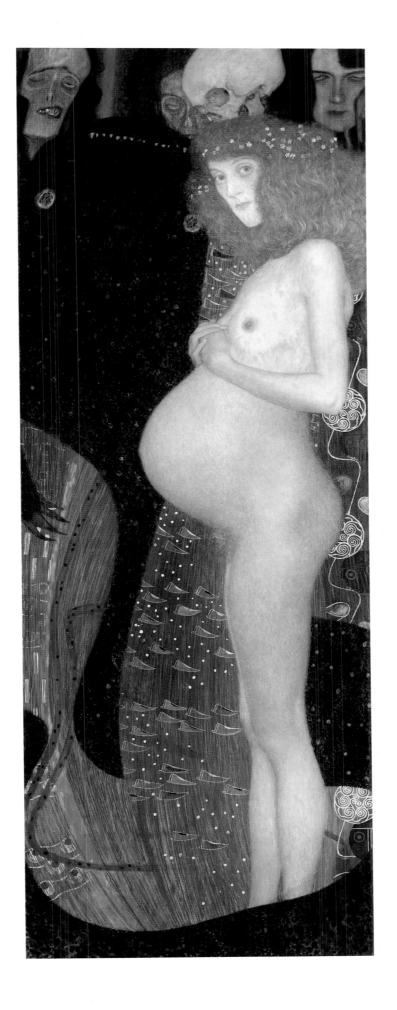

Gustav Klimt
Hope I
1903
Oil on Canvas, 181 x 67 cm
National Gallery of Canada,
Ottawa
(Novotny-Dobai No. 129)

Edward Burne-Jones
**The Tree
of Forgiveness**
1881–82
Oil on canvas, 180 x 111 cm
Inscribed: "E.B.J. 1882"
Liverpool, National Museum and
Galleries on Merseyside

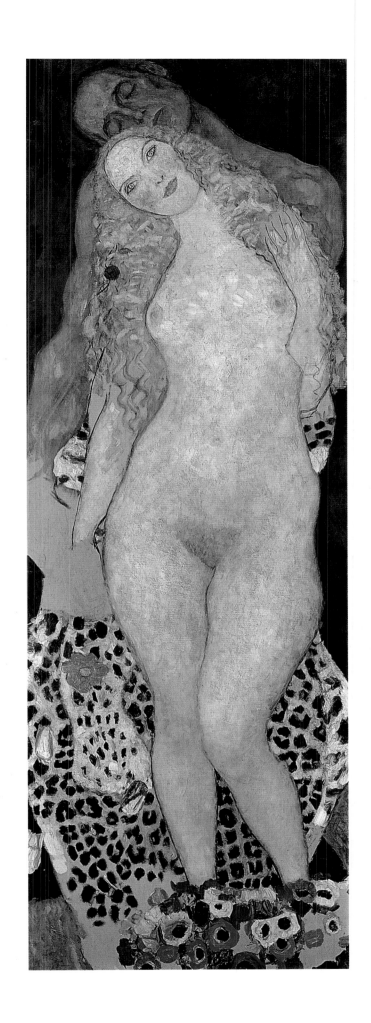

Gustav Klimt
Adam and Eve
1917–18
Oil on canvas, 173 x 60 cm
Vienna, Österreichische Galerie
Belvedere
(Novotny-Dobai No. 220)

247

Gustav Klimt
The Bride
1918 (unfinished)
Oil on canvas, 165 x 191 cm
Vienna, Österreichische Galerie
Belvedere/Private loan
(Novotny-Dobai No. 222)

rexic young wife Elisabeth (Sissi)—who would die by an assassin's knife, and their infant daughter Gisela—solicitously regarded by her older brother Rudolf, destined to commit suicide at Mayerling.

But beyond such precedents was the fact that Klimt shared with his coevils—from Schnitzler and Freud to Kraus and Loos—that voyeuristic fixation upon females, especially das "Kind-Mädchen," as mysterious, fascinating, frightening, and above all subject to the dictates of their anatomy. "In those days one could distinguish at a distance a young girl from a woman who had already known a man, simply by the way she walked," observed Stefan Zweig, speaking of Klimt's Vienna (*The World of Yesterday,* New York, 1943, pp. 78–79) "Woman's entire body is an accessory to her sexual parts," fumed the self-hating young Otto Weininger shortly before taking his life in 1903. For Freud, as put forth in the first of his *Drei Abhandlungen zur Sexualtheorie (Three Contributions to the Theory of Sex),* published the same year as Klimt's *The Three Stages of Life,* the erotic life of woman was, "partly owing to their conventional secretiveness and insincerity still veiled in an impenetrable obscurity" (Essay I, part 2, section a). Altenberg's judgment was compassionate, as he contemplated Klimt's "tired" young mother who "had given her noble strength to her little child." The child was "also tired," however; "it sleeps because it cannot live yet." The poet concluded with Klimtian sweep: "Es liegt alles in dem Bilde vom Tragischen und Romantischen des Frauendaseins, dabei das Nirwana und der Blick ins Leere" (It's all in the image of the tragic and romantic Woman-being, including Nirvana and the gaze into the abyss). That the central "Woman-being" in this case was that of a child-mother complies with Adolf Loos's explanation of the child-girl phenomenon in Vienna: "Das weibkind kam in mode. Man lechzte nach unreife. Die psyche des mädchens wurde ergründet und besungen" (The woman-child came into fashion. One yearned for immaturity. The psyche of the girl was fathomed and celebrated).

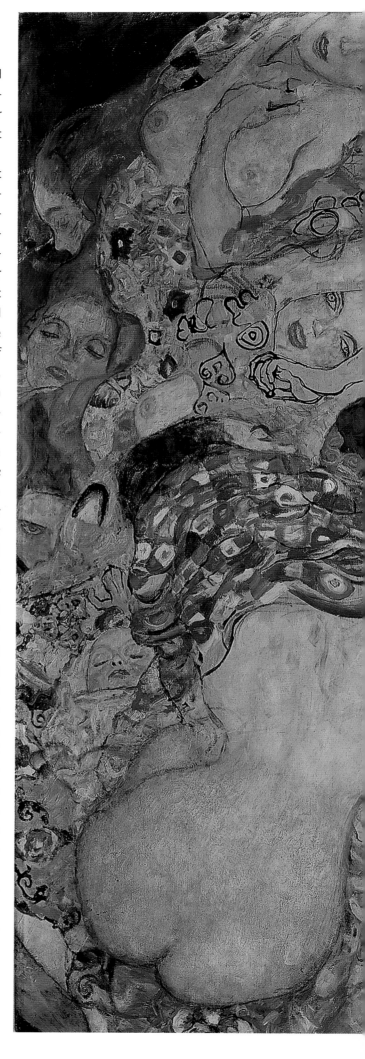

Detail, photograph of the Austrian imperial family, with, standing from left to right, Emperor Franz Joseph, his brother Archduke Max (later ill-fated emperor of Mexico) and his wife Charlotte; seated left, Empress Elisabeth with daughter Gisela on her lap, son Rudolf standing, and her mother-in-law, Archduchess Sophie seated on the right, 1861.

Photograph of three generations of Klimts: Gustav Klimt's mother Anna (left) with two grandchildren, their mother (second from right) and their aunt (far right), c. 1900.

What Freud had dared to address in his three 1905 essays—the existence of infantile sexuality—Klimt in *The Three Stages of Life* makes explicit, then abstracts his message of eternal Eros before our very eyes. Applying a private iconography of symbolic and cumulative decorative shapes which would climax in the ornate intercourse of circular and vertical forms of *The Kiss* of 1907–08 (ill. p. 231), the artist intersects the floating gold cocoon of his three females with a broad horizontal blue-black band at the top of the canvas. This organic form thrusts past the heads and injects a sense of phallic presence which is repeated in the eight smaller cucumber-like shapes horizontally invading the decorative fill of round cells (first observed by the artist through the microscope of his distinguished anatomist friend Emil Zuckerkandl, husband of Berta). To the lower right a jet of erect triangles infiltrates upward the fragile chrysalis of the three floating females, whose sexual identities and destiny are so suggestively symbolized by their reiterated emblematized surround. The inevitable drama of biological interaction enacted by Klimt's occulated spirals and stiff pyramids here would, because of their compelling ornamental beauty, elude the eye of the imperial censor, if not the modern eye. *The Three Stages of Life* thus not only merits characterization as Klimt's first purposefully subversive representation of the sexual imperative, but also as a kind of clandestine and triumphant (awarded a gold medal in Rome, 1911) revenge on the blind critics of the University panels—"Enough of censorship!"

Gustav Klimt
Mother and Children
1909–10
Oil on canvas, 90 x 90 cm
Vienna, Private collection
(Novotny-Dobai No. 163)

Biography

TOBIAS G. NATTER

1862   Gustav Klimt was born on 14 July 1862 at Linzerstrasse 247 in Wien-Baumgarten, at the time an independent suburb of the imperial and royal city of Vienna. Klimt's father, Ernst Klimt, an engraver from Bohemia, and his wife Anna, née Finster, found it difficult to provide for their seven children.

1876–83   At the age of 15 Klimt entered the Kunstgewerbeschule in Vienna. The intention was that he become a drawing teacher, like his younger brother Ernst, but in Professor Ferdinand Laufberger he found a patron who recognised and promoted his talent.

1881ff.   During their studies the Klimt brothers founded a studio community together with Franz Matsch. This "Künstler-Compagnie" soon became a viable enterprise receiving numerous commissions, in particular from the theatre architects Fellner and Helmer.

1886–96   His ceiling paintings for the splendid staircases in the Burgtheater (1886–88) and the Kunsthistorische Museum (1890–91) in Vienna made Klimt known to a wider public. Celebrated by many as a "new Makart", the successful late history painter stumbled into an artistic crisis. Gradually the production company with Franz Matsch was dissolved. Klimt's transition to being a modern painter came about during his work on the so-called "faculty paintings" for the University of Vienna (as of 1893).

1897–1905   With the foundation of the Viennese Secession on 3 April 1897 Klimt moved to the forefront of the art renewers, becoming their first president. At their own premises on Karlsplatz the avant-garde group showed top class European exhibitions. The eight heroic years ended with the Klimt group leaving the Secession in 1905.

1900   At the same time as Sigmund Freud published *The Interpretation of Dreams,* the relentless controversy surrounding the "faculty paintings" reached a climax. Klimt retired more and more from public life. Private commissions grew in importance. Klimt worked at a measured pace, doing meticulous preparatory drawings of each portrait. As of 1900 he produced one portrait of a woman per year.

1902   With his Beethoven frieze, created on the occasion of the Beethoven exhibition at the Viennese Secession, Klimt achieved a breakthrough, synthesising the monumental and the ornamental.

1903   The foundation of the Wiener Werkstätte by Josef Hoffmann, Kolo Moser and Fritz Waerndorfer was inspired by the concept of the *gesamtkunstwerk;* art and life were to be interconnected to form a unity. This dream was supported financially by Klimt's patrons and women collectors in particular. During a trip to Italy in 1903, Klimt was fired with enthusiasm for the gold mosaics in Ravenna.

1907   Egon Schiele knocked on Klimt's studio door in Josefstädterstrasse 21 for the first time. When that building was demolished in 1911, Klimt moved to Feldmühlgasse in Wien-Hietzing.

1908–10   Klimt opened the 1908 Kunstschau. Under Klimt's aegis Oskar Kokoschka and the new generation of expressionists confronted an indignant public. The Austrian state purchased *The Kiss.* A trip to Paris in 1909 meant important new inspiration for Klimt and the end of his so-called "golden period". The following year, Adolf Loos published *Ornament and Crime.*

1911   Klimt travelled to Brussels for the installation of his Stoclet frieze, which he had prevented from being exhibited publicly in Vienna.

1914–18   The First World War paralysed the art world.

1918   Klimt suffered a stroke on 11 January and died on 6 February 1918 of pneumonia. Egon Schiele made a drawing of the dead Klimt in the mortuary at the Allgemeine Krankenhaus: "I found him very changed," Schiele comments, "he had been clean shaven, I scarcely recognised him on the bier. Klimt looked sturdy, severe and tanned from the sun." Klimt is buried alongside his mother at the cemetery in Hietzing.

Literature

Index

Page numbers in *italics* refer to illustrations.

Czeike, 1992ff: Felix Czeike (ed.), *Historisches Lexikon Wien in fünf Bänden*, Vienna 1992ff.

Fischer 1987: Wolfgang Georg Fischer, *Gustav Klimt und Emilie Flöge. Genie und Talent, Freundschaft und Besessenheit*, Vienna 1987

Gmeiner/Pirhofer 1985: Astrid Gmeiner/Gottfried Pirhofer, *Der österreichische Werkbund. Alternative zur klassischen Moderne in Architektur, Raum- und Produktgestaltung*, Vienna 1985

Hevesi 1906: Ludwig Hevesi, *Acht Jahre Sezession (März 1897 – Juni 1905). Kritik – Polemik – Chronik*, Wien 1906. Re-edited by Otto Breicha, Klagenfurt 1984

Mahler: Alma Mahler-Werfel, *Tagebuch-Suiten. 1898–1902*, ed. by Antony Beaumont and Susanne Rode-Breymann, Frankfurt/M. 1997

Nebehay 1969: Christian M. Nebehay (ed.), *Gustav Klimt. Dokumentation*, Wien 1969

Nebehay 1979: Christian M. Nebehay, *Egon Schiele. 1890–1918. Leben – Briefe – Gedichte*, Salzburg 1979, Veröffentlichung der Albertina Nr. 13.

Novotny-Dobai: Fritz Novotny und Johannes Dobai, *Gustav Klimt*, Salzburg 1967

Sekler 1982: Eduard F. Sekler, *Josef Hoffmann. Das architektonische Werk. Monographie und Werkverzeichnis*, Salzburg/Wien 1982

Strobl Bd. 1–4, 1980ff.: Alice Strobl: *Gustav Klimt. Die Zeichnungen*, Bd. 1 (1878–1903) Salzburg 1980; Bd. 2 (1904–1912) Salzburg 1982; Bd. 3 (1913–1918); Bd. 4, Addenda, Salzburg 1984ff.

Adler: Heraldisch Genealogische Gesellschaft Adler, Wien.

IKG Wien: Israelitische Kultusgemeinde Wien

WStLA: Wiener Stadt- und Landesarchiv